D1322177

BECOMING CONSPICUOUS

BECOMING CONSPICUOUS

IRISH TRAVELLERS, SOCIETY
AND THE STATE
1922–70

AOIFE BHREATNACH

Published by the
UNIVERSITY COLLEGE DUBLIN PRESS
PREAS CHOLÁISTE OLLSCOILE BHAILE ÁTHA CLIATH
2006

First published 2006
by University College Dublin Press
Newman House
86 St Stephen's Green
Dublin 2
Ireland

www.ucdpress.ie

ISBN 978-1-904558-61-3 pb
978-1-904558-62-0 hb

CIP data available from the British Library

Typeset in France in Adobe Caslon and Bodoni Oldstyle
by Elaine Burberry
Text design by Lyn Davies
Printed in England on acid-free paper
by MPG Books Ltd, Bodmin, Cornwall

Contents

—

Illustrations

—

Tables

Abbreviations

—

CAI   Cork Archives Institute
DCA   Dublin City Archives
DH   Department of Health
DJ   Department of Justice
DT   Department of Taoiseach
GCCC   General Council of County Councils
ICA   Irish Countrywomen's Association
IFC   Irish Folklore Collection, Main Manuscript Collection
IFC S   Irish Folklore Collection, Schools Collection
IRA   Irish Republican Army
IRCHSS   Irish Research Council for the Humanities and Social Sciences
ISC   Itinerant Settlement Committee
ITM   Irish Traveller Movement
NAI   National Archives of Ireland
NCTP   National Council for Travelling People
NFP   Northside Folklore Project
NLI   National Library of Ireland
NUI   National University of Ireland
PRONI   Public Record Office of Northern Ireland
RCB   Representative Church Body Library
RDC   Rural District Council
RUC   Royal Ulster Constabulary
SJL   Sidney Jones Library, University of Liverpool
SMGC   Scott Macfie Gypsy Collection
SSVP   Society of St Vincent de Paul
TCD   Trinity College, Dublin
TD   Teachta Dála
UCC   University College Cork
UCD   University College Dublin
UDC   Urban District Council

Acknowledgements

—

This book has been brewing for so long that it is almost impossible to thank everyone who has brought it to fruition. The credit for awakening my original interest in Traveller–settled relations in 1997 goes to University College Cork History Department while De Montfort University funded the PhD thesis. The first attempt at rewriting was in the seclusion of Hertford College, Oxford. Maria Luddy in Warwick and Bernadette Whelan in the University of Limerick assisted me at various times. Finally, the book took shape in the generous and warm atmosphere of the Department of History at NUI Maynooth, where I was funded by the Irish Research Council for the Humanities and Social Sciences. Each institution and each mentor – Mike Cronin, Roy Foster and Vincent Comerford – has contributed to the emergence of this book, but the errors are entirely my own. A publication grant from the National University of Ireland is also gratefully acknowledged.

I pay particular tribute to the generosity of other researchers who, in the course of their own work, took note of material that was useful to my subject: Brian Covey, Drs Bronagh Allison, Anne Dolan, Niall Keogh, Robert MacNamara, Daithí Ó Corráin, John Walsh and Eric Zuelow. I also thank those who have allowed me to read their unpublished work: Nora Casey, Dr Sinéad Ní Shúinéir and Michelle Norris.

Many archivists and staff gave invaluable help as I travelled from archive to archive in search of scattered pieces of information: particular thanks to Liam Kenny who allowed me to access the uncatalogued collection of the General Council of County Councils; the archivist of the Dublin City Archive; Derek Phillips in the Representative Church Body Library; Sarah Smith in the National Photographic Archive; Brian Magee in the Cork Archives Institute; Dr Marie-Annick Desplanques, who directed me to the Northside Folklore Collection in Cork; Dr Bairbre Ní Fhloinn in University College Dublin advised on the Irish Folklore Collection and Kathy Hooper in Sidney Jones Library, Liverpool was very helpful. A number of county librarians and archivists responded extremely generously to my request for random information from their collections. Particular thanks to the staff in the County Libraries of Clare, Donegal, Leitrim and Meath. A very special thanks to Barbara Mennell and UCD Press for their hard work in preparing the manuscript for publication.

Lastly, my friends and family who counselled and consoled cannot be thanked enough. For enduring with relative stoicism the research, writing and rewriting, Peter Hertting receives my profound gratitude.

AOIFE BHREATNACH
NUI Maynooth, January 2006

Introduction

—

Most Irish people, who know little about Travellers' daily lives, often ask, 'Who are the Travellers?' In popular discourse, the term 'Traveller' remains interchangeable with 'itinerant' and 'tinker', two terms of varying antiquity that have recently acquired negative connotations. As there are three collective nouns, there are three official government examinations of Travellers, but only two reports were brave enough to attempt to define the community. In 1963, the Commission on Itinerancy defined an 'itinerant' as 'a person who had no fixed place of abode and habitually wandered from place to place, but excluding travelling show-people and travelling entertainers'.[1] Twenty years later, the Travelling People Review Body described the subject of its inquiry thus: 'They are an identifiable group of people, identified by both themselves and by other members of the community (. . . the "settled community") as people with their own distinctive life style, traditionally of a nomadic nature but not now habitual wanderers. They have needs wants and values, which are different in some ways from those of the settled community.'[2] In 1995, the Report of the Task Force on the Travelling Community, while recommending measures against racism experienced by Travellers, did not give a terse definition of the characteristics that set Travellers apart from settled people.[3]

No government report has ever produced a corresponding definition of 'settled', a label that exists to divide 'the rest' of the population from Travellers, 'us' from 'them'. 'Settled' is a category that is quickly qualified by urban and rural, rich and poor. Class, with its implications of status as well as relative prosperity, obfuscates any interpretation of the term 'settled community'. Indeed, the 'Traveller community' is no more homogeneous than the settled, but historical methodology cannot reveal much about the structure of a minority society that was, until recently, commented on by outside observers. So, how can analysis proceed when the collective nouns required are so tenuous? Their very fluidity has been placed at the heart of this study that chronicles different facets of the Traveller-settled relationship, suggesting the contingent nature of categories such as 'Traveller' or 'settled'. Both communities were profoundly affected by apparently unrelated social change such as the evolution of the rural economy, the rise of the welfare state and the development of urban planning. The boundaries between the two groups were more clearly demarcated as a consequence of altered social and economic circumstances.

I

Examining the effect of social change on Travellers and settled people, this book is the first attempt to assess the historical relationship between Ireland's indigenous nomadic minority and the housed population. Material about Travellers in Northern Ireland is not, however, included, but is published elsewhere.[4] The subject of much contemporary comment, publications on Travellers are dominated by present-day debates such as appropriate site provision and access to health care.[5] Scholars, drawn to the issue of racism in Irish society, have seen prejudice against Travellers as evidence of that evil.[6] It cannot be denied that Travellers provoke disproportionate levels of hostility from the majority population. A survey of attitudes in 1988–9 indicated that a situation of 'caste-like apartheid' existed, where Travellers were accorded rights 'so long as they do not come too close to Settled People in a personal capacity. Marriage, friendship and even next-door neighbourhood is ruled out by the majority'.[7] Inevitably, the question arises: was such antipathy a permanent feature of Traveller–settled relations?

In an attempt to understand the historical status of Travellers, this book examines developments in Irish society that affected attitudes to the nomadic population. Was the relationship between Travellers and settled people char-acterised by antagonism or tolerance at different times? What forces shaped and influenced minority–majority relations from 1922 to 1970? Was the pre-sence of the wandering beggar or boccough important for attitudes to mobility and alms giving? Robbie McVeigh has argued that Travellers suffer from a prejudice specific to nomads, termed 'sedentarism'. Such theoretical work has been influential in the field of 'Gypsiology', a sub-specialism dominated by anthropology and linguistics.[8] However, David Mayall's historical studies foreground the changing contexts that affected perceptions of, and reactions to, Travellers in England.[9] Yet most studies on vagrancy and poor relief ignore nomads, while scholars working on Traveller populations are not concerned with the majority government and society.[10] That division of interest is not maintained here, for it cannot be presumed that legislation, government policy and social change were mutually exclusive in their effects on Travellers or settled people.

While there are no historical studies of Travellers, there are also few his-torians writing about social change; modern Irish social history is profoundly underdeveloped in comparison with other countries and time periods that can boast of monographs on popular culture, religious practice, and gender relations to name but a few.[11] The best modern works to date have been produced by historical geographers such as Jacinta Prunty and Ruth McManus.[12] Scholarship on the development of the welfare state is sketchy while the existence of the urban working class is barely acknowledged.[13] Of necessity, this survey depends upon primary material to describe Irish society in general as well as Travellers in particular. Of course, examining broader issues in Irish government and society was an approach dictated in part by archival material that did not feature Travellers prominently. Unfortunately, the reaction of Travellers to government or the majority community was extremely difficult to discern, since their voices were never recorded.

As for many other Irish people without literacy or status, it was an arduous task to locate Travellers in the archival record. There was no undiscovered archive replete with Traveller material – readers will notice that the footnotes and bibliography are dominated by primary material drawn from recognised sources. Nomads appeared only when their actions affected the interests of government record keepers or when they impinged on public consciousness. In common with women and the working class, Travellers did not control the archival record, and contributions from the margins were not recorded directly. For example, when local authority tenants addressed Cork Corporation, their contributions were summarised rather than reproduced directly in the minutes. Similarly, 'tinkers' or 'itinerants' were described exclusively by outsiders concerned about the 'problems' they caused. A public problem often arises when 'there is a significant but not illegal deviation from societal norms'.[14] Their appearance in the record as problematic was also a consequence of record keeping, which lends itself to charting unwelcome or unanticipated developments, unsettling change or unforeseen expenditure. A civil servant, journalist or charitable individual will rarely write an extensive report on how all is well with the world. Neither will a politician raise an issue in parliament to comment on how satisfactorily the situation was handled. Therefore, the categorisation of Travellers in the archival record as a 'problem' should not unduly surprise us. The first government report on Travellers, the *Report of the Commission on Itinerancy*, published in 1963, was an excellent example of the tendency of government to problematise individuals or groups. The Commission was appointed in June 1960 by the Taoiseach, Seán Lemass, to obtain accurate information on the numbers of Travellers in Ireland and to recommend a solution to the problem of unauthorised encampments. As it devoted much consideration of the attitudes of the communities towards each other, it was particularly useful for analysing settled people's perceptions – official and popular – of Travellers. Popular opinion is hard to measure, although it is arguably no more demanding than discerning the personal opinion of evasive politicians or subtle civil servants. Popular attitudes to Travellers were analysed in newspapers and folklore material. The archives of the Irish Folklore Commission were a crucial source for understanding what settled people meant by collective nouns such as 'tinker', 'tramp' and 'gypsy' while newspaper coverage of significant events such as fairs indicated the social distance maintained between Travellers and settled people. Fundamental to

understanding the status given to Travellers by the majority is an examination
of what made Travellers different.

George Gmelch was the first scholar to argue that Travellers were quin-
tessentially rural, having no 'traditional' place in urban life.[15] That position
has become a truism, with even contemporary politicians and administrators
adhering to it,[16] but the historical evidence advanced here and elsewhere
proves that they were neither exclusively urban nor rural.[17] Since Travellers
were defined as a national, urban 'problem' in the post-war period, it would
seem that developments in the city environment played a significant role in
mediating Travellers' position in Irish society. Here, a detailed analysis of
Cork Corporation illustrates the effects of welfare policy, local government
administration and sanitation on social organisation. Cork city was chosen to
illustrate the urban situation in Ireland outside Dublin, because a capital city
experience is markedly different from that of provincial city life. However, the
focus on Cork is not exclusive: Dublin, Limerick and Galway also feature.
Changes in official and popular definitions of land use, as well as evolving
attitudes to public and private space, rendered Travellers alien to post-war
Ireland enshrining rigid social norms. As David Sibley has argued, the status
of non-conforming minorities worsens considerably as the state extends its
remit.[18] In this study the catalyst for change in modern Ireland is not the
economic dynamism of Seán Lemass and T. K. Whitaker, but mundane legislation on planning and welfare that was passed in the 1930s. Outright
hostility to Travellers emerged as the allocation of two interconnected
resources was determined by the government system: money and status.
Local officials who distributed welfare benefits were reluctant to help
Travellers while the working classes who received such financial support were
antagonistic to their inclusion in the greatest welfare project of twentieth-
century Ireland, public housing. Superficially, both official and popular
opposition arose from a perceived threat to financial resources. But much
more than finite finance was at stake for the urban working class, who sought
to advance their claims to status by firmly assigning the lowest rung of the
class ladder to Travellers. Government intervention alternately supported and
stymied that cause. The evolution of the Irish class system, which increased
the social distance between Travellers and settled people, is thus central to
this study. Attempts by settled people to provoke government action to solve
the 'itinerant problem', and the government policies formulated to address
those complaints, are interlocking narratives in the second half of this study.

Chapter 1 describes, within the limitations of the sources, who Travellers
were and how they were different from settled society. The distinctions, real
and imagined, made between Travellers and Anglo-Romanies, are also analysed. The importance of fairs in determining the position of nomads and the

perceptions of their society is discussed. Chapter 2 examines the position of homeless men and women in urban and rural Ireland, and whether attitudes to begging and alms-giving were shaped by the decline of the wandering vagrant, and the extension of welfare benefits. Chapter 3 goes on to describe some of the most important developments in Irish society that affected the position and status of Travellers. Much of this chapter will not discuss Travellers directly, but will focus instead upon the increased state control over the lives of all of its citizens. One consequence of developments in state and society from 1922 to the 1950s was the alienation and isolation of Travellers. The planning process, public housing and compulsory education all served to widen the gap between Travellers and the working class. Niches occupied by Travellers were eroded not by increasing intolerance, or a wave of vast impersonal 'modernisation', but by persistent government regulation of various aspects of Irish social organisation. Such regulation also served to make Travellers increasingly distinctive and, often, unacceptably different.

Chapter 4 examines why, although government departments sometimes tried to control Travellers, they were not noticed as a social problem until the 1960s. The division of responsibility between voluntary charity and state welfare ensured that nomads evaded close scrutiny: the Society of St. Vincent de Paul and the Legion of Mary ministered to Travellers while local government often denied them welfare services. Occasionally, efforts were made to target Travellers for public health reasons or on the basis of problems caused by vagrancy and homelessness; those sporadic attempts to control Travellers are outlined in detail. Administrative structures were not the only reason Travellers evaded state intervention, as chapter 5 demonstrates. How and why the reluctance to address the problems attributed to a small, but visible minority was overcome is analysed here. The composition, methods and aims of the first government report on the community, Commission on Itinerancy, is also explored. Whether the Commission's report marked a shift in the relationship between voluntary charity and state welfare is discussed.

How the Commission's recommendations were implemented demonstrated that the state was unable to offer Travellers even basic services. Although the report was accepted by national and local government in principle, the provision of facilities for Travellers proved politically impossible. Local politicians called on the government to solve the 'national problem' that was Traveller accommodation while the Minister for Local Government firmly placed the onus for halting sites and housing on each local authority. Voluntary agencies stepped into the breach, working to convince settled people that Travellers deserved housing and campsites, while helping Travellers to access welfare and health services. Continuing a pattern established since the foundation of the state, the voluntary sector provided facilities for the most marginalised members of society. This chapter and the book conclude at the stage when Travellers began to participate in the voluntary groups that sought to improve their lives. After 1970, the voluntary and public sector began to consult Travellers themselves about measures designed to aid their community. The epilogue addresses the themes that have dominated Traveller–settled relations since 1970, revealing profound and welcome changes as well as dispiriting continuities.

Finally, it is essential to state that this study cannot offer any 'solutions' for any difficulties that Travellers and settled people experience in their contact with each other. Neither does it provide a template for contemporary or future relations between settled people and Travellers. Rather, it is an attempt to explain the historical foundations of that relationship and how it changed over time. But this book does document hate, fear and intolerance, and how they were expressed. Conversely, it also explores generosity, open-mindedness and charity. For the relationship between the Traveller minority and settled majority in Ireland was subject to multifarious influences at different times; the battle between prejudice and tolerance was complex, contingent and occasionally contradictory.

ONE

'GIPSIES' AND 'TINKERS'

IDENTIFYING NOMADIC GROUPS IN IRELAND

—

It is popularly assumed that Travellers were the only nomadic community in Ireland. Although the migration of Irish Travellers to Britain has been recognised, there has been little attempt to discern the extent of similar patterns in Anglo-Romany families.[1] One scholar has advanced the view that Travellers are split into distinct groups, the boundaries of which delineate families who are indigenous Travellers from those descended from Anglo-Romany stock.[2] The historical evidence certainly indicates that Romanies frequented Ireland, as the term 'gipsy' appeared often in newspaper accounts of nomadic visitors to an area. The Commission on Itinerancy was told by some authorities that Gypsies travelled Irish roads and six such families were recorded in the census. These families came from Wales and travelled in the eastern counties.[3] Some Romany families came to Ireland to escape the Second World War,[4] but earlier evidence suggests that travel between Britain and Ireland was well established.

In the *Irish Daily Independent* of July 1910, Maurice V. Reidy discussed Gypsies in Ireland, differentiating them from 'the Irish tinkers, who lead a somewhat similar wandering life'. He also carefully separated Gypsies from 'the ordinary tramp who infests the Irish country districts . . . sponging on the poor or country folk'.[5] *The Irish Times* in 1911 asked, 'why have the far travelling Gypsy-folk established no communities in Ireland? . . . The few Gypsies who cross the Irish Sea keep within the Pale I think'.[6] Pádraig Mac Gréine, a folk-lore collector, noted that Gypsies were 'rare' in Ireland. He divided travelling families into

> two classes, tinkers and gypsies. Between tinkers and gypsies there is little or no resemblance, save in the fact that they are itinerants; but there the resemblance ceases. They do not intermingle or intermarry, they speak different languages, or 'cant' as it is sometimes styled; and their religions are different.[7]

Most observers were not as certain as Mac Gréine and many references suggest that Travellers were mistakenly called Gypsies. Though there undoubtedly were Anglo-Romanies on Irish roads, Traveller material culture was readily associated with popular images of the colourful, roving Gypsy.[8]

Unlike Britain, where a cultural hierarchy placed pure-blood, authentic Gypsies above degenerate 'tinkers',[9] in Ireland the distinction between 'gypsies' and 'tinkers' was not absolute and suggested a degree of flexibility in attitudes to nomads, who were not definitively labelled and stigmatised. Nevertheless, the differences between Travellers and Gypsies enabled both communities (and occasionally settled people) to distinguish two separate, if similar, groups. What were the distinguishing features of these groups? Some deceptively simple questions must be answered. Historically, how many Travellers were there? How were they recognised as Travellers? Where and how did they live? Conventional wisdom is in thrall to the image of a campsite in a rural setting, with Travellers welcomed by settled people anxious to buy tinware from respected craftsmen. This harmony was disrupted by sudden social and economic change that destroyed craft skills and forced Travellers to live in undignified urban squalor. Clearly the reaction of rural Ireland to nomadic families must be considered although this chapter illustrates that the urban and rural dimensions to Travellers' lives cannot be easily separated.

NUMBERS OF TRAVELLERS AND GYPSIES, 1922–70

Determining the size of a nomadic population is no easy task. Possessing neither a fixed abode nor permanent employment Travellers and Gypsies were excluded from the state's conventional measurement techniques. There were sporadic and imperfect attempts to enumerate Travellers but these figures can only hint at the size of the nomadic population. In 1925, the gardaí were asked by the Commission on the Poor Law to count homeless persons and their dependants 'observed wandering on the public highways in a single night in November 1925'. Table 1.1 outlines the results of that census (the Metropolitan area refers to the County Borough of Dublin). There are numerous definitional problems with this survey. What age group is defined as 'Children' – up to 14, 16 or 18 years old? Are categories such as 'Habitual tramp', formally defined by the census collectors? Despite the limitations of this information, the presence of Travellers and Gypsies among the 'Homeless Persons' can be guessed at. Since family mobility distinguished nomads from lone vagrants and tramps, it can be assumed that the categories with high numbers of children – 'Habitual tramps' and 'Bona fide pedlars and hawkers' – contained nomadic family groups. Outside Dublin city, the proportions of men, women and children in each category varied significantly (Table 1.2).

Table 1.1   Number of homeless persons, November 1925

	Outside Metropolitan Area			Metropolitan Area		
	Men	Women	Children	Men	Women	Children
Travelling in search of Work	248	330	440	116	180	—
Willing to undertake casual labour but unfit/unwilling to work continuously	238	48	58	120	18	—
Habitual tramps	652	416	614	34	7	—
Old and infirm persons	150	63	14	34	7	—
Bona-fide pedlars, hawkers etc.	141	77	122	7	1	—
Total	1429	637	852	290	49	—

Source: Report of the Commission on the Relief of the Sick and Destitute Poor, Including the Insane Poor (Dublin, 1927), p. 17.

Table 1.2   Outside the Metropolitan area: categories of homeless persons

	Men %	Women %	Children %
Travelling in search of work	76	10	14
Willing to undertake casual labour but unfit/unwilling to work continuously	69	14	17
Habitual tramps	39	25	37
Old and infirm persons	66	28	6
Bona-fide pedlars, hawkers etc.	41	23	36

It seems that wandering homeless men were categorised as casual labourers, the vagrants who will be analysed in chapter 2. The more equitable distribution of the sexes and age groups in the categories of 'Habitual tramp' and 'Bona fide pedlar or hawker' suggest that Travellers and Gypsies were included under these headings, but as this survey was not intended to count Travellers, their inclusion was haphazard. The figures for Dublin city imply that no nomadic families were present in the borough, or perhaps Dublin police did not view caravan and tent dwellers as 'homeless'.

Families without a fixed abode were enumerated in 1938 by the gardaí. In the 26 counties there were 950 families with 900 children aged between 6 and 14.[10] On 6 September 1944, the gardaí again surveyed the Traveller population and counted 5,151 individuals, with 2,411 under 14 years of age. The survey did not include the County Boroughs of Dublin, Cork, Limerick and Waterford.[11] In the 1946 census of population, families were classified by type of residence and 'itinerant family' was included. In May 1946, 5,554 people were included under this heading. The category was retained for the 1956 Census but figures on itinerant families were not compiled.[12] This unwillingness to compile information on Traveller numbers perhaps reflects the administration's belief in the relative unimportance of the issue. Gardaí continued to count Travellers in the 1950s, although the purpose of these and earlier censuses is not known.

Table 1.3 Numbers of Travellers in the Republic of Ireland, 1952–61

Date	Number
30 April 1952*	6,275
10 September 1956	7,148
1 December 1960	6,591
1 June 1961	5,880

* does not include the county boroughs of Cork, Dublin, Dún Laoghaire and Limerick
Source: *Report of the Commission on Itinerancy* (Dublin, 1963), Appendix ii.

The figures in Table 1.3 pose a number of problems. Each census was taken on different days, at different times of the year. Oddly, the Carlow and Kildare Gardaí performed their census on 2 May 1952, but these numbers were included in the nationwide figure. The seasonal timetables determining Traveller life must have influenced any census. Furthermore, it is likely that those Travellers who crossed the border, or travelled between Britain and Ireland, were not included in these counts. Later statistics prefer to count families rather than individuals. In 1974 the population was placed at 1,690 families which was an increase on the 1960 figure of 1,198 families.[13] The numbers of Travellers in twentieth-century Ireland will never be accurately known because a nomadic lifestyle and minimal contact with organised structures of state and society made them statistically marginal. Finally, only camping Travellers or Gypsies were the focus of official interest since housed families were not considered problematic and therefore ignored. To appreciate the relative size of the Traveller community, it is useful to consider the figures in the context of the national population (Table 1.4). From 1951 to 1961, under three million people lived in the Republic of Ireland.

Table 1.4 Census of the Irish population, 1951–61

Year	Population
1951	2,960,593
1956	2,898,264
1961	2,818,341

Source: A. J. Fitzpatrick and W. E. Vaughan (eds), *Irish Historical Statistics Population 1821–1971* (Dublin, 1978), p. 4.

Travellers were counted in the 1956 census, but the recorded number of nomads did not even represent one per cent of the population. Ireland's indigenous minority comprised a tiny proportion of the Irish population. However, surveys of Travellers raise more questions than they answer. Who did gardaí and the census collectors decide fitted the term 'itinerant' and what determined this choice? Scholars have made little attempt to answer this vexed question in detail. In this chapter, however, I outline some significant features of Traveller culture which distinguished Travellers from the settled population, which led to the application of nouns such as 'tinker'. A fundamental need for a collective noun arises when individuals and groups are different in behaviour, occupational habits, material culture and appearance. Of course, these differences are expressed in the noun itself, but this information relies upon context and cultural definitions. To understand the historical application of nomenclature such as 'itinerant', 'tinker' or 'gypsy', we must consider the distinctive appearance and habits of these individuals. What set Travellers and Gypsies apart from the settled population?

DRESS AND APPEARANCE

Although the evidence is fragmentary, there was a perception that Travellers looked different. Labels were often ascribed on the basis of dress and appearance, but the criteria were rarely explained in detail. However, it is possible to speculate on the 'distinctive dress'[14] worn by Travellers. Women wore shawls, aprons and long skirts, a common feature of twentieth-century Irish dress in some areas until the 1960s. Large heavy shawls were worn by many Irish women in the country and cities.[15] In Cork city, shawls were a marker of social status. A middle-class Cork man remembered the stigma attached to the 'shawlies': 'There was always the worry that we might marry beneath ourselves, to a shawlie girl or someone living in the lanes'.[16] The conventions of twentieth-century Irish dress and the local, subtle gradations in fashion and social class still await comprehensive analysis. However, Traveller women retained the shawl even as mainstream fashion changed in the 1960s. The Commission on Itinerancy noted in 1963 that, 'The women dress in a manner that easily distinguishes them from the women in the settled population and usually wear a coloured rug across the shoulders, which apart from its warmth also acts as hold-all and infant-carrier.'[17] The dress of Traveller men was rarely referred to but Houlihan asserts that they wore 'bright neckerchiefs or shirts' and seldom wore the felt cap favoured by rural men.[18] Both men and women were often associated with red hair.[19] In Irish folklore tradition, red-haired women were bad luck and red hair was popularly associated with wild, ungovernable people. The proud bearing of Traveller men impressed one observer, who penned this elaborate description:

> Straight backed and light as their own ashplants, quick stepping as the ponies they drove before them, as Irish as the canabhan, hot-tempered and kind-hearted, hardy wayward clansmen and sloe-eyed pipe smoking women.[20]

Logan described how their 'swaggering, devil-may-care look' distinguished them from settled people.[21] Popular literature featuring Travellers also influenced perceptions of dress and appearance. A Traveller at Cahirmee fair was described as 'a character that might have stepped straight out of Maurice Walsh's *Road to Nowhere* or Bryan McMahon's [*sic*] *Children of the Rainbow* . . . Gay in multicoloured shirt and with a bright-hued neckerchief around his throat, he had the walk and the straight back of a tangler from Rathkeale.'[22] Interestingly, settled people expected Gypsies to be more flamboyant than 'tinkers', no doubt drawing on cultural expectations of the bohemian wanderer. Appearance seems to have influenced the term used by settled people to describe the camping families in their area. In Skibbereen, William J. Kingston remarked,

> In past years they were known as 'gipsies' but in recent years, they were more often called 'tinkers' which is more or less a term of contempt. . . . In past years gipsies looked very foreign. The men were swarthy with black straight hair and the women were blond with tow coloured or red hair. They were fond of bright coloured clothes and the women nearly always wore gay shawls. The modern gipsies or tinkers seem more ordinary in appearance and clothing.[23]

The colourful Gypsy who, strangely, never existed when contemporary wanderers were encountered is a common trope – perhaps this is an Irish example of this tendency.[24] It is clear that perceptions of appearance were determined by the standard images drawn from the European tradition of the flamboyant bohemian wanderer. When it was useful, Travellers themselves exploited this image. Women knew that fortune telling could be financially lucrative if an exotic appearance was assumed. When Nan O'Donoghue exploited her talents and the gullibility of house holders, she dressed specially.

> I tied a silk scarf on me head and went onto a little shop and bought cheap earrings – big, long, cheap earrings – and all the cheap bangles I could get and bracelets for me hands. And I put on rings. Not one was worth more than six pence. I went on then and got a good few bob.[25]

Such resemblance to the wild Gypsies earned Nan some money and confirmed popular stereotypes of 'gipsies' as exotic and 'tinkers' as plebeian. One woman from Newmarket, County Cork, commented on local tinkers, 'Some of the women, wearing long earrings pretend to tell fortunes, but as a rule we call these type "gipsies".'[26] When Travellers appeared colourful they were seen as foreign Gypsies. Similar confusion occurred when expectations of romantic Gypsy caravans were fulfilled by Traveller families driving ornate wagons.

ACCOMMODATION

Camping Travellers were easily distinguished from the settled population. Carts, tents and later horse-drawn caravans clearly set them apart as different. The mode of conveyance used by most Travellers was a light-springed cart,[27] which served as a shelter at night, often in addition to a tent. Pádraig Mac Gréine described in detail the construction and materials of tents observed in County Longford. The tent framework was wood, covered with canvas 'some of the more affluent families having a tarpaulin or waterproof cart cover for the purpose'.[28] The cover was long enough 'to form a lap at each end and so make the tent draught proof. Along the sides of the tent there is generally a foot or two of the cover to spare, which is weighted down with stones or sods'. The floor was covered with a deep bed of straw or hay and some Travellers owned mattresses or feather beds. The resulting accommodation was described as being 'snug and warm even in the coldest winter'.[29] To ensure separation of the sexes, male and female children slept in separate tents.[30] Horse-drawn, barrel caravans were used by more well-off families.[31] In 1934, caravans were observed to be spreading amongst Travellers who were abandoning their 'characteristic light-springed carts'. McEgill noted that '[the] caravan movement is spreading rapidly amongst our Irish nomads'.[32] Though McEgill viewed caravans as a Gypsy innovation, Patrick Logan disputed this, claiming that the Irish caravan was a traditional round topped, barrel-shaped tent built on a flat cart. He claimed that the English Gypsy caravans were square, built of timber and heavier.[33] When two separate sleeping quarters were required, a caravan was often augmented with a tent.[34] In December 1960, 64 surveyed families possessed both horse-drawn caravans and tents.[35] Until the 1960s tents were the second most common form of accommodation for roadside Travellers: 674 families owned horse caravans in December 1960, while 335 families lived under canvas.[36] But considerable variation in accommodation existed; Cork Travellers were relatively well off, with only one seventh depending on tent shelter alone.[37] For many Travellers, however, harsh winter weather made tents unpleasant.

Families commonly stayed in one place over the winter, often in heavy wagons or vans at the edge of urban areas. Nan Joyce's family returned to Belfast for the winter,[38] while families interviewed by Mícheál Mac Éinrí in 1937 settled around County Mayo's market towns of Ballina and Castlebar.[39] Travellers camped in suburban areas of Cork for up to six months at a time.[40] It also seems likely that empty or semi-derelict properties afforded shelter for Travellers.[41] A resident of Beara, County Cork even recalled when Travellers were offered accommodation by settled people:

> Long ago there were certain houses in each district where the tinkers used to stay – sometimes they used share their gatherings of the day with the people of the house – other times they wouldn't have enough for themselves.[42]

It is difficult to find any corroborating evidence for this practice. Some families rented accommodation in towns[43] while others turned to private lodging houses or to the publicly run County Home.[44] In 1952, the women of Kilbrittan's Irish Countrywomen's Association compiled a detailed list of Traveller families and their winter quarters: O'Driscolls wintered in Skibbereen, Foleys and O'Callaghans in Bandon, and Ryans and Sheridans in Limerick. Specific streets were associated with Travellers: 'Pound Lane in Bantry, Cat Lane in Dunmanway and Cork Road in Bandon were until recently the strongholds of the tinkers in these towns'.[45] The Briens, Coffeys and Driscolls who visited Newmarket were said to have houses in Kanturk.[46] (The nature of Traveller urban settlement is fully discussed in chapter 3.) Rathkeale was already associated with Travellers in the late 1930s when a respondent in the Schools Collection called it 'Tinkertown'.[47] The historical connection with Rathkeale of the Sheridans, Gammels, Quilligans and O'Briens is documented by Patrick O'Connor, who used census records, town plans, baptismal and marriage registers to write about an unusually distinctive Traveller population. His research revealed that the home base was as central to Travellers as nomadism itself. Regular return visits, burials and weddings in the town and the considerable investment in property testify to the importance of a traditional home base for these families.[48] Nan Joyce mused on the curious situation of Travellers without a fixed abode who nevertheless returned to the same place every winter: 'we always ended up there no matter where we came from because Belfast was like our home to us. Wherever you're reared you're always longing to go back there'.[49] Nan's winter headquarters were far from restful as they were 'hunted out' of camps in the city during the winter.[50] It was believed that winter traditionally ended on 17 March, when 'on Patrick's Day the stones turned over in the water and then the cold went out of the winter'.[51] Settled people also recognised the turning point that 17 March marked for Travellers. In 1964, the Department of Local Government asked Dublin Corporation not to evict a Traveller encampment until after St Patrick's Day, hoping that the families would move 'of their own accord'.[52]

Elderly Travellers often left the roads for housing or the County Home, the publicly run institutions for the care of the elderly.[53] In 1952, Mary Sheridan of Limerick moved into a house purchased by her sons. She was quoted in the *Sunday Press* as saying,

> at the age of 78 one does not mind settling down. All my life I have lived in a caravan, going from place to place, leading a respectable life. . . . For the rest of my days I will live in a small house but my heart will be in the caravan.[54]

Travellers were not averse to houses in principle and many maintained winter headquarters in towns. Clearly, Travellers did not want to live permanently in a house, when spring marked the beginning of the travelling season. Some families attempted to give up travelling but were isolated and ignored by their settled neighbours. Sean Maher remembered how his mother suffered intense loneliness: 'none of the neighbours would even talk to her, let alone come into our house for a visit or a cup of tea. To the townspeople we were dirty, begging tinkers and no respectable person would visit us.'[55] Housed Travellers lost touch with friends and relations because travelling facilitated contact between widely scattered family groups. Despite Maher's confessed hatred of the road, he could not remain in a house.[56] Thus not all Travellers were on the road at any one time: seasonal factors, age and personal choice determined accommodation patterns. The flexibility of accommodation patterns further complicated the state's attempts to enumerate nomads.

Although Irish Travellers lived in every part of the country, the extent of Anglo-Romany travel in Ireland is more difficult to assess. Some evidence suggests they may have preferred Leinster though they did venture beyond eastern seaboard. In 1933 the *Irish Independent* discussed the position of the Gypsy community in Ireland, North and South, noting the difficulties the economic war (an Anglo-Irish trade dispute, 1932–8) had brought to cross-border travel.

> At present, if a gipsy desired to enter Northern Ireland from the Free State, he must pay duty on his horses, ponies and dogs. There would be considerable difficulty with regard to the caravan and its furniture. In order to avoid these tariff troubles, the gipsies in both areas must remain where they are until the tariff problems are settled.

The principal Romany families in Ireland at this time were the Prices, Boswells, Lees, Lovells and Smiths, who met annually at Ballinasloe horse fair.[57] In Munster, the presence of Anglo-Romanies was also noted.[58] The Gentle family were photographed near Kinsale County Cork in 1955, suggesting that Romanies travelled far beyond Leinster.[59] Yet Gypsies appeared to be concentrated in Dublin city and its environs during the winter months. In 1936, the *Irish Press* ran an article on Gypsies living in the heart of Dublin city, in a court in Gardiner Street. Since the author, Sherley McEgill, clearly distinguished between Travellers and Gypsies in his various articles,[60] his identification of this group as Gypsies is important. Nine caravans were parked in the court 'which was spotlessly clean. All the caravans were brightly painted and the brassware shone in the winter sunshine.' Gypsy children attended the local National Schools while the adults earned their living by 'hawking linoleum to customers in the suburbs and the outlying villages in Dublin, Wicklow, Kildare and Meath'. Some also formed dance bands and performed on the streets: 'with their tiny stream-lined moustaches and Spanish apparel they bring a touch of romance and gaiety to the drab city streets in winter'.[61] Not all Gypsies parked in the city centre; a few 'preferred to spend the winter in sheltered lanes on the outskirts of the city'.[62] About 30 Gypsy caravans were noted in Terenure, County Dublin: 'it is convenient to the city and has all the amenities of rural life'. Close proximity to the new suburbs of Crumlin and Kimmage gave the women access to 'a ready market for the lengths of lino they sell at bargain prices'.[63]

It is also difficult to tell whether Travellers camped alongside Gypsies. In the 1930s, some Travellers disclaimed all contact with Gypsies:

> They are very definite on this point. They will tell you that gypsies are 'neither right not lucky,' and will stress the chief difference by adding: 'They aren't Catholics, sir and we never mix with them!'. Tinkers refer to them as gypsies, Romanies, gillies, and gillie-goolies.[64]

This may have been true of some families, but Anglo-Romanies did mix with Travellers. Nan O'Donoghue's brother married a Romany Gypsy,[65] while in

Britain, marriage between the two communities was common.[66] In Dublin city, the Society of St Vincent de Paul established a Gipsy Visitation Guild which sought out caravan dwellers with the intention of regularising marriages, and baptising and preparing children for the sacraments. It is difficult to tell whether Anglican Anglo-Romanies or Catholic Travellers were the primary object of the 'untiring zeal' of some Jesuit friars who supported the imitative, but that many of the families were from Wales is significant.[67] Since the 'Romany children' in Gardiner Street in 1936 were attending local schools and making their first Holy Communion[68] it seems that in Dublin at least, the St Vincent de Paul worked closely with Gypsies. The assertion that Travellers and Gypsies did not share the same religion is supported by a 1953 letter from a Church of Ireland clergyman, informing his co-religious that not all 'Gipsies' were Roman Catholics.

> I was formerly acquainted with a number of such families who parked their caravans on the outskirts of Dublin or even in half derelict lanes in the old parts of the city, in winter time . . . I have taken a Gipsy funeral . . . I have prepared a Gipsy girl for Confirmation. I know that several of my brethren in the vicinity of Dublin have had much experience of these people and of ministering to them.[69]

He acknowledged that it was 'difficult to distinguish the Gipsy at first from the other itinerants (the Tinkers of whom none are Protestant as far as I know)'. As most Gypsies had been in Ireland a long time, 'it is only the older ones who speak with that kind of North Wales accent which is an invariable sign of their origin'. He urged the Church of Ireland to take Gypsies 'who nominally or definitely belong to our Church under its wing'. He feared Catholic proselytisers would compromise the Protestant faith of Gypsies:

> . . . these people are being visited by Roman Catholics and Anglicans among them are encouraged to join the majority. In one encampment an energetic Roman Catholic curate was found organising a kind of 'mass confirmation' of most of the children in the caravans. An Anglican Gipsy stood out and declared that all her children would be 'done' in their own Church, no matter what happened . . . The situation was complicated by the fact that all caravans were under immediate notice from the police to leave the place; but the action was delayed until the confirmations were safely over.[70]

It seems quite possible, therefore, that the Society of St. Vincent de Paul was working with Anglican Gypsies as well as Catholic Travellers. In spite of their different and competing denominations, both groups, occasionally at least, camped together. It was the use of campsites that most distinguished both groups from the majority, housed population. Camping was also the source of the greatest conflict between nomads and property owners, with Travellers' land use patterns constrained by arbitrary policing and eviction orders. Yet apart from the limits imposed by the settled community, Travellers chose campsites to satisfy their priorities. In many ways, they exploited a landscape that was unfamiliar to settled people.

CAMPSITES: AN ALTERNATIVE GEOGRAPHY

Campsites scattered across the country formed an alternative geography for Travellers, who interpreted the landscape according to their needs. Campsites provided grazing for horses on the roadside ('the long acre') or a nearby meadow, wood for a cooking fire, shelter from strong winds and convenience to running water or to houses where water could be obtained. What settled people saw as waste or marginal land was a valuable resource for Travellers. Camps were usually set up on byroads close, but not immediately next to, houses and villages: 'They take some by-place which is not far from houses, but not exactly close by'.[71] The same places were frequented regularly – three crossroads near Mallow, County Cork, were known to the settled community as Traveller campsites.[72] In Navan, County Westmeath, Travellers still remember the names of camps that no longer exist.[73] Campsites had 'colourful nicknames that bring them to life, and perhaps serve to keep their locations fixed in the Traveller's memory'. Jody Joyce remembered camps in County Offaly called 'Saps Conderans', 'Saps Bridge', 'Hill of Clara', 'Bogtown', 'Gillan Bridge', 'Sandy Road of Ferbane', 'River Road of Birr'.[74] Patsy Joyce recalled a camp in Longford which Travellers called 'Ballrange' though the official name was Stonepark.[75] The availability of campsites was also heavily determined by the tolerance or otherwise of local gardaí, who could break up camps with impunity. Dinah Duke recalled

> It was hard at that time, because you might only have moved in, when the guard would come and tell you, you have to move on. When the guard came you would have get the children out of their beds and go looking for another camp.[76]

Campsites were not confined to idyllic rural settings; in the 1930s caravan and tent dwellers occupied vacant lots in Dublin city centre until they were evicted by Dublin Corporation.[77] Many families were forced from stable accommodation in the city to camps in the suburbs from which they were constantly moved.[78] Those who could afford to pay rent for vacant yards remained in the city, while poorer families were forced to live outside the city or leave Dublin altogether.[79] The vulnerability of Travellers to arbitrary policing and their increasingly precarious access to accommodation in post-war Ireland is well illustrated by the priority given to the motor car.

Campsites near main roads exposed Travellers to the dangers of motor traffic, an increasingly common feature of Irish roads in the post-war period. During the war years, the numbers of cars dropped significantly, from over 52,000 in 1939 to only 7,845 in 1945.[80] Once wartime restrictions ended, car numbers rose dramatically, to 44,489 licensed vehicles in 1946.[81] In 1945, James Dillon TD asked the Minister for Justice to ensure that Travellers camped on byroads rather than trunk roads. Fianna Fáil Minister Gerry Boland replied that the Garda Commissioner had been instructed 'to take all possible steps to prevent obstruction of the roads by itinerants' encampments'. Dillon was careful to clarify that Travellers should not be hounded from all roads, merely main roads:

> The poor itinerants have to live like the rest of us but the dangers attendant on their camping beside a road, involving danger to their children who run about the encampment and involving danger to the drivers of motor vehicles as a result of their wandering live stock, are far greater on the trunk road than on the by-road.[82]

In 1951, Dillon was concerned that Travellers were once again camping at the side of main roads: 'Would the Minister remind the Guards to insist that they should not make encampments on main roads for the protection of their own children?' The Minister for Justice assured the House that he would bring the matter to the attention of the gardaí as, 'the protection of the children' from road accidents was necessary.[83] The danger to children from passing traffic remained in 1957, when Dillon once again raised the matter.

> For two or three years, by a process of tactful persuasion, and perhaps something stronger, the tinkers were persuaded to abstain from setting-up camp at the side of trunk roads. In the last two or three years the practice of camping by the side of trunk roads has manifested itself very strongly again to the grave danger of the tinker's own children and to the great anxiety of passing traffic. I would ask the Minister to direct the attention of the Commissioner to that fact and to suggest to him that the Guards be asked once more to persuade these people, when they camp, not to camp at the side of main roads.[84]

Wandering animals and children on the roadside were not a significant danger until motor traffic increased; in 1957, 135,013 cars used Irish roads.[85] When horses and bicycles were replaced by the motor car, campsites on the verges of busy roads, delaying traffic, became problematic. The growth in

motor traffic and the consequent obstruction created by campsites meant that
Travellers were a visible nuisance in post-war Ireland. Motorisation is a part
of the modernisation process that has been blamed for the economic marginalisation of Travellers in post-war Ireland.[86] How Travellers and Gypsies
made a living, and the impact of 'modernisation' on the rural economy therefore deserve some consideration.

OCCUPATION

A nomadic lifestyle was well suited to the occupations preferred by Traveller
men and women. Travellers were self-employed, selling skills, items and their
labour in accordance with the demands of the market. They exploited niche
economies, and tailored their work to local circumstances. Once the chances
for work in one area had been exhausted, families could move on to pastures
new. Contemporary Travellers believe that 'what you actually work at is of
very little importance, you look for opportunities and make the best of them'.[87]
Travel patterns therefore depended on the potential for trading and begging
in an area. Micil de Paor in County Waterford said of 'na tuincéirí', 'Fhaid
agus go gheibhdís aon phoic oibre ar aon chor thimpeall an pharóiste do
dh'fhainidís thimpeall'.[88] ('As long as they could get any bit of work at all
around the parish, they would stay on'.) In an economy founded on home
production there were ample opportunities for exploiting different trades and
local demands. E. Estyn Evans's *Irish Folk Ways* brilliantly evokes the rhythm
of a society where itinerant craftsmen supplied specialist trades to scattered
settlements.[89] Settled populations needed the skills of Travellers and accorded
them a degree of respect for their craftsmanship. Travellers were popularly
associated with tinsmithing,[90] and the decline in this trade is cited as the
reason for their increased urbanisation in the post-war period.[91]

But the decline of the 'real tinker' had long been forecast: in 1913 it was felt
that 'ere long their existence will only live in tradition'.[92] The end of 'tinkering'
was lamented in 1937 with *Ireland's Own* citing enamelware as the reason for
its demise.[93] Among the Travellers interviewed by Mac Gréine, there was considerable pride in the tinsmithing trade as a 'family trade, handed down from
one generation to another'. However, a tinsmith would also deal in donkeys, or
sweep chimneys when the opportunity arose.[94] According to the Commission's
report, 30 tinsmiths also claimed to be sweeps. Among the other trades and
crafts claimed were carpenter, flower-maker, shoemaker, basketmaker, wait-
ress, tailor, dressmaker, mechanic, umbrella repairer, brushmaker, blacksmith
and welder.[95] When plastic finally usurped tinware in the 1950s, Travellers
turned to other ways of making a living. Indeed, they had always filled changing

needs in rural communities, from furnishing the poteen trade with stills to making rings from a half crown.[96] The tin trade was but one aspect of the Traveller economy; making a living on the roads depended on the ability to turn a hand to anything. When certain sources of income vanished, Travellers adapted accordingly. Judith Okely has challenged the belief that the Traveller economy suffered profound dislocation following the decline of craft skills, stressing the adaptive nature of a nomad's exploitation of niche economies.[97] For example, before the introduction of myxomatosis, men caught and sold rabbits to earn extra money.[98] Labouring work was also undertaken; the family income was supplemented with seasonal work such as potato or beet picking.[99] Farmers employed Travellers on a 'contract basis for an agreed sum per acre, or for the job'. This arrangement suited Travellers since the whole family could be employed on a task and the hours could be flexible: 'The itinerants apparently prefer this type of arrangement to working regular hours for wages'.[100] By the 1960s, most Travellers were dealers and collectors of scrap or any waste material with resale value.[101] Seasonal migration for temporary agricultural work in Britain continued among Travellers from the eastern counties.[102]

Another trade popularly associated with Travellers was horse dealing; their skill with horses was well known, though not always trusted. One County Limerick farmer never bought a horse from Travellers because he felt they were 'doped' or 'dosed', so that 'the horse would do anything he'd be asked for two weeks after'.[103] Donkeys were also traded, because 'many Irish farmers were much too proud to breed or deal in donkeys, so the trade was left to travellers'.[104] Horse dealing was the primary trade of certain families who were differentiated from the 'tinkers' by this occupation. On the Beara peninsula in County Cork, the Harringtons were not considered 'tinkers in the same sense as the Coffeys – they were horsedealers'.[105] The horse-dealing Sheridans from Limerick only visited parts of County Cork for the Cahirmee Horse Fair.[106] When tractors replaced farm horses, Travellers bought up old horses for slaughter.[107] Horses and donkeys were essential for travelling and trading, but caused the greatest tension with the settled community. On 28 August 1965, in Johnstown County Kilkenny a Traveller man was shot dead by two farmers' sons in a dispute over grazing horses.[108] The Commission hoped that the adoption of cars and vans would improve relations between Travellers and settled people as the 'trouble and injury' caused by wandering donkeys and horses would vanish.[109] However, the horse has remained an important part of Traveller culture, and central to the identity of many Traveller men. Dealing in horses remains a serious business for Traveller men and the present-day Ballinasloe horse fair is testament to its centrality.[110]

The economic activities most associated with Traveller women and children were hawking and begging, the mainstays of the subsistence economy.

Opinions of the settled people on begging varied in the sources from hostile to sympathetic, with many expressing no opinion on the practice. Mac Gréine wrote that 'they are very persistent, and present such a doleful appearance that the country people usually give them something to get rid of them'. If the proceeds of begging did not suit their requirements, they discarded these immediately 'generally a short distance from the house at which they received them'.[111] This practice would not have endeared them to alms givers, but beggars on foot could not carry large loads. A beggar could not refuse the charity offered, even if it did not match his or her needs. The relationship between supplicant and alms giver was a complex one and shaped popular opinion of Travellers. Begging and selling could 'torment the housekeepers'[112] and assertive behaviour by Travellers may have challenged perceptions of 'charity cases'.

> The country people never regarded tinkers as objects of charity as they did the poor old beggar-men and women of the old workhouse days. These poor creatures *begged*. The tinkers just *demanded* and God help anyone who left one of them leave the door empty handed. This obtains in the case of the tinkers up to the present day. They wish all kinds of ill-luck to the house and to the crops and to the cattle if they are refused their demands and people are sometimes afraid of their curses.[113] (Emphasis in original)

On the other hand, another respondent to the 1952 questionnaire noted that 'in the very act of begging they set up a feeling of superiority in the minds of those they beg from'.[114] An English visitor expressed his distaste for Travellers begging at Puck fair, but his attitude was not shared. "'And why should they not?' I was told sharply enough. 'It's a free country. It's their way of living and they've a right to that surely if they can. And they don't live on the rates. Sure, they cost nothing at all unless you like to give it.'"[115] The relationship established between those seeking and those distributing alms was intricate, drawing equally on cultural sensibilities and pragmatism.

For Travellers seeking food, clothing or money in order to survive, resorting to curses and petitions was essential and, in the context of their relatively powerless position, understandable. Moreover, that their curses were not taken too seriously is suggested by the saying 'its not worth a tinker's curse'. Prayers and blessings were companions to curses. Nan O'Donoghue knocked on the door of a house with the words "'God save everybody in'", saying "I'll say three Hail Mary's for you ma'am if you make us a cup of tea'".[116] Nan felt that householders in the West of Ireland would not give to Travellers unless God were mentioned.[117] In Nan Joyce's and Nan O'Donoghue's auto-biographies, their dislike of begging is clear. Nan Joyce commented that

'Travellers begging had to make themselves all miserable-looking before they'd be given anything but when you were selling something it was different, you felt better.'[118] But begging was unavoidable.

> Then we would start begging off the houses, a grain of flour and anything the woman would give us. A bit of meat, spuds or cabbage, lock of onions, tea or sugar or a bit of butter; we would get a bit in every house. We had to do it, we all begged with the black shawls, the children in our arms, breast-feeding them . . . The times were too hard; it was all begging.[119]

Many Travellers hawked handicrafts such as artificial flowers.[120] Nan Joyce hawked *Old Moore's Almanacs* in Belfast city.[121] Small items were peddled in rural areas, 'brooches, hair-grips, tie-pins, beads, laces and pictures'. There was a ready market for these goods among remote rural households. A basket of 'swag' would contain many small items, 'little pictures, hair combs, strainers, scissors, needles, thread, nearly everything you could mention . . . shoe laces, polish'.[122] These small articles would be sold, and food begged from the householder in the process.

It seems that the occupations pursued by Gypsies distinguished them from Travellers and may have helped settled people to identify them. While Travellers were popularly associated with tinsmithing and horse dealing, Gypsies made baskets and wickerwork furniture.[123] In County Cork, 'their principle [*sic*] work is making baskets, tables, chairs etc of twigs. They pitch their camps near places where they can get the twigs, the articles are sold from door to door. They also sell such stuff as floor covering, mats and brushes'.[124] Like Travellers, their craft skills came under pressure from changing markets and tastes.

> In former years, the gipsies who toured Ireland specialised in the sale of basketware. They still sell wickerwork but this trade is no longer lucrative. They now tour the country with rolls of linoleum. There is always a brisk demand for this article in rural areas and very few cottagers can resist the appeal of the eloquent Romany saleswoman when they display their goods.[125]

However, Gypsies followed a similar pattern of self-employment to Travellers and varied their trades to match local circumstance and commercial expediency. Men unable to prosper in basket making turned to collecting 'wastepaper, rags and scraps'.[126] In common with Travellers, it was women, rather than men, who sold door-to-door.[127] It was not the decline of the craft economy alone that distanced Travellers from settled people, for the tin trade was replaced with alternative ways of earning a living. Changing attitudes to their position in Irish society cannot be attributed to economic obsolescence alone. As their subsistence economy was also heavily dependent upon the generosity of the settled community, the questions of charity, and alms-giving cannot be ignored.

Before the spread of the cash economy in the 1940s, farmers and smallholders grew their own vegetables, reared chickens, cured bacon, kept milk cows and made butter. Food, not cash, was given as alms. Since every household produced a small food surplus, there was ample available for Travellers who called to the door. The growth of the rural bus service and motorisation has been blamed for ending the market for Traveller hawkers[128] but the increased monetarisation of the rural economy had other effects also. As farmers specialised and concentrated on commercial production, they ceased to produce their own food.[129] Households purchased goods in market towns, replacing farm produce with food from the grocery shop. There was no longer a potato pit in the back garden, or a side of bacon hanging from the rafters to share with Travellers. Government regulations also discouraged home production. Rules on pig slaughter made it illegal to kill a pig on an unlicensed premises and James Dillon sprang to the defence of the marginal rural economy. He asked the Fianna Fáil Minister for Agriculture to 'bear in mind that in certain parts of the country there are thatchers, weavers and itinerant persons who earn their living sometimes – not exclusively, but largely – by going around doing services for their neighbours'. He hoped that this practice would not be outlawed by new legislation; 'If you make it quite clear that the person who comes to my house, kills a pig, cures it, takes a cup of tea and gets a present, is not committing an offence, it would do.'[130] These developments in the rural economy did not affect all areas of the country equally[131] and Travellers may not have been immediately and dramatically worse off. Another fundamental shift in Irish society that is imperfectly understood is the decline of fairs and markets. However, this change in the social and economic calendar of town and country had considerable implications for the status of Travellers.

SPECTACLE: FAIRS, FIGHTS AND FUNERALS

Fairs and markets were central to Irish life. From weekly or monthly markets in towns and villages to the great annual fairs, it was by these gatherings rather than the calendar that the rural community measured time.[132] Religious festivals, called 'patterns' because of their association with patron saints of an area, also hosted great fairs until they were suppressed by Church authorities.[133] Markets in town and city centres drew country people and Travellers seeking a bargain or a chance to trade. Traveller caravans and wagons were often parked in the Coal Quay market in Cork city's Cornmarket Street.[134] At such gatherings, people of all classes and origins met and mingled, among them Travellers and Gypsies. Wealthy farmers and dealers rubbed shoulders with beggars, ballad singers, fiddlers, pedlars, and gamesters. Markets in large county towns also attracted the urban working class: Macroom, Fermoy, Mitchelstown and Mallow in County Cork drew Cork city street traders anxious to do business.[135] Even into the nineteenth century, cock-fighting and bull-baiting were part of the sport of great fairs; games and horse racing survived into the twentieth.[136] Historically, fairs such as the infamous Donnybrook fair were occasions for lawlessness and bloodshed.[137] Fairs in Munster and South Leinster gave faction fighters occasions to renew their ritualistic violent antagonism.[138] A great seasonal gathering of people from near and far was licence for a cathartic 'moral holiday' that was often linked to fertility magic.[139] By the twentieth century, the excesses of faction fighting had ended but ritualistic elements survived. Arensberg and Kimball observed the 'elaborately conventional'[140] economic aspects of fairs in County Clare, detailing the relationship between the small farmer and the cattle dealer rather than the social significance of the gathering for the local community. 'Luck money' was exchanged between buyer and seller after the conclusion of the deal while the 'tangler', often a Traveller man, acted as intermediary to secure a sale. Historians seeking information on class and communal relationships cannot ignore these great social and economic occasions, which were not exclusively rural. Cork city hosted horse fairs within its boundaries at least until 1921[141] and the Munster Agricultural Show was a significant social event for town and country. Fairs were particularly important for Travellers, who renewed friendships and allegiances with families seen only once or twice a year while trading and begging among the large crowds. The patterns that had survived – Clonmacnoise, Knock, Lough Derg, Croagh Patrick – also attracted large numbers of Travellers. Similarly, race meetings at Galway, Mallow and Fairyhouse were highlights of the Traveller calendar.[142]

Travellers congregated in large numbers at the edge of the town hosting the fair. One Cork man commented that Travellers 'never fail to make the days more interesting for their presence'.[143] For a number of days, Travellers and settled people traded and drank together in a confined space. Fair gatherings of Travellers demonstrated the enduring success of their lifestyle as well as the coherence of their material culture. They were a routine part of every local fair, though they gathered in larger numbers at the great fairs of Spancil Hill, Ballinasloe, Puck and Cahirmee. Their presence in such large numbers was viewed with ambivalence by settled observers who were made uneasy by 'the great nomad army'.[144] In the run-up to Cahirmee Horse Fair in

Buttevant, County Cork, the countryside was described as 'infested with roving bands of humble horse dealers, gipsy vans and encampments'.[145] However, their presence also provoked poetic description and nostalgia for times past, which Travellers were seen to embody. Cahirmee had 'lost none of its ancient and "old world" glamour for the "travelling people" of Munster' whose 'gaily bedecked caravans' and piebald ponies converged on the town.[146] The colour and spectacle of Travellers' camps hinted at the gay abandon of an approaching holiday.

The centrepiece of Cahirmee fair from 1949 to 1958 was the Caravan Parade, called in 1955 the National Romany Caravan Parade. This competition for best caravan was organised by the fair committee and eagerly contested by Travellers, whose colourful caravans evoked images of roving Gypsies. The 'gay garlanded magnificence, the beribboned horses, the decorated caravans'[147] offered an irresistible opportunity for newspaper correspondents to romanticise Travellers. For the *Kerryman* reporter and the carnival organisers, Traveller material culture dovetailed with literary allusions to exotic Gypsies, with whom 'tinkers' compared unfavourably. The arrival of caravan and tent dwellers in Killorglan for the Puck fair was described thus: 'the gypsies with their gaily coloured wagons and their friends in less polite beggary, the tinkers'.[148] Yet this distinction was far from absolute, for 'gaily attired Romany youths' were part of the Cahirmee parade in 1953, yet the prizes were won by Sheridans from Cork, Rathkeale and Limerick respectively.[149] The strange contradiction in settled people's perceptions cannot be easily understood, but it suggests that the popular definitions of 'tinker' were relatively fluid. In certain contexts, observers were willing to see Travellers embodying 'the romance of bohemian life'.[150] In 1955, the parade attracted 21 caravans and more than 7,000 spectators. It was an event 'unique and strikingly impressive in all its richness of gay, brilliant, carefree nomadic life'. The *Kerryman* correspondent lauded the parade as 'a presence of the way of life that has kept Cahirmee of the Horses as, perhaps, the last surviving institute of times that are gone but can never be forgotten'. Remarkably, the task of maintaining tradition was laid firmly on the shoulders of 'the travelling folk and the horse dealing people of Munster'.[151] While Travellers were exoticised in descriptions of Cahirmee, it must be acknowledged that the fair itself was praised in terms that blended romanticism and hyperbole in equal measure. The *Kerryman* wrote of Cahirmee,

> It was a word that brought a breath of romance to the workaday world in which we lived. Entwined in every letter of it was an atmosphere that gave forth the exotic scents of the Orient, and the clink of Russian spurs and the rattle of French sabres.[152]

The glorious past when Cahirmee drew buyers from across Europe was constantly invoked in newspaper reports. The proud display of material culture in Cahirmee's caravan parade was unique to Buttevant, although Puck Fair's organising committee attempted to copy the successful tourist attraction in 1955.[153]

At most fairs Travellers were well known for fighting. This was seen as integral to the spectacle of fair day and since Travellers fought each other, settled people found it entertaining rather than threatening, 'It was a blood sport you watched in fascination and fear and when the ash plants came out the spectators retreated to a safe distance.'[154] The intervention of the gardaí was inevitable even expected: 'A fair day was no fair day without work for Guard Jordan and Jim Kennedy but a night in the cells cooled off everyone . . . There was an even predictable tenor to life.'[155] Grudges were rarely held and the combatants were often reconciled immediately. Thus people who quarrelled frequently but remained friends were said to be 'like the tinkers'.[156] In the context of a fair day, both street fighting and colourful caravans formed settled people's reactions to Travellers. The spectacle provided by exotic, wild and carefree nomads was a vital part of the fair. Spectacle permitted admiration but maintained distance; it acknowledged difference while containing it as harmless entertainment.

Other Traveller rituals conducted during a fair could also grab the headlines. A spectacular Traveller funeral in 1945 popularised the idea of the 'King of the Tinkers'. John Ward's funeral in May 1945 coincided with the sheep fair in Ballinasloe and 10,000 people were estimated to have attended.[157] Travellers came from Counties Leitrim, Offaly, Roscommon, Tipperary, and Clare to attend the service. Members of the general public also attended as the Wards were 'associated with the life of Ballinasloe for generations'.

> The final tribute of his tribe was a moving spectacle, with women in many coloured shawls and dress and the traditional red petticoats and men of wiry fibre and physique set up a keening around the grave.[158]

John Ward had apparently earned his crown by a combination of descent and pugilistic abilities. In the Ward family, male fighting prowess earned the title of 'King of the Tinkers', a role that fascinated settled observers. Lawrence Ward succeeded his father John as King and his crowning drew media attention across the British Isles.[159] Lawrence was reportedly proclaimed King by 400 members of the Ward family, who offered £100 as the prize in a challenge fight. No one accepted the challenge and Ward, who had already won 13 free fights defending his title, was acclaimed King. The ceremony was watched by several hundred people visiting Ballinasloe who 'gushed and jostled each other . . . in a frantic effort to get a front line view of the crowning of the

"Tinker's King'". The ceremony concluded when Ward was presented with six white horses and a new caravan.[160] Cultural rituals conducted in public at large fair gatherings demonstrated Travellers' distinctive appearance and behaviour. Funerals, wakes, fairs and fights played an important role in determining perceptions of Travellers.

For Travellers, the true importance of fair day was the opportunity it afforded to meet friends and relations, and celebrate weddings and baptisms.[161] This social function was of little relevance to settled observers, who saw a pageant of colour and carefree abandon. The cultural function of fighting in Traveller society remains poorly understood. Outside interference in these fights was not appreciated: 'The travellers have a strict code with regard to these fights. They see it as their own business to be settled by themselves.'[162] Keening, which remains an important part of Traveller burial rituals, was for the outside observer merely a 'Moving Spectacle'.[163] Within specific contexts, Travellers were rendered picturesque by settled people. Perceptions of Travellers as colourful and exotic may have played a significant role in mediating relations between the two communities. Romanticisation can be disparaged but it could counter pejorative stereotypes. Since close contact between Travellers and settled people was confined to certain limited contexts, settled people could hardly avoid romantic constructs of a culture they saw, but did not understand. Spectacular occasions such as fairs, fights and funerals gave ample opportunity for observation but little for participation. The conclusions drawn from these observations were determined by settled values that were not static; attitudes towards street violence appear to have altered dramatically. Houlihan said of Traveller fights at Puck, 'Before opinions changed it was something of a sideshow at the fair, which drew, rather than scattered crowds.'[164] After the Second World War, contact between the two communities at fairs declined as tractors replaced horses, and cattle marts on the edge of towns made traditional street fairs redundant. These developments took place suddenly 'without anybody realising what a difference it would make'.[165] Possibly Travellers continued to adhere to an obsolete calendar of fairs, visiting certain towns because of old associations. Nioclás Breatnach recalled Travellers from Tipperary visiting Dungarvan County Waterford after the horse fair that had originally drawn them had ended.[166] The decline in these regular, formulaic often ritualistic gatherings, ended a vital social outlet for Travellers as well as another niche economy. For settled people, Traveller visits may have seemed an intrusive nuisance without the structural justification of a fair.

CONCLUSION

The meeting of urban and rural at fairs in a market town encapsulates the interdependent nature of two societies that are often seen as mutually exclusive. Travellers have been portrayed as inherently rural, but in their famous study of peasant society in County Clare, Arensberg and Kimball cast doubt on this truism. 'Tinkers' were a 'special case', 'whose ties are with the towns and whose visits to country districts are short and predatory'.[167] Historical evidence demonstrates that both Travellers and Gypsies earned their living in urban and rural areas, but their position was not secure in either milieu. The nature of a nomad's economy, which depended on self-employment and niche markets, was always vulnerable to changing tastes. The twentieth century witnessed a number of economic developments that forced craftsmen to almost wholly abandon craft skills in favour of dealing and waste collection. By focusing on this development, popular and scholarly opinion has ignored the contribution of women and children, whose selling and begging were essential elements of the family economy. Those skills also came under pressure from social and economic change, particularly as rural dwellers were drawn away from subsistence agriculture by monetarisation. The rise of the motor car and the decline of the fair also greatly affected the visibility and acceptability of Travellers in rural Ireland.

Throughout this chapter, the term 'Traveller' has differentiated indigenous nomads from families with Romany origins. Although Anglo-Romanies are no longer popularly distinguished from Travellers, the historical application of the two terms was significant. While the confusion in applying labels such as 'tinker' or 'gipsy' reflected a complex interplay between social attitudes and popular images of exotic bohemians, it also described two nomadic groups. The confusion of the terms often reflected observed differences that were imperfectly understood. Travellers in expensive, ornate caravans may have appeared to be Gypsies, but it is likely that those families were more economically successful than tent dwellers. Perhaps settled people were using those terms to describe class difference in Traveller society, an issue further discussed in chapter 5. However, the ambiguous use of such collective nouns also illustrates the breadth of social distance between nomads and settled people. With the addition of long earrings and cheap bangles, Nan O'Donoghue could, in spite of her accent and name, be transformed from a lowly tinker into a foreign bohemian. Since both groups lived in caravans and tents, they shared a form of accommodation that set them apart from settled society. Travellers and Gypsies were also separate from vagrant men and women whose position and status in Irish society were unlike those of nomads.

TWO

INTIMATE STRANGERS

THE PEOPLE OF THE ROADS

—

Alongside Travellers and Anglo-Romany gypsies, an amorphous group of individual wanderers took to the roads for subsistence. This chapter will describe the vagrants who travelled Irish roads, outlining the social contexts of their dealings with the majority, housed population. In common with many European countries, Ireland's mobile population included the poor and tradesmen as well as Romany or indigenous nomads.[1] Beggars, the wandering insane, pedlars, traders, ballad singers and entertainers went from place to place, earning their living from the communities they visited. However, the reactions to urban and rural vagrancy were separate and distinct phenomena. Alms giving to regular, familiar beggars was a feature of rural County Cork while street begging in Cork city was decried as a 'nuisance'. Homeless people in urban areas were accommodated in hostels run by charitable organisations; in the countryside a bed by the fire was offered. In order to clearly distinguish the label 'vagrant' from 'tinker' or 'gipsy' we must understand the survival strategies of homeless men and women in twentieth-century Ireland. Whether wandering beggars were accepted or ostracised by the housed population must also be analysed. Examinations of popular nationalism argue that mobile communities are constructed as the antithesis to a bourgeois, respectable body politic.[2] The social implications of political nationalism, enforced by gunmen representing the 'local community', has been discussed by Peter Hart, whose analysis reveals much about the confusion between labels such as 'tramp' and 'tinker'. This chapter describes how individual beggars and nomadic families did not receive the same reception from the settled population. However the progressive decline in the numbers of the mobile poor left Travellers alone in exploiting niche economies and the charitable spirit of house-dwellers.

THE HOMELESS IN TWENTIETH-CENTURY IRELAND

Vagrancy in Ireland has received little scholarly attention, apart from Caitríona Clear's brief outline of the situation pertaining in Galway in the late nineteenth and early twentieth centuries. Clear is careful to point out that the 'tramps and vagrants' featuring in police reports and workhouse registers were unlikely to be Travellers, as 'Complete families of travelling traders and craftsmen were never identified as a public order problem by the police or poor law authorities in this period'. Nomadic families had 'transport, tools of a trade . . . and most importantly of all, the travelling man was seen to be supporting his wife and family'. From 1850 to 1914, it was 'unaccompanied men in their 20s', who gave rise to political and police concern.[3] Vagrant men were often seeking labouring work and, with no skills or trade, they struggled to subsist in a society with limited employment prospects. Women were a minority among convicted vagrants, as destitute females were more likely to be offered aid by voluntary and statutory agencies, and also more likely to be placed 'in a workhouse, hostel or asylum'.[4] The profile of twentieth-century vagrants remained overwhelmingly male, as able-bodied men took to the roads to eke out a living.

From the foundation of the state, the homeless were excluded from official consideration and often denied basic services. The Commission examining the Poor Law commented, 'although this class are not recognised we know that they exist'.[5] Although it was outside its terms of reference, the 1927 Commission report briefly alluded to homelessness. As detailed earlier, a survey revealed that 3,257 people were without accommodation on a single night in November 1925.[6] Men represented 53 per cent of those homeless, women 21 per cent and children 26 per cent. Since the number of homeless people was small, the Commission merely recommended that 'it may be necessary in Cork, Dublin, Waterford and Limerick to set aside special accommodation for this class'.[7] This provision was necessary because 'these people complained of the great loss they suffered by the closing of the workhouses. In the old days they always got a few nights lodging in such institutions.'[8] The exclusion of the homeless from public institutions was part of the new state's reform programme for the poor relief system. The Department of Local Government and Public Health explained that hatred of the workhouse sprang from its association with vagrants and 'the physical wreckage of the population'.[9] Vagrants were unwelcome in the newly respectable county home (a new name for old institutions) where people availing themselves of indoor relief would not be expected to associate with 'the undesirable elements of humanity'.[10] When the respectable poor were accommodated in the county home, the homeless were excluded. The policy of the independent state was to deny homeless men and women entry to public institutions, expecting voluntary organisations to provide for them.[11] The role of these organisations and the general public in supporting destitute individuals will be analysed here.

RURAL HOMELESSNESS

The paucity of knowledge about the lowest levels of Irish society has led those writing about Travellers to ignore other individuals living on the roads. From the Schools Collection gathered by the Folklore Commission in 1937–8, it is clear that Travellers were not alone in using nomadism to maximise subsistence living opportunities. Children's accounts from County Cork under the heading 'Travelling Folk' are peopled with colourful, often tragicomic local characters 'Paddy Wheel About',[12] 'Dan the fiddler'[13] and 'Jerry the Quality'.[14] As information was sought under the heading 'an lucht siúil' (literally, the walking people), this source should not be taken as a comprehensive survey of Travellers alone, who would have been more readily identified as 'na tincéirí' (the tinkers). The interpretation of 'an lucht siúil' as beggars or Travellers varied from school to school though the majority of teachers and pupils chose to discuss the vagrant homeless. From the information contained in the Schools Collection, we can roughly identify three different categories of traveller: those who sought lodgings, those who sought alms and those who sold items or a skill. These wanderers were largely separate from Travellers and Gypsies.

Male tramps seeking lodgings travelled a regular circuit, staying with the same families for one night before moving on to the next household on their route. Many were not wholly sane, some were ex-soldiers[15] or former inmates of Industrial Schools.[16] What is striking about these individuals is that although sometimes unconventional and occasionally of questionable sanity, they were written about with considerable affection and sympathy by the school children. They were part of the local population; their dress, habits and family history were well known. This mostly male vagrant population was integrated into the local community and though they lived on charity, one child described them as 'respectable travellers'.

> These men do not ask for alms. They usually call at dinner time or at tea time. We invite them to join us and they regale us with stories of their adventures while the meal is in progress. They give us news of our friends in Kilkenny, Waterford or Limerick.[17]

Though they did not ask for assistance, these men were offered shelter and food. In exchange they told stories, brought news, sang songs or played an instrument.[18] This was a legitimate currency in a society where entertainment was largely self-made and any diversion from routine gossip welcomed. Women were increasingly rare visitors and one woman said 'Travelling women often came around but [now] no women come except gypsy and tinker women'.[19] Some informants believed that the numbers of beggars had declined within living memory.[20] Beggars may have been less numerous, but they remained part of the community, where they were 'generally welcome in the houses because they are like old friends of the family'.[21]

   Those seeking alms rather than lodging depended on a popular religious culture that praised unquestioning generosity offered to a nameless, unknown wanderer, who was later revealed to be the Mother of God or Christ himself.[22] In a similar way to Travellers, men and women seeking alms sought charity with prayers and blessings: 'He began his prayers and petitions before reaching the house and continued them for some time after entering the kitchen, in a continuous stream of words.'[23] A beggar would receive alms with blessings such as 'May God spare your health', or 'May God increase your store'.[24] The elaborate ending of a petition used by a Mrs O'Donoghue from Macroom was recalled by one informant:

> Ná fhaghad-sa bás go deo go mbéarfaidh mé solas na Nodlag liom! Go saoraidh Dia ó bás i ndorchacht na h-oíche sinn! Go dtugaidh Dia grásta na foidhne daoibh-se is domhsa chun trioblóidí an tsaoghail seo imochar go fulangach foidhneac, agus beannacht Dé le h-anmann na marbh agus le nbhúr n-anam féin ar uair bhúr mbáis![25]

> May you not die at all until I return with the light of Christmas! May God save us from death in the darkness of the night! May God give the grace of patience to you all and to me to carry patiently and passively the troubles of life and God's blessings be with the souls of the dead and your own souls on the hour of your death!

The practice of generous hospitality was also upheld by a secular folklore tradition that told of liberality rewarded and meanness punished.[26] One child recounted a local apocryphal tale in which a beggar woman refused lodgings brought a plague of rats upon a family that ended only when she was granted £10 and lodgings for the rest of her life.[27] Despite the overwhelmingly positive depiction of tramps in this source, not everyone was welcoming; 'some people like to see them coming but others have no welcome for them'.[28] The authorities were not necessarily sympathetic to the plight of these vagrants; in 1925, the persistent begging of a 'deaf, dumb imbecile' in County Cork was suppressed by gardaí.[29] Yet police action was not necessary to suppress mendicant begging as the numbers of rural vagrants were diminishing. Their passing was regretted by 'some of the older people [who] were actually glad to welcome them and offer them food and shelter'.[30] The state pension was cited as one reason for the decline in the numbers of elderly people on the roads.[31] Improvements in the welfare system no doubt affected settled people's opinion of begging and alms giving. Universal unemployment benefit was codified in the Public Assistance Act 1933, but it was 1938 before benefits were sufficiently generous to improve the lot of the Irish poor (see chapters 3 and 4). As state subsistence was seen to improve, tax and rate payers may have felt that individual alms giving was no longer needed. Under these circumstances, tolerance for begging may have declined. For the poorest, more generous benefits probably ended the need for begging. The decline in the numbers of beggars left Travellers and Gypsies alone on the roads, and alone in exploiting begging as part of a subsistence economy.

Individuals with a trade also travelled the countryside to find a market for their skills and goods. For example, a clockmender visited rural parts of County Cork, staying in one house for a couple of weeks until the neighbourhood had exhausted the need for his services.[32] Ireland's sparse population and scattered settlements were unsuited to permanent retailers. Pedlars were able to earn a living from travelling the roads, selling to every house they passed.[33] Selling goods door to door was a licensed trade under the Hawkers and Pedlars Acts. In March 1924, 186 hawkers' licences were issued.[34] James Dillon was anxious to protect the hawker from criminalisation under new legislation in 1938, which gave the Minister for Industry and Commerce increased power over trading and retailers (see appendix). Urban hawkers who sold fruit, vegetables fish and flowers were excluded from the Bill's provisions but the 'ordinary wares' traded by the rural hawker, 'tin pannikins, caps for pipes' were not also exempt.[35] It was unlikely that all travelling sellers were licensed and, for some hawkers, trading was a pretence to cover the solicitation of alms. Beggars whose hawking was a little more than a legal fiction were vigorously defended by Dillon.

> If the Minister lived in a country town, as most Deputies do, he would know that he had three or four very good friends amongst that class – familiar friends who have come in collecting twopence or threepence on one day per week. They come most religiously on that day and would be ashamed to come on any other day. They have a regular route. They are old friends and they circumnavigate the regulations prohibiting their activities by selling studs or bootlaces or something of that kind, so that if a Civic Guard came on the scene you can grab a pair of bootlaces and protest that you were engaged in a commercial transaction; that there was no eleemosynary element in operation at all. I know that it sounds

absurd to be talking about these things, but these people will be guilty of a statutory offence if they offer these commodities, and they will be caught.[36]

Dillon's passionate advocacy defending the rhythms of rural life was not supported by any other Dáil deputy. Whether the legislation was enforced against rural beggars posing as hawkers, or Travellers selling tinware is impossible to judge, but legislation criminalising unregulated trading was on the statute book.

URBAN HOMELESSNESS

Although the homeless were found in higher concentrations in large towns and cities, their place and function in society are difficult to determine.[37] The Society of St Vincent de Paul became concerned for homeless men following the closure of the workhouses after independence. The workhouse casual ward and the accommodation it provided for men travelling to find work or those too poor to afford lodgings vanished. The local Public Assistance Officer was expected to make provision for poor travellers and Society members were urged to bring cases to the attention of the authorities or to find lodgings for the poor. The Society's President, Sir Joseph Glynn, stressed that 'most of these men are looking for work and should not be allowed to sink into the mendicant classes'.[38] The South Cork county home was the only institution to officially provide for casual inmates who stayed for a night or two, although their numbers were small.[39] Homelessness in urban areas was largely ignored by government relief agencies who left accommodation for 'casuals' to private charity. One reason for this neglect was the contrasting forms of relief offered by the state and voluntary organisations. Rate and tax-funded relief agencies perceived their task as offering assistance in securing the essentials of life, rather than the reform or rehabilitation that vagrants needed. The Commission on Poor Relief believed that government agencies were not suited to the task of rescue work among the vulnerable in society. Voluntary schemes were successful precisely because they were 'voluntary and actuated by higher motives than the provision of material necessities'.[40] Better results could be achieved by voluntary charity and this division of responsibility was accepted by the private and public sector. Yet the state sector, however reluctantly, continued to offer temporary accommodation to homeless men and women.

Casuals in county homes constituted a tiny fraction of the population receiving indoor relief, so small in numbers that they were not annually categorised in the figures for indoor and outdoor relief.[41] In March 1950, they represented just 139 people out of a total population in county homes of

8,585.[42] However occasional their appearance, the casuals were problematic for some institutions. The Health Bill 1952 contained a clause[43] specifically written in response to the perceived problems caused by casual admittances. The Fianna Fáil Minister for Health, Dr James Ryan, cited the rowdy and disruptive behaviour of tramps and casuals, which necessitated legislation that branded a patient a criminal if he or she did not obey institutional rules. The Minister claimed that county homes which admitted drunk casuals the night before a local race meeting required additional powers to cope with them.[44] Indeed, Dr Ryan could not see 'how a county home could be run without the powers laid down in the sub-section'.[45] Deputies argued that a power designed to counter exceptional troublemakers should not be applied to all patients in the county home.[46] Mr Thomas Kyne, simultaneously striving for hyperbole and horror, called it 'the Belsen Camp section of the Health Bill'.[47] Dr Ryan was unmoved, wondering 'why Deputies should go absolutely berserk on the idea of the liberty of the individual and allow our old people to be disturbed in their night's rest in the interests of this sort of theoretical liberty'.[48] Following a lengthy debate, the Minister modified his position and offered to redraft the section,[49] perhaps conceding that legislation based on the drunken antics of a few 'blackguards' represented poor law.

In addition to county homes, common lodging houses provided accommodation for homeless men in urban Ireland. Liam O'Flaherty's use of a lodging house in his fictional work, *The Informer* (1925)[50] and George Orwell's painful account (1933) of 'doss houses' in England[51] show the world of the casual lodging house, where rooms were rented by the night. An individual lodging house in Cork city could accommodate between three and 45 men, with a Salvation Army hostel offering 79 beds in 1919.[52] The number of beds available changed annually as lodging houses were demolished, sold, closed for public health reasons or returned to domestic use. By 1943, only five common lodging houses remained in Cork.[53] The St Vincent de Paul maintained night shelters in Dublin city for men 'travelling from place to place'[54] and the Society's shelter for 'Catholic men' lodged between 80 and 90 men a night.[55] Society brothers also visited public lodging houses on Sunday mornings to provide breakfast and encourage prayer.[56] In Dublin, applications by casuals to the county home were discouraged as officials expected voluntary organisations to provide accommodation and services for homeless men.[57] The men using the county home or night shelters inevitably begged to earn enough money to survive.

When the poor resorted to begging, the law was not kindly disposed towards them. In Dublin, a man described by police as 'a regular nuisance' was sentenced to one month's imprisonment for street begging.[58] In 1924, police attention focused on homeless men begging in Dublin city. Their physical disabilities did not inspire much pity in *The Irish Times* editor whose comments bore an uncanny resemblance to Ebenezer Scrooge's infamous entreaty on workhouses and prisons.

> We hold that these poor cripples have a moral right to assistance in their unequal battle with life. Their place, however, is not upon the streets and their deformities ought not to be a tax upon the city's impatient and promiscuous charity. There are hospitals and homes which they are entitled to enter, and we are sure that the police and municipal authorities will not invite the aid of such institutions in vain.[59]

Dublin policemen had instructions to move 'deformed mendicants' from the streets although they were present only in limited areas of the city.[60] The extent to which these beggars actually caused a nuisance is questionable. A city centre police sergeant told his Superintendent: 'It is however difficult to get rid of this class of people as invariably they do not beg or importune passers-by and are most careful not to cause obstruction.'[61] Their very existence and the tactless exposition of their deformities in Dublin's public streets were the only nuisance they appeared to create.

Cork city in 1926 was described as 'The Beggar's Mecca'. A *Cork Examiner* columnist maintained that begging was now 'open and undisguised, without the least cover or excuse' whereas in the past, beggars had been 'so closely watched by the Constable that he or she always covered the begging trade with a pretence of selling boot-laces, shirt-buttons or some other thing'.[62] The writer felt that no 'deserving person' would need to beg in Cork as 'such splendid provision for the relief of the poor is made by the citizens of this most charitable city through the organisations chartered to fight the want and misery that will always be with us'.[63] Yet St Vincent de Paul members in Cork found 1925 particularly difficult because of the 'unprecedented amount of local distress'.[64] In 1926, the Society 'sought to protect its members from the danger of regarding their Society as a philanthropic society, [and] the public from the risk of looking upon it as a municipal or public relief organisation'.[65] In February 1926, Superintendent Mansfield described begging in the city as 'a thorough scandal'; 'Mendicants were coming to the city from all parts of the Free State and were doing a thriving business in Cork'.[66] The presence of beggars was unsurprising given the distress and poverty present in the city and county. There was such 'exceptional distress' in the city and surrounding districts in 1926, that the authorities abandoned the gospel of fiscal rectitude and sought to borrow to cover the cost of increased relief.[67] Conditions only began to ameliorate in 1941 'mainly owing to increased public assistance, and to the employment of a large number of men at high wages in England'.[68] Begging remained a feature of the Cork streetscape until at least 1945.[69]

In times of persistent poverty, homelessness and begging must have been the fate of many.

TRAMPS OR TINKERS?

Although Travellers exploited mobility, niche economies and charity, they were received differently from individual tramps. The position of vagrants serves to illustrate the status accorded nomads by the settled population. Possessing tents and caravans, Travellers remained outside the intimate family circle that admitted tramps yet both groups depended on charity offered by householders. As government regulation and social welfare expansion reduced the numbers of wandering beggars, the tolerance accorded to Travellers who continued to seek alms may have diminished. There were differences and similarities in the reception extended to vagrants and Travellers by the settled population. Reflecting a certain ambivalence, householders were not always definitive in their application of the terms 'tinker' and 'tramp'.

The extent of the differences in attitudes has been discussed by Peter Hart in his work on the Irish Republican Army (IRA) in County Cork from 1916 to 1923. His powerful account of the victims of IRA violence and how they were perceived as irredeemably different by armed revolutionaries became an instant classic of Irish historiography. He documents how the marginal status of a chronically poor underclass made them vulnerable to class-inspired violence, arguing that the violent nationalism unleashed in County Cork targeted the marginal and 'unrespectable' with the tacit compliance of the wider community. The 'first and most obvious targets' for the IRA were, according to Hart, the 'tramps' and the 'tinkers'. However, he was forced to acknowledge the positive portrayals of wandering men in the Schools Collection. Thus 'familiar tramps' were welcomed in farmhouses but 'itinerant strangers' or '"tribes" of tinkers' were resented.[70] Despite acknowledging the differences between tinkers and tramps, Hart seems anxious to equate the labels. For example, his table of victims has one category – 'tinker/tramp' – for two groups he had earlier asserted were received very differently by 'respectable' society.[71] The deaths of lone tramps suggests that the IRA did target individual vagrants but the author does not clarify how this violence was reconciled with the welcome afforded to 'familiar tramps'.

Hart's analysis covers many complex issues of social organisation without referring to the problems of categorisation that are exacerbated by the dearth of significant Irish social history studies. The real difficulties in interpreting collective nouns or class labels are rarely alluded to. No doubt the sources were not clear or consistent in their application of the terms, 'tinker' and 'tramp'.

Indeed, by citing the killing of Mick O'Sullivan in detail, the author reveals the ambiguous use by the gunmen of the label 'tinker'. O'Sullivan was a street-singer and cattle drover, an ex-soldier, 'a very raggedy individual, a kind of tinker and hard nail'.[72] The description of O'Sullivan as a 'kind of tinker' is odd. Whether 'tinker' in this context refers to a Traveller or a tramp is impossible to say. His army background also made him vulnerable; although eight per cent of those shot by the IRA were categorised as 'Tinker/Tramp', 29 per cent and 36 per cent of victims were ex-servicemen and Protestants respectively.[73] How were victims who fitted more than one category, for example a tramp or Traveller with a service record, treated in Hart's categorisation? A flaw in Hart's work is his fluid use of nomenclature in the narrative and the final, decisive categories presented in the statistics. The difficulty of picking out Travellers from tramps, and tramps from ex-servicemen is not fully explained. What of the ubiquitious urban cornerboy, often an ex-serviceman and occasionally a tramp? The indistinct boundaries between labels is not foregrounded, as Hart's primary narrative concerns violent political mobilisation rather than the messy categorisations that distinguish Irish social organisation. Finally, his statement that 'as the IRA often killed tinkers, tramps, and other loners and outsiders who might never be missed, some of the killings will surely never come to light'[74] must be also challenged. Travellers may have been outside settled society but they were not necessarily 'loners'. The family of a Traveller shot by the IRA would have sought a body for burial. Therefore, questions of definition and categorisation dog any consideration of the status of Travellers and individual beggars.

As part of the effort to determine who is a Traveller, the question of origins must be raised. How can Travellers be distinguished from large numbers of homeless individuals or families? Examinations of the mobile population are complicated the inconsistent use of collective nouns by record keepers whose primary concern was not social differentiation among the people they documented. Charitable organisations and government officials were preoccupied with questions of entitlement and welfare, not the differences between nomads and vagrants. Gmelch and Gmelch have proposed that Travellers' developed an ethnic identity owing to increasing isolation from the settled community and the growth of a distinctive material culture. Controversially, they propose that an established Traveller population – its origins lost in the Celtic mists – absorbed dropouts from the settled community.[75] Sharon Gmelch has modified this view somewhat,[76] without acknowledging the contradictions in the original argument. Although they believed that Traveller identity developed as the social distance between the settled community and those without a fixed abode grew from 1850 onwards, their argument also assumes Travellers, in some form, pre-dated this period. Their analysis describes the social ostracisation of a mobile population that the fluid settlement patterns of the poor refute. How can Travellers be deemed isolated when they were often joined on the road by varying numbers of 'settled' or non-nomadic people? The survival and accommodation strategies of the poor make it difficult to identify an homogeneous 'settled' community developing in opposition to a 'travelling' one. In addition, Gmelch and Gmelch side-step the inevitable question: how did some, but not all, vagrants become Travellers? According to the Gmelches, tramps and beggarmen did not join Traveller society but single mothers did.[77] There is no historical evidence advanced to support these arguments, yet this article remains an influential and widely read piece of scholarship. Regrettably, conventional historical sources may never be able to offer significant insights into the development of Traveller society.

Travellers' stories about their origins are legion and rarely consistent, as would be expected with an origin myth from a largely non-literate society with little experience of political mobilisation. Interestingly, some reference to a settled past is made but those stories acquire a powerful meaning in the context of dominant nationalist myths. In one account, settled ancestors were the victims of dislocation arising from two central events in the canon of English perfidy in Ireland: the Cromwellian plantations and the Famine. Nan Joyce asserted that 'some of my ancestors went on the road in the Famine but more of them have been travelling for hundreds of years – we're not drop-outs like some people think'. According to the Joyce, native Travellers mixed with Spanish immigrants and acquired Norman names such as Power by marrying English travellers. Some settled people 'burned out during the Cromwell evictions' or made homeless by the Famine married Travellers already on the road.[78] Rathkeale families justify their attachment to the town with an oral tradition locating them firmly in the local history of religious and ethnic dispossession, the Palatine plantation.[79] Claiming a place in this history of eviction gives the 'local bona fides' of Rathkeale Travellers 'immemorial depth'.[80] In addition to allying their history with the nationalist saga of invasion and conquest, Travellers posit their origins as pre-colonial.[81] These stories 'reveal simultaneous acceptance of the dominant themes of Irish nationalism and Catholicism, [and] an active rejection of stigmatisation of the Traveller way of life'.[82] Helleiner considers Traveller nationalist origin myths to be 'part of larger post-colonial nationalist discourses in which Irish citizenship, identity and culture are opposed to the colonial past'. Helleiner also asserts that these myths divert attention from 'the economic and political processes and relations of power' that produced and sustained Travellers.[83] If this is the case, Travellers are complicit in this denial. The origins question is one of the most controversial issues relating to Irish Travellers.

For some Traveller activists the origins question is vitally important. Michael MacDonagh writes:

> I feel it is very important when people talk of Travellers to look at their origins, because this will not only condition the way people think about Travellers but will also dictate what kind of services they will provide and the way these services will be delivered. It is important to show the origins of Travellers so that people's mind-sets and way of thinking changes. No longer is it acceptable to say that Travellers were settled people and therefore it's perfectly alright to resettle or reassimilate them.[84]

The political significance of the origins question proves the centrality of nationalism to Irish society. MacDonagh is anxious to convince settled people of the antiquity of Traveller origins. He rebuts popular myths held by settled people about the emergence of the Travelling community from amorphous wandering poor, preferring Eoin MacNeill's explanation that Travellers were descended from industrial communities that lived in Ireland in Celtic and pre-Celtic times.[85] Clearly, MacDonagh believes that historically proven origins can combat prejudice and justify the provision of culturally sensitive services for Travellers. In appealing to a halcyon Celtic past, he uses conventional nationalist tactics by asserting an 'Irish' identity for a separate ethnic group living parallel to, but separate from the majority population. Curiously, Traveller's ethnicity both supports and challenges 'Irishness'. By describing themselves as 'Irish' they validate popular assumptions about identity, while simultaneously demonstrating the reality of cultural difference in Irish society. In locating their history within a recognisable nationalist canon, Travellers claim ownership of the 'Irishness' that is fostered in popular culture by tales of British oppression. Jim MacLaughlin's account of a 'blood and soil' nationalism that demonised nomadism should be qualified by an Irish context that gives pride of place in the pantheon of victimhood to the dispossessed and exiled.[86] It is that Irish nationalist tradition that Travellers have used to explain their place on the margins of society. However, the significant gap between the origins claimed by Rathkeale Travellers and the Celtic beginnings advanced by MacDonagh suggests that, collectively, Travellers have yet to agree on their history. Overall, the origins issue provokes complex and contradictory responses from academics and Travellers alike. The significance of the boundary between Travellers and mendicant men or women is highly political. Although the distinction between homeless individuals and nomads was not hotly contested in the past, it was no less significant for what it indicated about attitudes to charity and mobility.

CONCLUSION

The debate over what defined a Traveller was not a notable feature of pre-
Second World War Ireland. However, it seems that distinctions were made
between tramps and tinkers. The popular perception of vagrants was relatively
positive and many families invited regular visitors to stay overnight. Travellers
with tents or caravans did not seek accommodation; the relationship between
settled and nomadic families was appreciably more distant as a result. Although
the gardaí and officials occasionally targeted vagrants, wanderers were mostly
left to subsist on voluntary charity, both organised and individual. The position of vagrants in Irish rural society was therefore determined by many of the
factors outlined in the previous chapter that affected Travellers. State intervention, social and economic change, and the extension of welfare benefits
altered the contexts for vagrants' interaction with the housed community.

The presence of vagrants also complicates attempts by scholars to seek the
roots of 'anti-Travellerism' in Irish nationalism. How did exclusionary
nationalism, harnessed to the cause of bourgeois property owners, co-exist
with the charity extended to mendicant men and women? Mobility and
begging were common among Travellers and vagrants, and social change
affected both groups in a similar fashion. The increase in social welfare
benefits ended the immediate need for begging but may also have contributed
to a decline in the practice of individual alms-giving. As subsistence farming
decreased, households had fewer goods to dispense as alms. Nationalism had
little to do with these changes, but the ideology's attraction for scholars is partly
explained by the dearth of Irish social history. No one ideology, no matter
how powerful, can fully explain the development of attitudes to Travellers in
twentieth century Ireland. The extension of state regulation in a number of
areas profoundly altered the context of Traveller–settled relations. In addition
to the developments already outlined, such as the decline of fairs and the
monetarisation of the rural economy, the status of Travellers in urban society
must be considered. In the following chapter, an overarching ideology such as
nationalism rarely appears, as it emerges that the status of Travellers was
entangled with intricate mechanisms of social change in urban environments.

THREE

TRAVELLERS IN URBAN AREAS

LANDSCAPE AND COMMUNITY

—

The marginalisation of Travellers should be placed in the context of the evolution of civic society. Much of this chapter will therefore focus on the extension of state control into the daily lives of its citizens. As a result of the developments in state and society from 1922 to the 1950s, Travellers became more isolated and alienated. This chapter will outline the importance of public space to communal definitions in Irish society. The use of land for campsites was (and continues to be) the focus for conflict between Travellers and settled people; this tension results from legal strictures on land usage that were enacted in the 1930s. Planning legislation redefined public space and transformed the character of urban areas, while introducing the concept of an amenity, a landscape designed and maintained for popular and (often domestic) tourist consumption. Pre-empting the planners, the police force extended its surveillance of streetscapes in the 1920s. Unconventional or inappropriate public behaviour was increasingly defined as criminal, which had considerable implications for the relationship between Travellers and settled society.

In addition to evolving attitudes to space, Irish society was experiencing significant changes in a number of areas, for example family work practices and housing. The social status and living environment of the urban working class were transformed, often as a result of government intervention. This chapter will analyse the changes in urban areas, with particular emphasis on Cork city, which rendered Travellers conspicuous and visibly different from a working class that had seemed similar to Travellers in socio-economic structure and working habits. For, to an extent that has not been recognised, it was government intervention that moulded Irish society and its social norms. Those laws, regulations and policies often had unforeseen consequences, for the social standing of Travellers was eroded not only by impersonal forces of 'modernisation' but by persistent government regulation of various aspects of Irish social organisation. Such governance also served to make Travellers increasingly distinctive and, often, unacceptably different.

POLICING PUBLIC SPACE

Since the foundation of the state, efforts to improve society have been made through the criminal justice system. Certain behaviour has been codified as criminal in an ever-expanding body of legislation and regulation. For instance, non-attendance at school was a serious offence under the School Attendance Act 1926. Parents were fined if their children avoided school, the final sanction being committal of the offending child to an industrial school.[1] Byelaws on parking, street trading and littering were enforced through the courts. Anyone selling goods on the public thoroughfare had to apply for a licence under the Street Trading Act 1926. The consequence of such regulation was, as Rottman has noted, 'a constant expansion in the range of behaviour that can be classified, at least formally as criminal. But are people who break such laws criminals?'[2] If we accept that the criminal law embodies 'a particular concept of crime and criminals'[3] the prospects for the marginal and unconventional members of society deteriorate when definitions of unacceptable or abnormal behaviour are enshrined in criminal law. Sibley has argued that non-conforming minorities suffer as the state extends its remit[4] – whether Irish Travellers were affected, directly or indirectly, by interventionist government policies will be analysed here. Increased policing of streetscapes in addition to closer regulation of the family economy of the poor changed Irish society after independence. Evolving social norms – often dictated by police and administrators – curtailed the ability of the urban and rural poor to make a living. The evolution of attitudes to, and legislation on, the division between public and private space also affected Traveller–settled relations by narrowing the definition of acceptable uses of public areas.

Urban working families lived in overcrowded unsanitary slum conditions in the decayed heart of Ireland's cities.[5] 'Huckster shops' selling small quantities supplied cash-strapped families with a penny's worth of tea, a halfpenny worth of sugar and a half pound of butter.[6] In pawn shops, 'the poor man's bank', good clothing was pawned until Sunday when it was redeemed for Mass.[7] Unemployment among unskilled labourers was endemic and there were few opportunities in the trades. Since poor relief was available only for short periods, men and women sought part-time work or became self-employed. In Cork city, families worked hard to make a little extra. Vegetable gardens, fowl and pigs were essential to the economy of the poor. Any surplus could be sold on the streets for cash. Street trading was women's work; customers and stallholders were female.

All up Shandon Street would be full of stalls. Apples, fish vegetables. Sunday mornings there'd be a woman sitting on a stool down at Shandon. She'd be selling sheep's feet, trotters. Then during the week that same woman would sell the crubeens, pig's feet and the cabbage.[8]

Small producers from the rural hinterland of Cork city sold their produce on the city's streets.[9] The market towns of Cork county provided a similar facility for small holders to sell surplus produce. Children were an integral part of the subsistence family economy. For the poorest families on the edge of hunger, the potential labour of children could not be overlooked. Upon reaching 10 or 12 years, an eldest daughter was an effective baby sitter for working parents. Children as young as 12 left school in order to work.[10] In rural areas, children's work on the land was equally important for the family income.

The marginal economies of the rural and urban poor were dependent upon and characterised by family labour and vibrant street markets. In 1926, the government passed two acts which had a considerable impact upon the poor. The School Attendance Act compelled all children of 6 to 14 years to attend school, while the Street Trading Act empowered local authorities to suppress and regulate traders. Those acts restricted the ability of poor working-class families to exploit the subsistence opportunities available to them. Street trading was almost eliminated in Dublin city in spite of rampant slum conditions and meagre welfare provision. Restrictions and regulations imposed on stall trading in Dublin city centre controlled the economic lives of the poorest, and overwhelmingly female, citizens of the city. In Cork city the use of streets as a marketplace for sellers of food, clothes and chandlery was curtailed by the application of the Street Trading Act to Cork County Borough in 1929.[11]

The idea for the act originated from the Dublin Metropolitan Police commissioner who sent drafts of possible legislation to the Cumann na nGaedheal Minister for Home Affairs, Kevin O'Higgins. Commissioner W. R. E. Murphy was frustrated with the legislation in place[12] and he suggested regulating the activities of any 'pedlar, hawker, tinker, vendor of any class or description of goods or wares'. 'Going from house to house' was also to be controlled by the new legislation.[13] The government did not legislate until 1926, despite complaints from Murphy in 1924 that 'during the past few years the number of traders have increased very considerably and numerous and repeated complaints have been received from traders, the Citizen's Association and other public bodies in Dublin'.[14] Casual trading was legal and licensed[15] but the legislation was intended for migrant salespeople, and was inadequate for dealing with established street traders in an urban area. The Street Trading Bill was a response to the situation in Dublin County Borough, though it could have been adopted by other local authorities. The minister described the bill as legislation which 'while permitting street trading and thus preserving the means of livelihood for the persons engaged therein, would regulate and control traders, so that there would be no undue interference with traffic on the highway or with those engaged in carrying on business in shops and in premises throughout the city'.[16] The bill licensed two types of trader: individuals moving from street to street and those trading from a stall. Dáil deputies disagreed with restricting the legislation to towns of 5,000 people or more and were eager for all urban areas to be allowed adopt the measure. It was hoped the bill would solve fair-day problems in small towns, but O'Higgins reiterated that it was designed with Dublin in mind, and said the Department of Home Affairs 'have no great evidence that such a bill is required outside the City'.[17] However, by the third stage of the bill, O'Higgins had himself received letters from local authorities asking him to remove the population restriction.[18] The minister agreed with the change but remarked:

> Of course, one feels cynical about the enthusiasm to adopt this Act, because the local authorities through the country . . . have a great many powers, by the judicious use of which they could improve the amenities of their areas of charge, and they do not use them. This power, which is simply to banish . . . competition in the open to the local traders is enthusiastically taken up as something that is a mighty measure that will bring calm to Kerry and balm to Ballydehob.[19]

Dáil deputies supported the bill for a reason that O'Higgins had highlighted – the protection of ratepayers from 'the unfair competition of street traders'.[20] O'Higgins himself scrupulously outlined the intended uses of the bill, rejecting a general interpretation that its powers were to be used to suppress competition.[21] If elimination of competition was the aim of the bill, the minister would not have exempted sellers at markets or fairs from the regulations. O'Higgins felt that existing powers were sufficient to deal with congestion on market days.[22] He was determined that the local interests responsible for unconfined fairs on the main street should endure the accompanying casual trading.[23] Clearly, TDs were representing the interests of shopkeepers rather than small farmers or craftsmen who traded small surpluses to supplement subsistence incomes.

Interestingly, the act when passed differed significantly from the draft version suggested by Commissioner Murphy before 1924. The categories 'pedlar, hawker, tinker, vendor' and traders going from door to door, were not included in the regulations. Specifically excluded from police control were those who carried goods for sale 'only to persons in, at or immediately outside the house or other place in which they reside'.[24] Therefore legislation that disadvantaged self-employed urban residents spared Travellers who called from house to house selling goods and trinkets. Arguably however, strict controls on city streets limited the entrepreneurial opportunities for Travellers as much as the urban poor. Though regulation may have been O'Higgins's intention, when the Dublin Commissioners prohibited stall trading in over 250 streets, the byelaws seemed to be a determined effort at elimination. The Minister for Local Government and Public Health, James Burke, refused to hold an inquiry to address the 'widespread dissatisfaction' amongst street traders, as appeals were only permitted before ministerial approval was granted.[25] Dublin's street traders went unheard and some 'honest women'[26] were deprived of their livelihoods. As the first major statute since independence regulating the use of urban space, its impact upon poorer and more marginalised citizens deserves some consideration. The act made a significant contribution to constructing definitions of public space in an urban environment.

Street trading was also common in Cork city, particularly along one of its oldest thoroughfares, North Main Street. Some women had been trading for as long as 30 years.[27] Stalls, barrows and boxes were used to display goods, or produce was simply spread on the ground. The money earned might not have been substantial, but for families in poverty small contributions were essential. Rural producers also sold on the city streets, avoiding the chain of purchasers and shopkeepers unfavourable to smallholders. Oral history evidence also suggests that Travellers traded in Cork city centre markets.[28] Despite the depressed economic conditions and poor employment prospects for most of Cork's working class, Philip Monahan introduced the Street Trading Act to Cork County Borough in January 1929.

The corporation considered the obstruction caused by street trading in 1924, but found it impossible to reconcile the interests of ratepayers with the established tradition of trading.[29] The Council's failure to fix the irksome issue of street trading was criticised in the inquiry report which led to the dissolution of the authority in October 1924.[30] Shopkeepers were not the only Cork citizens discomfited by street trading. Motor cars were becoming increasingly common in the city centre, creating logistical problems in relation to parking, pedestrian crossings and traffic flow that remain today. In 1923 there were 9,246 private motor cars licensed in Ireland. This grew to 13,380 in 1924 and 19,848 in 1926. While Dublin County Borough had the largest number of car owners with over 5,000 vehicles in 1930, Cork County Borough was next with 1,670, while in Limerick, only 594 cars were registered in the borough.[31] A letter writer signing himself/herself 'Motor Owner' painted a vivid picture of bustling city streets that obstructed private cars.

> The most congested centre in Cork is Daunt's Square, being a passage to the markets, garages, SS Peter and Paul's Church and Presbytery and Schools and we find at times impossible to pass owing to the dumping of onion boxes, stands,

itinerants (cheap jacks) [*sic*] and singers. The footpaths are obstructed by boxes, women and children, and sometimes a perambulator is dumped across the path with a baby enjoying its bottle. Respectable citizens are loath to pass this thorough-fare. Numbers of women and children range themselves along paths poking handfuls of onions into people's faces. On Saturdays, cars, motors etc. are often held up owing to congestion. With the help of the Civic Guard and Corporation officials this nuisance could be removed in a day.[32]

The City Manager, Philip Monahan, finally tackled the problem in 1929. Monahan claimed that byelaws under the Street Trading Act were 'not intended to abolish street trading in the City but to regulate it in such a manner that it shall not be an obstruction to the ordinary traffic of the City nor to the business of other traders'. If found trading in an unauthorised street, a stallholder was liable to have her goods seized by the Civic Guards. Monahan described street trading in North Main Street, at Daunt's Square and on the North Gate Bridge as 'a serious obstruction to traffic'. He acknowledged that 'it may be a hardship on traders to move to other places' but warned that unless trading ceased in prohibited areas, the full powers of the act would be used. Trading was allowed to continue in designated city centre areas.[33] Also, a trader had to purchase a licence and display a badge to prove legitimate, licensed status. This was a yearly license and may have resembled rates enough to placate shop owners. Licensed and labelled, street trading was allowed to continue in a small area of the city.

In order to assess the impact of this act, it is necessary to examine where many of the stalls were located. On 18 October 1928, approximately 120 women traded in the South district of the Garda Síochána. All had permanent addresses and traded largely in Cornmarket Street, North Main Street, the Coal Quay and Kyle Street. In the North district, 29 people were listed, trading mostly in Shandon Street, Blarney Street and Wolfe Tone Street, areas later at the centre of slum clearance schemes.[34] Though the byelaw schedule listed every street in the city except those specifically exempted, the enforcement of the act was not uniform or severe. Monahan had originally raised the matter to clear traders from 'three streets of the city considered unsuitable for such purpose'.[35] Traders on the North Main Street, Daunt's Square and the North Gate Bridge were targeted by the byelaws and the initial problem solved. However, defining the appropriate use of street space was soon beyond the control of Cork Corporation or the City Manager. The opinions of ratepayers and public representatives were superseded by those of the gardaí who gained more control over public areas than any other group. When the issue of street trading was raised again in 1938, it was the Chief Superintendent for Cork, not the City Manager, who decided on regulation and enforcement.

Motorised transport brought a corresponding need for police supervision of traffic, the most important increase in police duties in the twentieth century. The power to control vehicular traffic was wedded to the regulation of pedestrians and the surrounding streetscape. In 1928 the *Garda Síochána Code* stated that the purpose of legislation on road traffic was 'to increase the powers of, and to establish a system of supervision by, the Garda Síochána over the general traffic so that . . . it would be almost impossible for an accident to occur'.[36] An officer was to discourage 'the practice of pushing perambulators side by side' on a busy footpath and to move on groups standing on the footpath or at corners. Gardaí were to 'deal firmly with flower sellers or others who stand on sidewalks, or annoy respectable persons by persistently following them'.[37] Orderly, docile and respectable streets patrolled by the gardaí were envisaged. But in municipal areas, policing on the streets was split between the corporation and the gardaí. In the 1920s, street inspectors employed by the local authority inspected obstructions of the thoroughfare and vehicular traffic.[38] When the Road Traffic Bill 1931 was introduced, Cork's City Manager suggested to the Borough Council that power to make traffic byelaws be transferred from the corporation to the Garda Commissioner. Monahan suggested that the gardaí retain powers 'to deal with all forms of Street Nuisances, such as, those caused by the exposing for sale of goods on the footway, the dumping of refuse or sweepings in the public street, defective eaveshoots and downpipes etc'.[39] The Road Traffic Act 1933 gave sole responsibility for traffic conditions to the Garda Commissioner (see appendix). Gardaí now possessed more control over the regulation of traffic than at any time in the history of the police force[40] and there was a corresponding increase in police surveillance of public street space. For example, under the Shops (Hours of Trading) Act 1938, the policing of shop opening hours was transferred from local authorities to the gardaí (see chapter 1).[41]

In 1938, street trading was again raised when the Chief Superintendent for Cork J. J. Hannigan wrote to Monahan on the forthcoming Cork Traffic Byelaws.[42] Hannigan wanted to open up Cornmarket Street and adjoining thoroughfares to traffic and suggested the corporation make byelaws under the Street Trading act of 1926. Monahan consulted the City Solicitor who wrote 'since street trading is entirely a matter for the Guards, if they think there is a need for regulations, I suppose we should have them'.[43] The renouncing of regulatory powers by the local authority and their transferral to the gardaí were significant. Policy making within a bureaucratic framework, conducted without due regard to the consequences of legal prohibition and law enforcement, became the norm. While local politicians might not have behaved any differently, that they were denied the opportunity to voice public opinion reflects the deeply unrepresentative character of technocratic power.

The Minister for Justice signed the Street Trading (County Borough of Cork) Order in 1941, prohibiting trading other than the sale of newspapers in city streets. In November 1942, Alderman D. G. Buckley moved that the byelaws be rescinded 'considering the fact that they have caused unnecessary hardships on the street traders of our city who have been carrying on such businesses (handed down from relatives) for over 150 years, without being a hindrance or obstruction to traffic'.[44] However, nothing came of this protest and trading remained curtailed in the city centre and surrounding suburbs, with the new schedule also listing streets in newly built estates.[45]

Controls on street and stall trading were just one example of the impulse to order public streets. Letters to the *Cork Examiner* complained of children (and occasionally adults) playing ball, one correspondent describing it as 'a growing evil in our streets'.[46] Parents of children over eight years old who obstructed the thoroughfare with ball playing were fined in the Cork District Court.[47] Such was the problem of children on the streets that Rev. Dr Thomas of St Peter and Paul's Church condemned it from the pulpit.[48] The corporation was asked to make byelaws preventing 'persons using . . . shop windows as back rests' and to discipline 'itinerant street musicians'.[49] The complainants may not have represented public opinion as a whole, but those registering their dissatisfaction succeeded in portraying themselves as such. Nowhere in the records did members of the public support the rights of citizens to use public streets as play areas or marketplaces. The use of public space by men, women and children challenged interest groups such as shopkeepers and offended the sensibilities of some individuals. Errant ball-playing children and their careless parents needed guidance on proper behaviour, advice that was administered primarily by the police service and courts in the form of fines or arrests. This examination of street trading illustrates the extent to which social and economic life of the poor could be transformed by legislation. Working-class women attempting to supplement their incomes by trading were licensed and regulated to appease the embodiments of the middle class – ratepayers and car owners. The interests of the police in controlling streetscapes were also served by the 1926 act and subsequent byelaws. Since this act did not affect Traveller women and children hawking goods door-to-door, their subsistence economy survived while street traders lost their livelihoods. In the same year as the Street Trading Act, compulsory school attendance was introduced. This act further restricted the informal working-class economy by penalising families who supplemented their income with children's part-time work. The Street Trading and School Attendance Acts should be considered together since concern about children's work and education were closely related to conceptualisations of the public street.

1 Caravans on the Long Mile Road, Dublin, 3 April 1957
Courtesy of the National Library of Ireland

2 Camp in County Wicklow, 1930–50
Courtesy of the National Library of Ireland

3 Smith working at Sheridan and O'Brien campsite, Loughrea, County Galway, May 1954
Courtesy of the National Library of Ireland

4 Caravan at Cahirmee Fair, Buttevant, County Cork, 1954
Courtesy of the National Library of Ireland

The Dáil passed the first School Attendance Act for the independent state in 1926. The act updated the attendance provisions of the Irish Education Act 1892, making attendance compulsory for children aged between 6 and 14 years. Exemptions were granted to children 12 years and over for 'light agricultural work for his parent on his parent's land'.[50] Employment of children of school going age could be prohibited by ministerial regulation.[51] Upon a second conviction for truancy, the courts could commit a child to an industrial school or to the care of another relative[52] The act was deemed an immediate success by the Department of Education when enrolments and attendances increased nationwide. A preliminary scrutiny of attendance records suggested increases from two per cent to ten per cent in certain areas.[53] Sporadic school attendance was widespread among nomadic Traveller families, yet, for a variety of reasons, they evaded prosecution. The School Attendance Bill 1942 was drafted to address the difficulties posed by 'vagrant children', suggesting that Travellers successfully avoided the terms of the 1926 Act (see chapter 4). Working-class settled children and their families were not able to escape the interventionist zeal of local authorities.

In urban boroughs, where school attendance committees enforced the legislation, attendance was among the highest in the country. Unlike their rural counterparts, urban children were not granted exemption from attendance to contribute to the family economy. Part-time work by children on city streets was decried by some in authority, who viewed the public street as a dangerous corrupting influence on young people.[54] Dublin children involved in street trading were vulnerable to the evil moral and physical effects of the activity. Dr Myles Keogh, who administered trading licences in Dublin city, considered that regulation was but 'a method of legalising an evil'.[55] He recognised, however, that prohibiting children from street trading would cause 'great hardship' to the poorest families in Dublin city dependent 'on the scanty earning of the children for their livelihood'.[56] Civil servants in Cork city's employment exchange hoped the corporation would regulate street trading to prevent 'the unseemly and undisciplined conduct of young boys and girls around the city streets and outside the cinemas late at night'.[57] In 1932 Monahan felt that restricting juvenile street trading would be 'imprudent' given the economic circumstances of the city. He estimated that 200 children traded after school hours; a number of these were girls aged between 8 and 14 years. Wisely, Monahan believed that alterations in the economic circumstances of parents were more likely to affect juvenile employment than municipal byelaws.[58] Yet in 1937 Cork Corporation regulated children's trading activities with byelaws under the Employment of Children Act 1903 (see appendix). The byelaws prohibited girls under 16 years from trading altogether, giving permission only to boys between 14 and 16 years old.

Licences were given only if there was no other 'suitable' employment available. Street trading included 'the hawking of newspapers, matches, flowers or other articles, playing, singing or performing for profit, shoe blacking and any other like occupation in streets or public places'. A licence could be suspended if used 'as a cloak for begging, immorality, imposition or other improper purposes'.[59] In 1938, litter byelaws[60] and regulations on parking[61] signalled an increasing concern with the management of public streets. Regulating the employment of children on the streets was thus a statement about the character of public space as well as the nature of childhood and the family. While Travellers themselves escaped direct intervention, the society around them was transformed by such legislation. A working-class dependant on self-employment and family labour found the informal economy constrained by legislation. Travellers alone were largely unaffected by this legislation and succeeded in maintaining their distinctive social and economic organisation. However, the implications for the status of Travellers of the changing nature of public space and policing could not be avoided.

Streetscapes were subject to increasing surveillance by the gardaí in independent Ireland. The criminalisation of street activities did not immediately or obviously affect Travellers, but the erosion of official tolerance for unconventional use of public space signalled greater intolerance towards Travellers. Once official respectable standards for public behaviour were set, all had to conform to those rules. Arguably, by eroding street life in Irish towns and villages, the criminal law and its enforcement agents widened the gap between Traveller and settled attitudes to public and private space. However, it was the large-scale building projects of local authorities that most definitively shaped Irish spatial geography. The 1930s saw the embryonic beginnings of town planning in Ireland, while administrators grappled with the reality of developing and defining uses of public and private space in publicly owned housing estates.

PUBLIC HOUSING AND THE NEW WORKING CLASS

The provision of public housing marked the most significant intervention by local authorities into the lives of citizens. While housing the poor began in the nineteenth century under the Labourers acts and the Housing of Working Classes acts, there were major policy changes in the twentieth century.[62] The Housing (Miscellaneous Provisions) Act 1931 was intended to increase government assistance to those in the greatest need – urban slum dwellers. However, in the period 1932 to 1942, twice the number of planned labourer cottages were built while only two-thirds of the targeted urban houses were constructed.[63] This expansion in labourers' cottages occurred despite a hostile reaction from landowners who were forced sell an acre per cottage to local authorities.[64] Grants for new houses and reconstruction were overwhelmingly taken up by farmers. By 1939, subsidies for private housing totalled £3 million, almost 75 per cent of the amount spent on local authority housing in urban areas.[65] Thus in rural areas, private property was redeveloped and improved, while county councils increased the supply of public housing for the rural poor. In the cities of Cork, Dublin and Limerick progress was slower as high land and labour costs strained municipal balance sheets. Urban slum clearance finally gained momentum in the 1930s; the long-term consequences for Traveller–settled relations of granting local authorities wide-ranging powers over the urban environment were certainly unintended.

Under legislation introduced in 1931, public health and poor housing were conclusively linked. The ill-health long understood to be a consequence of poor living conditions was finally deemed unacceptable by the government. Slum clearance was about the eradication of disease: a precondition for generous government funding was that a Medical Officer of Health declare whole streets 'unhealthy'. Under the Housing (Miscellaneous Provisions) Act 1931, rehousing families from a clearance area would secure central funding for two thirds of the loan charges incurred. Once the Medical Officer of Health certified properties as 'unfit for human habitation', local authorities could acquire land in and adjacent to an unsanitary area with a Compulsory Purchase Order. This legislation encouraged demolition since public housing for families from substandard but not 'unfit' housing secured funding of only one third, as opposed to two thirds if the former residence were demolished. In Cork city, where 614 houses were built from 1922 to 1933, the new legislation enabling slum clearance had a dramatic effect. Between 1932 and 1944, 2,044 houses were constructed.[66] However, as there were 3,500 to 4,000 families in need of housing in 1938,[67] construction lagged behind demand.

How significant were a better environment and cleaner surroundings for social attitudes? For slum dwellers from overcrowded tenements the new, modern, plumbed accommodation must have been a revelation. Large gardens and green spaces for public use were novelties for many from the inner cities. Living conditions were transformed: in 1926 there were 73 slaughterhouses within the Cork County Borough, including one knackers yard, 12 tripperies, 8 sausage factories and 6 guthouses.[68] In 1934, Monahan hoped to erect a public abattoir to replace tripperies cleared with the slums and restore employment for rehoused slum dwellers.[69] It subsequently emerged that the Council could not spend public money on replacement piggeries and tripperies[70] so rebuilt slum areas became almost exclusively residential, with 'offensive trades' no longer conducted in the vicinity of housing. Suddenly, the poor no longer lived with the stench and filth created by trades such as bone boiler or tripe maker. Such changes in physical geography must have altered citizens' perceptions of their status as well as their living environment. Work patterns were also influenced by increased availability of unemployment benefit. After the Unemployment Assistance (Amendment) Act 1938 benefits were more generous, a fact that surely compelled those earning marginal wages to depend on welfare instead. As eligibility for the dole depended upon unemployment, casual or part-time work would preclude benefit.

Those Travellers who lived – seasonally or sporadically – in slum housing, were eligible for rehousing but, as the following chapter details, this raised questions about the nature of welfare entitlement. Also, Dr Michael Flynn, County Medical Officer for Westmeath in the 1950s, believed that the demolition of cheap, private, rental accommodation restricted Travellers' opportunities for voluntary settlement.[71] For not all Travellers were on the roads at any one time: elderly Travellers moved into housing or institutional care; families made sporadic attempts at settlement, and living in rooms or a house for the winter months was common. In County Cork, Travellers lived seasonally in the lanes of county towns such as Bantry, Dunmanway and Bandon (see chapter 1). The urban areas where Travellers lived were redefined by slum clearance. Old Chapel Lane, in Rathkeale County Limerick, strongly associated with Traveller settlement, was condemned by the Board of Health as unfit for human habitation.[72] The crowded lanes and alleyways that offered cheap, short-term or seasonal accommodation for Travellers vanished in slum clearance programmes. One former resident recalled lanes that were 'teeming, teeming with people. . . . Some of them houses were so small they'd say you could stick your hand down the chimney and pull a tea cup off the table'.[73] The term 'lane' was itself a significant class signifier. When the cleared areas were rebuilt, they were also renamed, though this tendency pre-dated the 1930s.[74] (It is worth noting that lanes in the countryside also vanished before the tide of middle-class suburbia: Cáit Shea's Lane in Bishopstown became O'Donovan Rossa Avenue.)[75] One study on residential segregation in Cork city revealed that from 1901 to 1946, 36 per cent of streets with a high proportion of lower-class residents contained the 'lane' suffix.[76] Travellers occupying houses in the lanes therefore lived in close quarters with the urban working class. Travellers and certain classes of the settled population did not always live separately. Local authority building programmes begun in the 1930s eradicated areas in towns and cities where both communities lived side by side. This was undoubtedly an unforeseen development, since administrators gave little thought to the social lives of slum dwellers. One Cork man remembered slum clearance thus:

The people had to move. They had no option, no back-up. Who was going to fight for them? When you're poor, you'll find very few friends, especially people of influence. . . . Within 20 years, the Middle Parish was levelled off, nearly completely, so that 25,000 people dropped to about 1,000. The city centre lost its vibrancy. It became a cold, heartless place.[77]

In spite of the superior facilities in new estates, relocation was a traumatic experience involving dislocation from familiar surroundings, family and friends. The St Vincent de Paul Society provided beds and furniture for new tenants with few possessions, and tried to ameliorate the loneliness arising from the break-up of local communities.[78] Though the new houses were a vast improvement on tenements, occupiers were not shy of criticising their surroundings. Houses in Capwell were altered as tenants disliked the ranges, preferring open grates.[79] Tenants complained of the remoteness of Churchfield and Fair Hill from the city centre and their employment, while slum dwellers in Shandon Street refused new suburban homes, hoping to secure tenancies in nearby Wolfe Tone Street.[80] Each year, a 'considerable number' of the 110 families who vacated public housing returned to poor conditions, and subsequently reapplied for new houses.[81] The Rev. R. J. Dalton wrote about the 'natives of Cork' adapting to the disappearance old neighbourhoods; 'They pine for the old friendliness and the gossip and the lost homeliness; and it is not strange and unintelligible that many of them find their way back to the squalor and the friendliness of their old homes'.[82] Citizens sought to exploit public housing according to their circumstances, with significant factors being school-going children, old or infirm relatives, community support networks and local loyalties. Tenants also began to mobilise to improve their new communities. In the new suburb of Gurranabraher a Parochial Improvement Society was established and lobbied the Council for a grant to build a parish hall.[83] While the parish priest was probably central to this initiative, residents understood the concept of articulating their rights after receiving their houses through a bureaucratic process that defined and validated their claims. The Cork Corporation Tenants Protection and Development Association approached the Council on many issues, from establishing differential rental systems to Traveller campsites.

Most complaints from corporation tenants did not detail what it was about Traveller encampments they objected to, preferring to encapsulate their protests in a simple, resonant word, 'nuisance'. Encampments in Cork County Borough were concentrated on the north side, adjacent to corporation houses. In 1958, a deputation from the Cork Corporation Tenants Protection and Development Association complained to the corporation of the 'nuisance caused by itinerants'. The Lord Mayor (Richard Valentine Jago of the Civic

Party) responded by calling on the manager to institute proceedings 'each
week against owners of caravans trespassing at Fair Hill until caravans have
been removed'.[84] Prior to the expansion of public housing on the north side,
Fair Hill had been a rural area remote from the city centre. One consequence
of slum clearance and low density urban sprawl was the encroachment of the
city on a rural hinterland where Travellers had camped seemingly unnoticed.
And as cheap accommodation in the inner city was demolished, the numbers
of Travellers camping in one place during the winter months might have
increased. As housing swallowed traditional campsites, Travellers and public
tenants came into conflict. Except for one reference to the Carrigrohane
Road on the south side,[85] all complaints in the corporation minutes about
Traveller camps cited parts of the city dominated by public housing schemes.
Tenants mobilised to lobby the corporation, founding an association[86] and a
rather ominously named Protection and Development Committee.[87] From
the Council minutes alone, it would appear that Travellers camped only in
the vicinity of Churchfield and Gurranabraher. Perhaps campsites were
concentrated on waste ground in public housing estates, but the silence from
the residents of Model Farm Road and Blackrock can be explained in another
way. (As chapter 6 shows, middle-class homeowners were capable of vociferous opposition to Travellers.) Local authority tenants were accustomed to
lobbying the corporation who acted as their landlord and represented their
interests. When Travellers camped on public land, Cork Corporation, as the
landlord, received complaints from residents adjacent to the land. Since the
corporation owned little if no land in the expensive southern suburbs of the
city, it would not receive complaints from tenants living there. Travellers
camping on private land could be moved on by the gardaí or by local residents forcing a landowner to clear the site. Tenants of public housing were
accustomed to dealing with local politicians and officials. In addition, local
authorities exercised considerable regulatory control over public housing, so
tenants naturally turned to the administrators of byelaws to police open space
in their housing estates.

Local authority tenants were themselves subject to much regulation,
which varied according to administrative area. Tenants' opportunities for
self-employment and subsistence food production could be restricted by
regulations circumscribing uses of the house and garden. Many local authorities encountered problems in developing adequate facilities for tenants. In
Dublin city, tenants wanted small workshops where they could continue to
operate businesses that had been located in tenement basements. Although
Dublin Corporation officials were sympathetic, it was impossible to implement
under planning regulations. Council tenants in Nenagh, County Tipperary,
wished to keep pigs in their back gardens, while Westmeath County Council

wanted to provide cow parks for labourers' cottages.[88] Local authorities in built-up areas enforced byelaws regulating the keeping of animals, particularly pigs, which were considered especially dangerous to public health.[89] The housing acts therefore forced local government to define and police urban space. The formal planning process instituted in 1934 further politicised the appropriate uses of public space.

PLANNING: REDEFINING A LANDSCAPE

The Town and Regional Planning Act 1934 attempted to control and regulate development to advance 'social betterment and industrial progress'.[90] The minister and his department hoped that local interest in 'greater cleanliness and brightness' would replace the 'general apathy and inertia' regarding the appearance of towns and villages across Ireland.[91] Clearly defined plans, formulated and implemented by local authorities, would promote the need for planning in the public mind. The minister acknowledged that change would discomfit certain members of society, cryptically stating,

> A great deal might be done inexpensively without recourse to legal measures, and, indeed without offence or annoyance even to delinquents.[92]

What exactly is meant by this brief reference is impossible to say, but it could be an admission that marginal people also inhabited public space. The minister outlined how local authorities bore a heavy responsibility for the appearance of towns and villages, since they controlled large public buildings as well as open spaces and parkland. The department urged local authorities to landscape public recreation grounds with 'suitable flower beds', though acknowledged that this was not directly dependent upon planning powers in the new act. In concluding, the minister reminded local authorities that their functions had 'a very intimate bearing on public welfare', particularly in the context of spending on housing, school medical services and child welfare schemes.[93] This advice on planning from the department is intriguing, ranging from cleanliness, delinquents and flower beds to welfare schemes. While castigating a widespread lack of interest in public space, the department seemed to imply that even 'delinquents' had a stake in streetscapes. It concluded that neat, well-maintained public space was a corollary of rising living standards made possible by preventative medicine and slum clearance. Yet, according to John Collins, the Town and Regional Planning Acts 1934 and 1939 conferred 'few if any positive powers' on local bodies or the central authority.[94] Planning did not gather momentum after this legislation;

uncertainty over compensation for private landowners gave local authorities cause to hesitate.[95] Despite the failure to implement the act, the language of amenity had entered the administrative and public consciousness. Landscape could be viewed as a resource, a product to be consumed by local people. The appearance of public space was considered as important as its cleanliness or safety. By viewing the environment as an amenity, the government promoted the appropriate usage and development of a valuable, consumable resource. Residents of an area could see public space as integral to and reflective of the values of their community. Although local authorities did not create detailed plans for future developments as envisaged by the acts, they possessed powers to veto certain uses of private property. Ownership of property was no longer absolute; permission for development rested not with the landowner but with representative local government. Greater involvement of local communities in planning the appearance of their areas brought about a revolution in public space in Ireland.

Initial moves towards improvements in public space were made during the Second World War or 'the Emergency'. Parish councils were created by the government in response to wartime conditions. These bodies interested themselves in the 'social and economic welfare' of their communities. Some 1,133 parish councils were formed, undertaking specific emergency work but also organising the tillage campaign, ploughing matches and cultivating allotments. Others concentrated on improving their local amenities by 'removing rubbish dumps, cleaning neglected graveyards etc'.[96] Those councils did not survive after the war, their services being quickly dispensed with in favour of professional local government. The Acquisition of Derelict Sites Act was also passed in 1940. Legislation already empowered local authorities to compulsorily acquire dangerous derelict sites, but the 1940 Act was the first to define unsightly appearance and ruinous condition as dereliction. Sites that were 'unsightly and detrimental to the amenities and appearance of a town and its surroundings' could be acquired by a local authority and improved. Central funding was available to fund these improvements.[97] The Taoiseach, Eamon de Valera, was anxious that local authorities would 'proceed energetically' with the acquisition and development of derelict sites.[98] The Department of Local Government and Public Health encouraged the use of the act, noting that the clearance of derelict sites would provide employment over the winter months.[99] De Valera had attached 'considerable importance' to the poor relief aspects of the act and hoped that local authorities would make 'full and early use of their powers' under the act.[100] Wartime stringency curtailed the finances of many local authorities and progress on the acquisition and clearance of derelict sites was slow.[101] After the war, the Department of Local Government once again urged the clearance of derelict sites 'to improve the appearance and amenities of any parts of their districts'.[102] The Minister for Local Government wrote to the Taoiseach 'I feel keenly myself on the eradication of these ruins and derelict buildings to be seen in some of our towns and villages and strewn along the main country roads'.[103] Reclamation of waste and marginal land had implications for Traveller camping there. When Dublin Corporation reclaimed derelict sites in the city centre, Travellers and Gypsies were evicted (see chapter 4). It is not unreasonable to assume that reclamation projects in urban and rural areas across the country would have had a similar effect. The Commission on Itinerancy noted that Travellers camped on 'undeveloped building sites, the residue of ground left over after building operations – unfenced, open or derelict areas whether public or private'.[104] Fencing of open land in Dublin and in Cork, 'in places where itinerants encamp or are likely to do so', closed recognised and potential campsites.[105] Those barriers could be erected the day after Travellers had vacated a site,[106] demonstrating an extraordinary potential for rapid response within local bureaucracy. Availability of campsites would have been considerably reduced as the landscape was redefined. Works carried out under the Employment and Emergency Relief Scheme could have had similar effects. In Cork city, the City Engineer funded the landscaping and fencing of open space used by Travellers under this scheme.[107] Public relief works remained popular with local and central government throughout the period under review. Demanding manual labour in exchange for unemployment assistance revealed the tenacity of nineteenth-century attitudes towards the able-bodied male, seen as less deserving than women, children, the elderly and the sick. Works that required unskilled labour and cheap materials were funded under unemployment relief schemes. The exclusion of Travellers from publicly owned space was probably facilitated by relief works but since the reasons for such works were not stated, validation for this theory is difficult to find. Yet apparently innocuous relief works and the development of public amenities were not always innocent. In 1960, the creation of a public park in Dublin's hinterland was urged because Travellers were camping on private ground from which the county council had no authority to remove them.[108] A council acquiring land for a public park is unremarkable, until the covert reasons behind the development of this 'amenity' are considered.

The concept of a public amenity that was introduced into the street and landscapes by the Town Planning acts acquired more significance in the context of tourism. Bord Fáilte Éireann encouraged local interests to abolish eyesores in order to attract more tourists, while also improving the environment for local consumption.[109] In 1959, Bord Fáilte inaugurated a tidy towns and villages competition, a scheme which initiated the creation of a uniquely Irish streetscape.[110] The Department of Local Government urged local authorities to enter the tidy towns competition stating, 'It is clearly in the national interest that maximum number of towns and villages should participate, so that there may be widespread awakening of civic consciousness in the direction of making and keeping towns clean, tidy and generally attractive.'[111] The minister stressed the importance of the leadership offered by local government: 'It should not be necessary to point out how discouraging it may be to local residents if negligence or lack of interest on the part of sanitary authorities results in dirty streets and littered unkempt open spaces'. Local authorities were also reminded of their byelaw powers over litter.[112] Increasingly, public spaces were managed according to tourist and amenity needs, as well as public health considerations. Improvement grants for derelict sites may have been sought with the express purpose of excluding Travellers from familiar camping grounds, or this may have been an unlooked-for consequence of reclamation. Financing and the incentive of attracting tourists facilitated a redefinition of public space at local level.

Undoubtedly, the promotion of neat, orderly public space landscaped and tailored for public consumption further denigrated Travellers by rendering their encampments unsightly to the all-important tourist. A mythical tourist figure appalled by the existence of Travellers occasionally appeared in the post-war rhetoric of politicians. In the Dáil, deputies complaining about the 'tinker nuisance' did not refer to tourism until 1949.[113] Deputy Tadhg Manley feared that tourists would find Travellers dirty and presumably draw conclusions about the cleanliness or otherwise of all Irish people.[114] Travellers annoying tourists by begging was most frequently mentioned, particularly by a Galway deputy who criticised government inaction on the problem.[115] Only Brendan Corish sought to present Travellers as a tourist attraction in themselves saying 'the tourists almost break their necks looking out the windows of cars or trains to see what they describe as attractive nomads'.[116] The disgusted tourist was convenient, a useful and publicly acceptable justification for outrage, but also indicated a growing consciousness of appearance of landscape and people as a consumable product. The nuisance to tourists of begging Travellers in Killarney formed the gardaí's case against Nora O'Brien and Mary Faulkner in 1955. The vicinity of the new tourist office was 'haunted' by beggars and the gardaí described streets of beggars 'lined up by the hundred'.[117] Begging was illegal, irrespective of whether natives or foreigners were approached but the gardaí clearly believed that begging from tourists was a greater evil and expected the courts to support this assessment. A Cork councillor also complained of beggars causing a 'nuisance' to tourists in the city.[118] Whether those tourists were domestic or foreign is unknown.[119] The question of domestic tourism must be raised – what did Irish people as tourists, travelling in their own country, expect? Munster people flocked to see the caravan parade during the Cahirmee Horse fair suggesting that Traveller culture could be a domestic tourist attraction (see chapter 1). We can but speculate on the experience of Irish people as tourists travelling and consuming Irish public space. As domestic tourists took to camping and caravanning during and after the Second World War, local authority control over unauthorised campsites was strengthened. This issue was crucial for relations between Travellers and settled people. When central government legislated for the growth in seaside caravanning, some local authorities applied the legislation against Travellers.

CONTROLLING CAMPSITES: THE LOCAL GOVERNMENT (SANITARY SERVICES) ACT 1948

Outdoor holidaymaking increased in popularity during and after the Second World War. A little-known effect of the war on Ireland was an increase in camping and caravanning since travel to the Continent was impossible.[120] In Britain, motor caravanning had become popular in the 1930s and continued to grow throughout the 1950s.[121] Unlike its parent organisation, the Irish branch of the Caravan Club of Great Britain and Ireland was politically inactive and did not lobby the government for facilities for its members.[122] To control the growing practice of holiday camping the government enacted the Local Government (Sanitary Services) Act 1948. The powers of this act formed the basis for the reactions of many local authorities to Traveller campsites. This act combined a desire to protect public health from unserviced campsites with the concept of a public amenity. Interestingly, as growing numbers of Irish people were taking to caravanning or camping after the Second World War, the publicly expressed antipathy towards Travellers intensified.

The Local Government (Sanitary Services) Act 1948 was a major statute that extended and amended public health legislation dating from 1878. It regulated the maintenance of graveyards, the provision of sewerage and water supplies, public bathing facilities and temporary dwellings. According to the minister, the powers over temporary dwellings were drafted to deal with the sanitary consequences of the 'considerable growth in the practice of holiday camping in tents, huts and caravans'. Section 20 of the Local Government Act 1925 contained regulatory powers over temporary dwellings but those were unsuitable as 'this Section was framed primarily, . . . to apply to those itinerants who are in the habit of dwelling temporarily on road margins'.[123] Balrothery Rural District Council (1928–9)[124] Bundoran UDC (1929), Howth UDC (1935)[125] and Galway Borough Council (1943)[126] had enacted byelaws to control temporary dwellings under the 1925 statue.

Helleiner states that Galway Borough Council drafted those byelaws 'to put itinerants out of the area'.[127]

The new legislation allowed local authorities to license camp grounds, regulate their development and completely prohibit camping in designated areas. Though originally intended to control temporary holiday dwellings, the powers of the 1948 Act were used to move Travellers continually on. Buncrana, Bundoran and Bray Urban District Councils, as well as Donegal County Council, almost immediately availed themselves of additional powers over temporary dwellings.[128] As popular seaside resorts, Bundoran and Bray may have needed to control temporary holiday accommodation. While Limerick city was hardly an important tourist destination, it was Limerick Corporation which eagerly embraced the legislative powers to prohibit camping under section 31 of the act. An order under section 31 prohibited all temporary dwellings if the authorities felt such dwellings would be 'prejudicial to public health or the amenities of the locality or would interfere to an unreasonable extent with traffic on any road'.[129] However, the prohibitive powers of this section were found legally wanting in 1952.

Following demolition of slum properties in Limerick city, Travellers set up camp on the newly created open spaces.[130] In order to evict those families, Limerick Corporation made an order under section 31 in late 1951. The order made temporary dwellings within 300 yards of any house or road in the confines of the city borough illegal. Once the order was passed the corporation lost no time in bringing Travellers to court for breaching the new byelaw. The defendants were fined nominal sums but District Justice Dermot F. Gleeson was 'revolted' by the sweeping powers of the new byelaw. Mr J. J. Sexton, the solicitor who represented the defendants, sought legal advice on the constitutionality of the byelaw with a view to challenging it in the High Court.[131] The unsympathetic attitude of District Justice Gleeson towards the corporation's plight rendered the city authorities powerless. The manager, Mr Matthew Macken, described how such leniency meant that 'gypsies from all parts of the country are now facing towards Limerick'. The Mayor even offered to give evidence on the 'nuisance these people are causing'.[132] The city authorities pressed ahead with more prosecutions and District Justice Gleeson reconsidered the new byelaw in January 1952. He was not satisfied that the corporation could prohibit all caravans, tents, sheds and shelters in the city. Unwisely, Mr W. J. Dundon for the corporation submitted that 'until a person is prosecuted he may assume that he is not infringing the Order'. Gleeson responded that if the corporation were to 'pick and choose' the law would be brought into contempt. He believed his court had the power to decide if the order was *ultra vires*, because it was the only authority 'which stood between the executive and a particular section of the community'.

When Mr Sexton pointed out that his clients wished to state they were 'not tinkers but horse dealers', Gleeson replied, 'Let me say that I have always found tinkers to be well-conducted and well-behaved'. In February, Gleeson found the order to be bad in law and referred the case to the High Court.[133] On 16 May 1952 the High Court found the order under section 31 of the Sanitary Services Act to be *ultra vires*. If the order was good, 'nobody could camp out in a tent or a sleeping porch or in his own garden' without the corporation's consent.[134] The common law rights apparently safeguarded in the 1948 act would be undermined.[135] The President of the High Court described the order as 'manifestly unjust' since it involved 'such oppressive and gratuitous interference with the common law rights of those affected as could find no justification in the minds of reasonable men'. The High Court further declared that the legislature never intended the corporation to make such an order.[136]

The order was originally made in response to public outrage at the 'influx' of gypsies and tinkers to Limerick. Wise after the event, the *Limerick Leader* reflected, 'Obviously the Corporation went a bit too far'.[137] The case of Limerick Corporation *v* Mary Sheridan was circulated to all local authorities by the department, outlining the proper application of the 1948 Act. According to the High Court, a prohibition order had to be restricted in application, rather than covering to the whole or major part of a sanitary district. Future prohibition orders were to be drafted with regard to amenities, public health considerations and traffic: 'the less general the application of the Order the better'. Section 31 was therefore unsuitable if a local authority wished to remove temporary dwellings which they considered unsightly or unsanitary. The department drew the attention of local authorities to the nuisance provisions of sections 32 and 33, which 'were designed for dealing with individual temporary dwellings or small collections of temporary dwellings'. Sanitary authorities had preferred to use 'the more drastic powers of section 31 or 34' but it was hoped that this would become 'more sparing and discriminate' in the wake of the High Court judgement.[138] Mrs Mary Sheridan, who was prosecuted by Limerick Corporation for placing her caravan within 300 yards of a city-centre street, moved into a house just as the High Court gave its judgement. Two of her sons had bought their 78-year-old mother a small house in the Limerick Blackboy Pike. She was glad the courts had overruled the corporation, saying,

> My family is respected everywhere as horse dealers. For the rest of my days I will live in a small house but my heart will be in the caravan. My sons and daughters who have their own caravans will carry on the family tradition. Thanks to the Courts, they will continue to go through their own country as free people, not like caged birds as the Limerick Corporation and other Councils would like to have them.[139]

But the High Court decision did not silence Limerick's burghers for long. In 1955, a corporation deputation met the Minister for Local Government, Mr O'Donnell, to ask for new laws to '"crib, cabin and confine" itinerants'.[140] The shift in nomenclature from tinker and/or gypsy to itinerant in the space of two years is particularly noticeable, since it originates from the same body of men from the same area. The corporation sought power to control the 'filthy habits' of certain classes of itinerants who were 'a source of serious scandal and embarrassment to the neighbourhood'. What the corporation sought were special powers that would enable them to license Travellers living in the city. This licence could then be withdrawn and Travellers expelled if 'they did not conduct themselves'. The minister did not comment on this suggestion and instead asked if any powers conferred by the 1948 Act could be useful. The manager stated that the corporation felt that that any action it took under the act would be found *ultra vires* and the deputation urged the minister to amend the law 'so that effective control might be exercised over itinerants'. The minister was '100% in sympathy' with the corporation but he felt that legislation could not be introduced in the immediate future. O'Donnell also stated that the Church authorities 'expressed the wish on a number of occasions that these itinerants should reside in some area so as to enable the children to receive some reasonable education, and also to receive religious instruction'. However, he invited the corporation to prepare suggestions for the amendment of legislation which he would consider sympathetically. This the deputation undertook to do.[141] No legislation proposing to license Travellers was ever placed before Dáil Éireann.

Despite appeals to apply section 34 of the act sparingly, in 1959 it was in force in the County Health Districts of Wexford, Wicklow, Dublin, Clare (Killkee town), Galway, Cork (in coastal electoral divisions) and in the urban districts of Galway, Wicklow, Bray, Arklow, Youghal and Bundoran. Byelaws under section 30 in respect of the use of temporary dwellings were made in the county health districts of Wicklow, Monaghan, Louth, Sligo, Westmeath and Waterford and for the urban districts of Tipperary, Carrick-on-Suir, Thurles, Dundalk and Templemore.[142] Some of those byelaws probably applied to holiday camping, particularly in Bray, Youghal and Bundoran. Yet section 30 was enacted in urban areas far from the tourist trail, suggesting the powers were directed against Traveller rather than holiday campsites. The sporadic nature of the use of powers is the most salient point. Although Limerick Corporation felt the legislation was not drastic enough, many authorities had no need for its powers. After all, Travellers were illiterate and vulnerable; the observance of legal niceties was not a priority for local authorities who forced Travellers to move on. As not all local authorities acted within the provisions of the 1948 Act, their actions against Travellers were of dubious legal standing.[143]

CONCLUSION

The social developments in independent Ireland that adversely affected Travellers occurred for a variety of reasons. This analysis has focused on why Travellers became visibly distinct from the majority community in independent Ireland. Many families in urban and rural areas were characterised by family labour and self-employment and, in common with Travellers, they exploited seasonal opportunities and niche economies. Under the influence of increased government regulation, working-class families were transformed, and there is little evidence that they resisted the changes. When compulsory school attendance was enforced, urban families lost a valuable source of income. Trading was heavily regulated under the Street Trading Act, as business interests sought to stifle competition from hawkers and stallholders. Informal entrepreneurial methods of earning a living were heavily regulated partly because of their public character. The use of public streets by men, women and children as workplaces and play areas was increasingly confined; law enforcement improved once the gardaí gained sole control over the streetscape. Travellers largely escaped the consequences of the Street Trading and School Attendance acts, but definitions of public space and family organisation had considerable implications for their position in Irish society. Conventional behaviour on the street was enshrined in byelaws and regulations, reducing tolerance for unacceptable usage of public space. When trading and whole family economies among the poor were eroded, Traveller society remained characterised by those features.

The similarities in social and economic organisation between Travellers and the settled people were reduced still further by public housing. Suburban estates were entirely residential, the first time poorer members of Irish society experienced a physical division between work and home. Sanitation also raised living standards considerably. People who had secured tenancies were made increasingly conscious of their right to certain standards and services. However, those were not always forthcoming, as local authorities possessed neither the powers nor budget to fully develop new housing estates.[144] To secure greater facilities and to lobby their landlord, residents established neighbourhood organisations. Those groups also asked local authorities to break up Traveller campsites and eradicate the 'nuisance' they represented. Perhaps what local authority tenants hated most about Travellers was their resemblance to their own recent past. Before benefits, subsidised housing and compulsory school attendance, the Irish working class and Travellers shared many social and economic characteristics.

Yet the most important factor in Traveller–settled relations was land usage. To earn a living, nomadic families needed access to numerous campsites across the countryside. Reclamation projects during the Emergency reduced opportunities for access to marginal land, while planning and regulation instituted legal norms for development. Government officials began to view the environment in more aesthetic terms, perceiving it as a product in its own right. Tourism further encouraged officials and the public to regard the landscape as a marketable resource. Unlike the social transformation discussed earlier in the chapter, the commoditisation of landscape was not limited to poorer members of society. The pan-class appeal of the language of amenity represented the greatest threat to informal land usage by Travellers. As nomads were gradually excluded from a redefined landscape, the following chapter demonstrates that legislators and communities were ambivalent about a minority they had little wish to reform by conciliation or coercion.

FOUR

WELFARE AND ENTITLEMENT

—

Since the welfare system before the 1960s was not founded on universal entitlement, debates that centred on the entitlement of certain categories – the elderly, widows, children and mothers – to assistance was often heated.[2] As Lynn Hollen Lees states in her study of the English poor law, 'Cultural definitions of entitlement, rather than available resources, determined amounts and beneficiaries.'[3] Welfare as administered by local government therefore illuminates the extent to which Travellers were implicated in broader definitions of Irish society. This chapter will examine the system of welfare distribution that includes housing, education and health as well as income support. Could Travellers take up any of these benefits? The division of responsibility in welfare provision that allocated a reformatory role to voluntary charity meant that Travellers received financial assistance largely from the Society of St Vincent de Paul and the Legion of Mary. As already described in chapter 2, the care of certain groups such as homeless men and women was left to voluntary agencies. Travellers were characterised by the state as similarly difficult, suitable for reform rather than material aid.

Travellers were therefore largely ignored by the state before the 'itinerant problem' was identified in the 1960s. Both administrative divisions of responsibility and the prevailing welfare ethos explain this omission. Occasionally efforts were made to target Travellers for public health reasons or on the basis of problems caused by vagrancy and homelessness. These attempts were perfunctory and sporadic, reflecting the absence of a coherent attitude to Travellers among civil servants and politicians. Even as government intervention in society expanded, Travellers were both ignored and excluded. Since welfare was extended dramatically to the poorest in Irish society, why were Travellers not included? This chapter shows that Travellers sought to avoid certain welfare benefits (such as education), while both local and national authorities made little effort to include them. Indeed, some local authorities apparently refused to help Travellers. There were complex reasons for this, rooted in the organisation of welfare schemes, the relationship between the state and voluntary organisations, and the definitions of community that were expressed in entitlement to assistance.

WELFARE AND CHRISTIAN CHARITY

The twentieth-century welfare system inherited by the Irish Free State was grounded in the poor law of the preceding century, which was roundly condemned by the new ruling revolutionary class.

> The Irish Republic fully realises the necessity of abolishing the present odious, degrading and foreign Poor Law system, substituting therefor [*sic*] a sympathetic native scheme for the care of the Nation's aged and infirm, who shall not be regarded as a burden, but rather entitled to the Nation's gratitude and consideration.[4]

Significantly, the poor law was primarily associated here with care for the elderly although the system also provided material support for the able-bodied unemployed. The guarantees given to the working classes were less expansive. The Dáil determined to draft legislation 'with a view to a general and lasting improvement in the conditions under which the working classes live and labour'.[5] The poor law was not replaced but renamed: outdoor relief became home assistance and the workhouse was restyled the county home.[6] The most important change was that relief was more readily available outside the workhouse.[7] The department of local government and public health felt the reforms had 'revolutionised local government administration'.[8] For those applying for home assistance, the Board of Guardians had been abolished but, as before, entitlement remained at the discretion of the local authority. Vagrants and casuals denied entry to the newly respectable county homes hardly welcomed the revolution. The poor law system was now officially native: created and administered by Irish representatives, it was democratic in origin but no more sympathetic than its 'colonial' predecessor. Mary E. Daly has astutely noted that the reforms of local government were 'dynamic in matters which did not entail major expenditure such as administration and personnel reform, conservative on costly items such as housing'.[9]

Expanding welfare entitlement was not a priority for the first Cumann na nGaedheal government, which was preoccupied with financial retrenchment. Old age and blind pensions were cut while the private sector was expected to address the shortage of affordable housing for the poor.[10] *The Irish Times* urged the Free State government to abolish the dole – a 'feature of British rule' – since the system had a 'demoralising effect . . . on the fibre of the nation'.[11] In line with the poor-law tradition where medical treatment was universal, welfare entitlement in independent Ireland focused primarily on the health needs of the population. Cash handouts to the needy were avoided. The department responsible for administering the system considered relief to be potentially 'unnecessary or demoralizing'.[12] Cork's City Manager, Philip Monahan, commented on the 'strange anomaly' within welfare policy.

> On the poor law side Government policy would appear to be restriction and limitation of gratuitous assistance as much as possible. On what might be termed the public health side, liberality appeared to be encouraged. The provision of school meals and the organisation of child welfare and school medical schemes and the loose supervision over them by the central authority were instances of this.[13]

Monahan's allusion to schemes for children is significant: expanding welfare provision for children was a feature of the benefits system in twentieth-century Ireland. Contrary to its policy of fiscal prudence, from 1922–4 central government urged local authorities to provide free meals for school children.[14] The high mortality rates among illegitimate children worried the department which hoped that antenatal institutions for unmarried mothers would reduce death rates.[15] From 1932, free milk was distributed to 'necessitous children' at the discretion of local authorities who particularly targeted children under five years old.[16] By March 1933, 67,161 children were in receipt of free milk.[17] Free children's footwear was distributed from 1944–5.[18] The School Medical Service surveyed the 'general physical condition' of children in National Schools.[19] Generally, Traveller children would not have availed themselves of these benefits since they did not attend school or possess a fixed abode, both vital criteria for inclusion in these schemes.

The common element in all these schemes was their locally administered character. Universal access to assistance on the basis of clearly defined conditions was not available in the early years of the state. Some local authorities refused to distribute relief to those eligible for it and had to be reminded by central government of their duty to assist 'any poor person who was unable by his own industry or other lawful means to provide the necessities of life for himself or his family'.[20] In order to assist the unemployed during the war, the government intended to enlarge its programme of public works 'which would provide employment for unemployed persons instead of resorting to direct relief'.[21] Such works did not necessarily improve infrastructure since the schemes chosen used the maximum number of unskilled labourers and the minimum amount of materials.[22] Among the administrators of the reformed poor-law system there was a clear reluctance to distribute cash benefits to the unemployed. Believing that poor relief was damaging to the recipient reinforced ideas about the integrity of poverty promulgated by the Catholic Church. As defined by Catholic theology, charity was not a means to relieve the near starvation endured by the poorest in society but a supernatural manifestation of Christ's love.[23] Even aid from the Catholic brothers of the St Vincent de Paul Society was considered potentially damaging to the sanctity of the poor. Bishop Daniel Cohalan of Cork threatened to withdraw permission for church gate collections from the St Vincent de Paul. To cries of 'No' from an audience of Cork worthies he defended himself thus:

> If I thought in the least that charity, like the dole, was tending to corrupt the people, I would without hesitation and without a moment's delay, stop that collection at the doors. While there was undoubtedly necessity for it – the system of the dole was a necessity – at the same time he thought it had a very detrimental effect upon young men particularly.[24]

Until the establishment of the Department of Social Welfare in 1947, there was no definitive break with a poor law system that grudgingly supported the unemployed for short periods and demanded labouring work from able-bodied men on assistance. Despite revolutionary aspirations of reforming the benefits structure, Irish administrators never systematically removed poor law structures. The taint of pauperism lingered long: in 1949 the Department of Social Welfare noted that 'even today the stigma of the poor law has not been entirely eradicated from the public mind in regard to any form of State insurance or assistance'.[25] The pervasive poor-law attitude of minimal entitlement was sustained only because charitable societies relieved the ratepayer and taxpayer of 'financial burdens they could not otherwise escape'.[26] While the poor law continued to pervade official assistance, voluntary organisations supplemented state benefits with Christian charity. These groups also struggled, in the context of their spiritual mission, to define an appropriate response to the crushing poverty endured by many in independent Ireland. The conflict between spiritual aims and material aid experienced by the St. Vincent de Paul was expressed in their work with Travellers.

The Society of St Vincent de Paul was a nationwide, Catholic, lay organisation.[27] The society was composed of conferences located in parishes. Conferences reported directly to the Council of Ireland or to Particular Councils established at a diocesan level.[28] Until after Vatican II, it was an all-male society. The Ladies Association of Charity of the St Vincent de Paul established in Ireland in 1843 cared for households where the woman was the breadwinner and raised funds for their male counterparts.[29] The visitation of the poor in their homes was the fundamental tenet of the society, though no form of charitable assistance was prohibited.

The title of the poor to our commiseration will be their poverty itself . . . Neither class, politics, nor creed excludes anyone from claiming its help . . . In the care of the Catholic poor alone does it look to the observances of the duties of religion. But with all, of every creed, it seeks diligently to promote habits of temperance, cleanliness, thrift, industry and general morality.[30]

Though middle-class values – thrift, industry and general morality – were promoted by the society, the censorious attitude often encouraged by the differentiation between deserving and undeserving poor was absent. Most importantly, the society existed 'first of all, for the spiritual benefit of the members, secondly for the spiritual benefit of the poor, and in the third for the relief of the material needs of the poor'.[31] Though Catholicism was fundamental to the society's members, most of its work was not directly religious. Its members sought to promote religion by relieving families of crushing poverty, thus turning the thoughts of the poor from daily survival to spiritual welfare. Often, the society struggled with this spiritual mission in the face of overwhelming poverty. The possibility of misunderstanding the society's true spiritual purpose is hardly surprising when nationwide in 1926 it was estimated that 27,529 people had benefited from the assistance of the St Vincent de Paul Society.[32] A measure of its importance can be gauged by the fact that Sir Joseph Glynn, the president of the society, was a member of the Commission appointed in 1925 to report on poor-law reform.[33] In 1927, the importance of the society was noted in the *Report of the Commission on the Relief of the Sick and Destitute Poor, Including the Insane Poor*. The report acknowledged that private charity covered a wide field and relieved the ratepayer and taxpayer of considerable expense. For the most part, public and private charity 'functioned independently of each other'.[34] This distance from 'purely relieving bodies', suited a society with wider spiritual aims. The international headquarters of the St Vincent de Paul in Paris advised the Council of Ireland not to co-operate with other agencies.[35] Fiscal means differentiated voluntary charity from state aid but voluntary aims and strengths were also unique. Though a common end – the relief of poverty – was sought, the report clearly stated that the work of voluntary charity was often more effective than state aid, particularly in working with homeless men. While this charitable work benefited the state, the commission noted,

We however recognise that they owe such beneficial results as they may be able to accomplish primarily to the fact that they are voluntary and actuated by higher motives than the provision of material necessities. To bring them into any kind of even distant relationship to the Poor Law would probably mean their destruction.[36]

The contagion of officialdom could be contained if charitable societies worked without any state interference. The only acceptable relationship envisaged was if the state contributed initial capital costs and left the running of facilities in voluntary hands.[37] In 1927 the voluntary sector refused to carry the responsibility of relief and employ the bureaucratic methods of state aid. Believing firmly that the provision of basic necessities lay with the state, charities perceived their work as reformatory and thus primarily spiritual. The spiritual foundations of Catholic charities precluded analyses of the causes of poverty or a real belief that it could be eradicated. Along with much of Irish society at this period, the St Vincent de Paul fatalistically accepted the existence of 'the poor who are always with us'. The society often shared members with an organisation founded by Frank Duff in 1921, the Legion of Mary.[38]

A lay group 'at the disposal of the bishop . . . and the parish priest' it offered its services in the battle 'perpetually waged by the Church against the world and its evil powers'.[39] The Legion was established with the primary object of 'making its members holy'[40] rather than a specific mission to the poor. Work with Travellers and Gypsies was 'a comparatively small part of the Legion's work'.[41] It formed part of a remit that sought to 'work for the last ones of Christ',[42] seeking out the 'derelict or abandoned classes'.[43] Chief among these neglected groups were homeless men and women who were catered for in two Dublin city centre hostels, Morning Star (founded in 1924) and Sancta Maria (established in 1927) respectively. The St Vincent de Paul and the Legion of Mary both attempted to reach out to Travellers. The reasons for targeting Travellers and the methods used reveal much about perceptions of the minority as well as the operation of charity in the independent state. The relative generosity of the charitable organisations contrasts with the refusal of local and national authorities to extend aid to nomadic and illiterate Travellers.

CHARITY WORK WITH TRAVELLERS AND GYPSIES

Aiding Travellers and Gypsies first became a special work of the St Vincent de Paul Society in 1931. The initiative came from clergy who asked members of a Rathgar conference to visit the 'gypsies'. The activity was extended to other conferences and the committee for gypsy visitation, St John Francis Reggis, was established in Dublin in 1932. Brothers visited 27 families totalling 135 people in 1931–2. Many of these families were from Wales, which suggests that the term 'gypsy' refers to Anglo-Romanies rather than Irish Travellers. Some of these Gypsies may have been Protestant, as the complaints from the Church of Ireland minister in chapter 2 suggest. In contrast to other home visitation, material aid was given 'very sparingly, and only in extreme cases, as it might interfere with our spiritual work'.[44] This missionary activity was aided by the 'untiring zeal' of a number of Jesuit friars.[45] St John Francis Reggis members were exclusively concerned with the relationship of Gypsies to the Church and ensuring baptism of their children. The children were placed in local convent schools, while adults received religious instruction in their caravans. The Dublin brothers appealed to members across the country to include caravan dwellers in their work.[46] The conference was named the 'Gipsy Visitation Guild' in 1934.[47] Discussion among other conferences refers to 'tinkers and gypsies' suggesting that members outside the Dublin-based Guild ministered to Travellers. The spiritual aims of this particular work were heavily emphasised.

At the 1933 meeting of conferences, the question of gypsy visitation was discussed. No visits were paid to caravans in Ulster though a number of brothers expressed a willingness to bring the subject before their conferences.[48] Leinster conferences, excluding Dublin city and South County Dublin 'resolved that such work should be taken up without delay, especially from the spiritual side'.[49] A Cork member was not enthusiastic, believing that visitation would be of little advantage 'owing to the "Bohemian" tendency of the "Cork" gypsies'. In Thurles however, a conference had already begun work with Travellers and their efforts were rewarded with 12 Confirmations.[50] The conferences in Connacht had no prior experience of working with 'the "tinker" class', but the brothers were urged to 'do something for them and their children, especially with regard to the reception of the Sacraments and the attendance at Mass'.[51] Connacht members were reluctant to consider the work, prompting Sir Joseph Glynn to hope that 'my Connaught friends are not going to abandon the tinkers'. Glynn continued:

> They are decent people, who want a little attention from a society such as ours, so that they would take the pledge now and again. They want to be followed up, because when they are strolling around the country they are inclined to be careless about the children's welfare in not sending them to school or having them Confirmed. My experience is that if they are taken quietly they will do whatever is necessary.[52]

The society's aims in regard to Travellers and Gypsies were modest; reformatory missionary work did not include settlement. The extent of the society's work among Travellers and Gypsies is difficult to quantify. As a special work, the activities of the Gipsy Visitation Guild were reported annually. Work by individual conferences was published only as a general summary, describing principal activities. If contact with Travellers was incidental to the main work of a conference, it would not have been reported. The decision to work with Travellers and Gypsies was taken at a local level, by brothers responding to perceived need within a parish boundary. The influence of the parish priest must also be considered. Thus charity offered to Travellers by the society was dependent upon the interest of individual members. For example, a principal work of St Joseph's conference in Thurles was its efforts to teach Traveller children in 1934 and 1935. This was done during fair days, when conference members sought out Traveller children and taught Catechism for Confirmations.[53] The spiritual education of Traveller children was the most notable feature of this conference's work.

In 1936, the annual meeting of presidents discussed ongoing work with the 'Tinkers and Gypsies'. At the Munster group meeting it was noted that 'on the whole they are quite decent members of the community' and one brother reported that eight children were confirmed on one occasion.[54] Travellers in Connacht were assisted when they passed through Westport but the efforts of Galway conferences were impeded by the local authority. It was reported that 'as the authorities in Galway will not allow them to be within a certain distance of the city at weekends and this places them outside the areas of the different conferences, the work has been passed on to the Legion of Mary'.[55] As regional group meetings did not discuss work among tinkers or gypsies each year, the extent of contact cannot be accurately described. It seems likely that once brothers embarked on a programme of visitation it would not be easily abandoned. Nevertheless, Traveller mobility and the uneven geographic distribution of the St Vincent de Paul Society[56] would have made sustained visitation difficult. Work with Travellers and Gypsies in Dublin was more consistent, owing to the commitment of members and because some families lived in the city all year round.

The Committee of St John Francis Reggis reported that 64 families comprising 325 people were visited regularly in 1933. A curate and women volunteers taught classes because attempts to place the children in National Schools had failed. The role of local clergy who supervised National Schools on behalf of the patron – the Bishop – in denying education to Traveller children has yet to be assessed. Thirty or forty children, both boys and girls, learnt reading, writing, arithmetic and Christian Doctrine. Reform of the adults was proving difficult and inducements to 'lead better lives' were ignored. The brothers noted that,

> although anxious to send their children to school and give them a Christian education, they are slow to reform themselves. A great difficulty presents itself with adults as they are slow to take advantage of even instruction in convents. However, efforts are on foot to arrange a Retreat in the near future solely for gypsies or caravan dwellers.[57]

Its work was severely disrupted when, in early 1934, Dublin Corporation evicted caravan dwellers. Despite the brothers' efforts to prevent it, a large number of families encamped in the city were evicted. Many left Dublin for the country and classes for children and adults ended. Visitation was more difficult as those who remained were scattered throughout the city and suburbs. The brothers continued with their work, securing entry into convent schools for children and exhorting parents to attend Mass, though with limited success. Material help was given only in cases of necessity.[58] By 1935 the Committee, now called the Gipsy Visitation Guild, could claim that, except for those living far outside the city, the children of all the families visited were attending school. Forty-eight families were visited, totalling 200 people. The living conditions of these families varied.

> . . . the greater number . . . take up their abode in vacant yards throughout the city – outside the city their stay on the side of the road is very short because they are compelled to move frequently.[59]

Unfortunately, the St Vincent de Paul reports do not indicate if families living in yards travelled occasionally, if at all. However, it was noted that 'some families come for years to the same address, others do not remain for any length of time and are constantly changing from place to place'.[60] This does imply a pattern of nomadism centred upon a permanent address among some families.[61] Having succeeded in providing education for children, the brothers turned their attention to marriage traditions.

Irregularities or deviations from the Catholic form of marriage were now the focus of the brothers' considerable energies. Families visited by the brothers were encouraged, with some success, to conform to formal Catholic structures. Efforts to regularise marriage practices began to show results in 1936 when a number of young couples approached the Guild seeking their advice. Introductions to the clergy, baptism certificates and courses of instruction were provided. All children born to Catholic parents during the year were baptised.[62] The detail 'Catholic parents' suggests that there were other denominations among the families visited by the Guild. By 1938, the Guild was pleased to report that elopements 'without any idea of a religious ceremony' had ended, as young couples approached the Guild for guidance on a formal Church ceremony. The effects of lay missionary efforts on Traveller and Gypsy society may have been considerable. As the Guild's work was concentrated on a static population in Dublin city, the impact can be measured, if only from the perspective of the society members. Traveller reaction to the introduction of formal Church structures may never be known, but it seems clear that the community chose to change marriage practices. No doubt the

assistance of literate Guild members in the bureaucratic procedures for securing a marriage licence was appreciated. Since, despite the brothers entreaties,
Mass attendance did not noticeably improve, Travellers themselves made the
decision to participate in Catholic marriage ceremonies. The Gipsy Visitation
Guild did not force families to conform, as it had no power to do so. By not
distributing material aid, the brothers renounced a charity's most powerful
reformatory weapon. Without financial leverage, the brothers relied on per-
suasion and encouragement to change the habits of Travellers.

Yet spiritual work did not entirely preclude forms of material assistance.
Initially, the brothers were reluctant to give material assistance and yielded
'only in extreme cases'.[63] While provision tickets were not distributed as in
normal visitation, occasional grants were provided. By 1936, the attitude had
changed and criteria for aid were less strict. Provision tickets were given when
the wage earner was ill, for part-purchase of horses, for wood to build wagons,
for clothing, boots and marriage fees.[64] A cash grant for a horse and wagon
was given to a mother and five children who had been forced to live in halls.[65]
When sick or unemployed, Travellers often had no other source of support;
'[they] have no assistance from the state or otherwise, they are left absolutely
destitute'.[66] Brothers also provided secretarial services, writing to trace missing
relatives[67] and contacting parishes in England, Northern Ireland, Scotland
and Wales for baptism and marriage certificates.[68] The Guild also successfully
intervened to prevent evictions of families who received peremptory notices
to quit.[69]

The reports from St John Francis Reggis alter in tone, however, in the
mid-1940s. Work among caravan dwellers seems to have suffered a number of
setbacks particularly in relation to children's education. By 1945 the brothers
could not 'solve the difficulty of the children attending school'.

> Schools are usually full and even if there were vacancies, the roving life of the
> families would prevent their attending for more than a couple of weeks at a time.[70]

These problems with schooling suggest that Traveller children were being
denied the free National School education that was their right. However, the
increasing mobility of the Travelling community – whether voluntary or
forced – would also make school attendance more difficult. In 1943, the
annual retreat run by the Jesuits of Milltown Park was moved from Lent to
January 'because many families who make an early start on the road were
unable to attend'.[71] Visitation was arduous because families were widely scattered across the city. In 1947, this was compounded by Dublin Corporation's
closure of 'many yards and open spaces within the city which had been
frequented by travelling people, driving most of them to camps in the

suburbs'.[72] The exclusion of Travellers from the city continued in 1948, forcing families to the temporary camps outside the city.[73] From 1951, the work of the St John Francis Reggis Guild for Gypsy Visitation was no longer mentioned in the report of the Council of Ireland but this could be because the report was shorter and the work of individual conferences not so extensively reported. The Guild remained a special work of the society until 1958, when it was no longer listed among the principal special works in Dublin. Its disappearance was not explained, though declining numbers referred to in earlier years may have been a contributory factor.[74] This is also the period when the position of the Travelling community gave rise to public comment and interest. The society shared the belief of the community at large, that 'something should be done about these people'. The Council of Ireland felt that 'the matter had better be left to the authorities and that we should continue to assist them to the best of our ability, especially in the spiritual sphere'.[75] In 1960, following a request from the Commission on Itinerancy, the society consulted its conferences nationwide and submitted its conclusions to the Commission.[76] Regrettably, the records of the Commission did not survive and the society did not preserve its submission. The Legion of Mary also gave evidence to the Commission.

The Legion's work among Travellers was largely confined to the education of children in preparation for the sacraments.[77] In 1961, the Legion ran a 'school on wheels' in Dublin city: 'But until there are more of these mobile schools the open air "hedge schools" operated by the Legion all over the country and especially in Dublin will continue to be held.'[78] These *ad hoc* schools suggest that Travellers were still excluded from formal education. In a similar way to the St Vincent de Paul, the Legion attempted to encourage regular Mass attendance but this had little effect.[79] Travellers needed assistance from charitable mediators such as the Legion primarily in order to secure religious education. The high standards of sexual morality among Travellers conformed to the cardinal virtues of Irish society – chastity and fidelity in marriage. The Legion and the St Vincent de Paul were thus concerned with basic religious education of Travellers rather than rescue work among the deviant or immoral. The role of the female religious in educating and assisting Travellers was also significant but the extent of involvement of different orders and convents awaits further study.[80]

When considering charitable aid offered to Travellers, the strong local and personal factors involved must be considered. The assistance given by the Society of St Vincent de Paul and the Legion of Mary was decided by members in individual conferences or praesidia. This piecemeal assistance may have suited the lifestyle and requirements of Travellers who were anxious to see their children receive the Sacraments but not spend years in formal education. Travellers were not considered excessively vulnerable or needy by these groups, although it seems families had no support other than that offered by charitable organisations. Conformity to settled values was not the objective of lay charitable organisations who worked with Travellers. The St Vincent de Paul was not trying to reconcile Travellers to their poverty in order to promote their spiritual life. Neither were they encouraging frugality and respectability. Brothers believed that Travellers were 'thirsting for the Faith', therefore their work was missionary.[81] This was in spite of the fact that Travellers were not given the same benefits as other members of society: 'They cannot obtain assistance from the local authorities and eke out a sometimes precarious livelihood as best they may'.[82] By facilitating religious education and the bare minimum of formal education, both organisations appeared to accept nomadism as the basis of Traveller society. Thus contact between Travellers and charitable organisations was occasional, circumstantial and limited. In comparison to other defined categories such as the elderly or unmarried mothers, Travellers eluded the attention of voluntary charity organisations. Without a fixed abode, Travellers could not easily access welfare benefits. However, there was certain limited contact between Travellers and the benefits system. This contact occurred when Travellers were housed by a few local authorities, and when central departments noticed their non-co-operation with public institutions.

HOUSING

The importance of housing schemes in changing attitudes to public space among the Irish working class has been discussed in chapter 3. This section will explain the extent to which public housing developments restricted Travellers' access to housing, both temporary and permanent. Before the nationwide settlement programme was initiated in the 1960s, local authorities dealt with Traveller tenants on an *ad hoc* basis. The actions of each authority were conditioned by local factors such as the attitude of the county or city manager and the elected representatives. By 1961, the majority of local authorities had received tenancy applications from Travellers. Most lettings were successful although some Traveller families were ostracised by their settled neighbours, resulting in unhappiness for all.[83] This reaction by the settled community often made 'the new way of life unattractive, if not intolerable' for many Travellers who returned to the road to escape prejudice.[84] As chapter 3 showed, settled people also had difficulties adjusting to life in the new housing estates. Unlike settled people, Travellers could escape public housing by returning to the road.

Perhaps more significant than the troubles of adjusting to settlement were the unforeseen effects of slum clearance and the extension of garden suburbs, discussed previously, on Traveller accommodation patterns. Tenancies were decided by local authorities and prejudice against Travellers had a detrimental effect upon their chances of securing public housing. In Galway city a Traveller family were removed from the housing list 'on the basis that the Borough Council were not prepared to house families of the itinerant class'.[85] Apart from overt discrimination, securing a tenancy was a bureaucratic process, which undoubtedly alienated a largely illiterate population. Sean Maher's family were housed in Mulatty, County Kildare because he was able to write to the county council on his parents' behalf.[86] It also appears that compulsory purchase orders on which housing programmes depended may have been used to force Travellers out of urban areas. Dublin Corporation served an order in January 1934, acquiring 54 separate properties, 49 of which were described as 'waste ground'. Many empty spaces had been created by the demolition of property, but marginal land was also included in the purchase order.[87] Coincidentally, work by the Gipsy Visitation Guild of St Vincent de Paul was interrupted by the mass eviction of caravan and tent dwellers by the Corporation in early 1934. The compulsory purchase order may have specifically targeted land occupied by Travellers, securing their eviction while simultane-ously acquiring property for the housing needs of the city's population. As for the amenity and relief works discussed in chapter 3, the sources do not refer to unauthorised camping as a problem to be solved by public ownership of land, but evidence suggests that restricting informal land usage was an important factor in purchase decisions.

Nevertheless, Travellers in some parts of Ireland did benefit from the slum clearance policies initiated in the 1930s. The history of Traveller contact with the system of government reveals occasional and intermittent contact: some local authorities included Travellers for rehousing under slum clearance pro-grammes. St Mel's Terrace, in Athlone, County Westmeath was built in 1933, and housed 31 families 'the majority of which were semi-settled Travellers who had been living in shanties and run-down cottages on the edge of town'.[88] St Mel's and a similar terrace in Tralee, County Kerry had the largest concentrations of Travellers in one neighbourhood in the country.[89] From 1933 to 1972, 85 families, mostly Travellers, lived in St Mel's. This was three or four times the usual turnover for public housing. Reasons for this turnover varied: some families transferred to other public housing but many returned to the road or emigrated to England. Clearly, 'housed' Travellers did not necessarily view themselves as 'settled'. Travellers living in the terrace did not participate in the activities and institutions of the settled community, but this was considered to be largely the fault of settled people who discouraged their attendance. St Mel's tenants did not have any close friends outside the terrace, except among their own relations, and several of the families in the terrace were heavily intermarried.[90] Thus the premise that housing inevitably led to assimilation and an end to Traveller identity was proved unfounded even before the settlement drive of the 1970s.

In Mullingar, County Westmeath a different approach was taken to housing Travellers. Unlike in Athlone, no more than seven families were housed in any one street. The County Medical Officer, Dr Michael Flynn, helped house 32 of Mullingar's 41 resident Traveller families.[91] Flynn obtained funds from the local parish priest to purchase council houses on behalf of Travellers, who then paid back the loan. Such a fund was necessary because the council was reluctant to give Travellers loans under the Small Dwellings Acquisition Acts (see appendix).[92] Mediation by the parish priest and the St Vincent de Paul was therefore fundamental to Travellers' success in dealing with local authorities. The experiment was a success in that 25 families owned their own houses and all the children were attending school.[93] While the Travellers made strides towards respectability and the conventions of the majority community, they were not personally close to settled people since 'no one has yet forgotten that they were once "tinkers"'.[94] Mullingar Travellers restricted 'their close relationships to other Travellers in the town'.[95] Dr Michael Flynn described how difficult it was for families to make the transition to permanent housing: 'it was the rare family who stayed in their first house'. Many needed more than one opportunity to adjust to sedentary living and without a sympathetic local official securing another tenancy must have been difficult. These isolated examples of Traveller settlement in public housing point to the importance of influential individuals at a local level. Flynn commented, 'The individual who had a high level job with some clout could achieve something . . . I found that where the county manager, secretary, engineer or medical officer wasn't interested, nothing happened.'[96] Even nationally, the power of a committed and energetic individual to circumvent administrative niceties was considerable.[97] Sustained or large-scale Traveller settlement could occur if powerful figures in the local authority were supportive. Similarly, if a central government figure or department focused on the deviation of Travellers from the norms of the settled community, they could seek coercive powers to force conformity. Yet there is little proof that Travellers as a group were subject to sustained scrutiny by the machinery of the state. The small numbers of Traveller children committed to industrial schools are an example of their successful evasion of coercive state welfare.

EDUCATION: THE FAILURE OF COERCION

'Civilising' children through education was a strategy favoured by governments across the world when faced with an irreconcilably different minority group. In Europe, the Roma and Gypsy communities face particular obstacles in many national school systems.[98] The experience of minorities in state-run education systems is crucial to maintaining cultural difference. Therefore an examination of Traveller contact with an education system run by the majority community is essential. As demonstrated in chapter 3, full-time education did not affect all classes equally. Did the enforcement of school attendance affect Travellers particularly? Was cultural assimilation attempted in Irish education system, and, if so, how was it effected? A charge of cultural assimilation could be made if Traveller children were disproportionately subject to education in institutions such as industrial schools or reformatories. Industrial schools were detention and education centres for children established in the nineteenth century. Unlike reformatories, which detained juvenile offenders, children were sent to industrial schools because their homes were found to be deficient in 'sufficient protection and care'.[99] Scholarship on institutional care in Ireland, the intentions of its administrators and the experience of its 'clients' remain embryonic.[100] Assessing the extent of Traveller contact with the industrial school system is attempted within a simple sketch of the system itself.

After the foundation of the state, the numbers of children sent to industrial schools began to rise. Though from 1914 to 1922 numbers fell, by 1926 the numbers in care had risen to pre-war levels. A comparison by the Department of Education revealed that numbers in Irish industrial schools were significantly higher than in England and Wales. The Irish habit of using the schools as poor law institutions for the maintenance of the destitute largely explained this disparity. Out of 1,865 children committed to schools in Ireland in the 19 months ending 31 July 1926, 1,621 were committed for wandering or being destitute, whereas in the same period, of the 2,400 children committed in England and Wales only 280 were committed on these grounds.[101] County homes were being redefined as old age homes, so children, the mentally ill and unmarried mothers were reallocated to appropriate institutions.[102] The reorganisation of the county homes took some time to effect but the post-independence trend was to send children to industrial schools; this served to swell numbers annually. Institutional care was not a cheap option: national school pupils cost public funds approximately £8 per annum while an industrial school child cost more than £28.[103] Despite this financial disincentive, the numbers of children in industrial schools continued to rise.[104] The most common grounds for committal were 'begging' and 'wandering' as defined by the 1908 Children's Act and 'destitution' under the 1929 Children's Act.

Table 4.1 Legislative grounds for the committal of children, 1928–31

Year	Begging %	Wandering %	Destitute %
1928–9	21	60	*—
1929–30	9	37	37
1930–1	9	30	43

*Act of 1929 not operative in 1928–9
Source: *Report of the Department of Education 1930–1*, p. 81.

The categories of begging and wandering would suggest that Traveller children were well represented among industrial school committals. Indeed in 1927, the Commission on Poor Relief recommended that the boards of health take the children of vagrants into their care

> . . . when they are satisfied that the accommodation provided for such children affords no sufficient protection against the weather, and that owing to the migratory habits of the parents the children are not attending school or that the surroundings in which they are living are morally bad.[105]

Such children would then be transferred to industrial schools.[106] Yet there is every reason to believe that this recommendation was ignored. District justices were unwilling to commit Traveller children to industrial schools since families clearly had reasonable means of subsistence.[107] The cost of industrial school education was also a major factor. Local ratepayers paid for committed children and rising rates were deeply unpopular. Local authorities struggled to strike a low rate that would simultaneously keep voters happy and fund infrastructural improvements, sanitation schemes, road works and poor relief. Unsurprisingly, committal of Traveller children was 'stoutly opposed' by local authorities conscious of 'the burden on the ratepayers'.[108] Even Traveller children with physical or mental handicap found it difficult to enter institutional care; one family needed the intervention of the St Vincent de Paul before a local authority would sponsor a deaf and dumb child.[109] Louth County Council in 1937 protested that Traveller children with no right to local funds were chargeable on the rates. The Louth representative to the General Council of County Councils (GCCC) requested that the GCCC ask the Minister for Local Government and Public Health about 'the problem of children of the vagrant class wandering into a county and becoming a charge on the local rates by their being committed to Industrial Schools'.[110] The Council believed that 'as the children in question are not usually domiciled in any particular county it appears . . . that the chargeability in respect of them should fall on the general taxpayers and not on the ratepayers'.[111] What the Department of Local Government thought of this exception is not recorded, but figures from the Department of Education do not list any detained children paid for by central funds. In July 1940 there were 2,904 boys and 3,530 girls in industrial schools paid for by local authorities.[112] Cork Corporation supported 218 children in industrial schools; the County Council funded 505.[113] Without a fixed residence, Travellers were not entitled to locally funded welfare services. In the opinion of local representatives, rootless nomads did not qualify as deserving members of the local community. This official refusal to contemplate Traveller entitlement contrasts with popular recognition of Travellers' connections to a local area where they maintained winter head-quarters, as outlined in chapter 1. On an unofficial level, Travellers were seen as part of a geographically defined local community but their rights as citizens under the welfare system were rejected. Although authorities possessed the powers to detain vagrant children, the welfare of Traveller children who were 'wandering' did not concern local representatives and officials. Travellers were arguably more fortunate in this neglect than settled children who were committed to institutional care.

In 1942, 16 years after the introduction of compulsory school attendance, the Department of Education attempted to increase coercive powers over Travellers who successfully evaded primary schooling. From 1934 to 1937, an average of six per cent of committals to industrial schools were under the terms of the 1926 School Attendance Act.[114] As Traveller children attended school sporadically and only for short periods, committal to institutional care for non-attendance could have unduly affected them. But the gap between legislation and enforcement was considerable. District justices did not con-sider failure to attend school sufficient reason to remove Traveller children from parental guardianship.[115] The drafting of a School Attendance Bill in 1942 to address the difficulties posed by 'vagrant children' suggests that Travellers successfully evaded the terms of the 1926 act. The Minister for Education, Thomas Deirrg, presented the bill to the Dáil in October 1942.[116] The department felt legislation targeting 'vagrant children' was necessary since Travellers had evaded conviction. Figures from 1938 estimated that there were 900 vagrant children of school-going age in Ireland.[117] Derrig believed that 700 of these children received no schooling at all. Section 21 of the School Attendance Bill 1942 was designed to bring these children and their parents 'faoi'n smacht', under control.[118] The measures outlined in the bill represented a wide ranging attack upon the Traveller family. The powers envisaged for the gardaí and the school attendance officer were extensive and aimed only at 'vagrants', singling out Travellers for particular attention. On 1 May each year, a vagrant was required to register in a garda station the names, ages and educational particulars of his children. Failure to register or supplying inaccurate information was punishable by fines. Children of vagrants were required to take educational tests at the behest of the minister and failure to do so was punishable by fines and/or imprisonment.[119] A school attendance officer could question any vagrant he encountered[120] while a garda could arrest without warrant anyone 'who appeared to him to be a vagrant and whom he suspected of having committed an offence' under the school attendance acts. Any child between 6 and 14 years in the custody of the arrested vagrant could be taken into custody and removed 'to a suitable place of detention'. A vagrant who did not send his children to school could be fined or sent to prison while vagrant children were automatically removed to industrial school or the care of a relative after the first conviction for truancy.[121] Derrig apparently envisaged Traveller children staying with settled relatives or friends while their parents continued to travel.[122] This suggests that the bill was not intended to regulate the whole Travelling community or to end nomadism, although it would have had that consequence in practice. Naturally, Derrig did not declare his intention was to commit all Traveller children to industrial schools, since legislation that increased local rates would not have been welcomed.

Some of the extra powers granted to enforcement authorities also applied to settled people. A school attendance officer could challenge any child found on the street during school hours and further question the parents if necessary.[123] John Marcus O'Sullivan, who as minister had drafted the 1926 act, worried that the rights of parents guaranteed in Article 42 of the constitution[124] were being infringed. He had no such scruples about the rights of vagrant parents who were certainly not 'ordinary parent[s], settled definitely in the town or country'. Vagrants neglected their duty as parents[125] and were thus unworthy of constitutional protection. James Dillon steadfastly defended the family in the face of bureaucratic regulation but he did not decry the specific attention paid to vagrants.[126] Deputy Timothy Linehan commended the legislation:

> I am satisfied that, no matter what some people may think about the divine right of parents, it is a good thing that the State is now being given power to remove the children from the care of those vagrants if they are not treating them properly and giving to those children the opportunities which they should get in a State like this.[127]

Linehan even suggested that the term 'no fixed abode' be removed from the definition of vagrant as many families owned or rented a house to which they returned for the winter.[128] The bill passed both Houses of the Oireachtas but was found unconstitutional by the Supreme Court in April 1943.[129] Section 4 of the bill[130] was found unconstitutional because it interfered with a parent's right to determine the provision of education for their children.[131] The department privately conceded that the 1926 School Attendance Act was probably also repugnant to the constitution.[132] The finding of the Supreme Court protected Traveller (and to a lesser extent, settled) families from a state willing to make drastic interventions into its citizens' lives. In contrast, Northern Ireland legislators passed a statute with remarkably similar coercive powers in 1950 (see appendix). Exactly why the Department of Education chose to target Traveller children in 1942 is not clear. Without access to Education files we can only speculate, but a possible reason could have been the increasing attention paid to Travellers during the Emergency. In general, administrators rarely noticed Travellers as a group with particular needs or problems. For example, Traveller children escaped the expanding preventative remit of public health by not attending schools where medical examinations detected childhood illnesses. It was only when some Travellers apparently threatened the health of the general population in 1940 that the Department of Health legislated for them.

PUBLIC HEALTH: INFECTION AND ISOLATION

In certain contexts, Travellers did make use of the state medical services. Women in childbirth were assisted by midwives, the district nurse or the local doctor.[133] With no fixed abode, families could not receive public health sub-ventions such as free milk. Naturally, the state did not encourage Travellers to avail themselves of their entitlements or change the application criteria to reach nomadic families. This should not be seen as deliberate exclusion since penny-pinching local relief agencies even categorised charity from the St Vincent de Paul as 'means' when assessing eligibility for benefits.[134] Application procedures were drafted to suit the needs of the administration and the less money paid out in benefits the better.

Vagrants were first blamed for the spread of typhus in the 1931 report from the Department of Local Government and Public Health. The epidemiology of the disease proved difficult to trace so a medical inspector speculated that 'the disease is in some cases spread by vagrants who harbour infected lice'.[135] Yet public health officials were not unduly concerned with vagrants spreading typhus. The disease was recognised as an outcome of unsanitary, overcrowded conditions that were endemic to the poorer classes in Ireland. Improvements in housing were the foundation for the gradual elimination of typhus.[136] The department noted with satisfaction the increasing attention devoted to sanitation schemes by local authorities who implemented expensive schemes owing to 'a public health consciousness and a deeper knowledge of the questions at issue'.[137] Most public health professionals were sufficiently astute to acknowledge that the source of infectious disease lay in serious infrastructural deficiencies, poverty and bad living conditions rather than a handful of Travellers. Also, notifiable infectious diseases included only a fraction of the deaths from communicable illnesses each year.[138] For example, infant mortality in 1936–7 increased because of non-notifiable respiratory and alimentary diseases, a situation caused by increased poverty and distress after a succession of strikes.[139]

However, typhus, known as 'the Irish ague', lingered on in the Irish population after its eradication in Europe.[140] Eight cases occurred in Cahirciveen, County Kerry in 1937 but no blame was attached to Travellers.[141] In 1938, no cases of typhus were recorded, the first time since records began that the disease had not occurred.[142] But this triumph was short lived and five cases occurred in 1939.[143] Under the conditions of the Emergency, typhus represented a serious threat to the Irish population. Perhaps more importantly, the British administration knew that endemic typhus in Ireland was a grave threat to its war effort. From 1943 to 1947, 55,000 prospective emigrants to Britain were examined and deloused before travelling.[144] With increased hardship due to restricted food and employment, a typhus epidemic would have had disastrous consequences. In August 1940, an outbreak of 12 cases in County Donegal was traced to 'a band of itinerant tinkers'.[145] Public health officials attempted to persuade the group to be deloused and isolated for a period in order to prevent further infection but 'before effective measures could be taken the itinerants had disappeared'.[146] After this case, the department sought additional powers of detention for individuals who represented possible sources of infection. Submitting his case to government, the minister outlined how a 'crisis situation' would be rendered more serious for the military and civil authorities by an epidemic of typhus that could infect the army. Wartime conditions justified the extension of powers sought.

> The minister is of the opinion that in the interests of public safety more drastic measures must be taken than can be justified under the present law and that persons who are dangerous sources of infection should if necessary be detained until themselves and their clothing are rendered innocuous.[147]

The Emergency Power (Number 46) Order made on 27 August 1940 empowered the minister to issue a warrant for the detention and isolation of persons likely to spread disease.[148] Medical Inspector Dr P. Ronan Fanning noted the considerable difficulties of dealing with the 'tinker class' and welcomed the new powers to help officials 'fight this menace'.[149]

Probably as a result of this public health scare, Travellers and wanderers on Irish roads were discussed in August 1940 by the cabinet committee on

Emergency problems. The committee wished to ascertain if the numbers on the roads had increased during the Emergency and whether suspicious activity harmful to the war effort could go undetected. The Minister for Justice assured the committee the gardaí had 'standing instructions' to question and monitor the movements of 'vagrants and campers'. Garda reports did not indicate 'anything abnormal about the number or character of the persons who are at present camping and "caravaning" [*sic*] on the roads'. An increase in camping always occurred during the summer months and this was particularly so in 1940 because foreign holiday destinations were regrettably inaccessible.[150] During the Second World War, government involvement in all levels of society increased. This was an inevitable consequence of the disruption caused by the collapse of imports and efforts to create a self-sufficient economy and society. To maintain stability and distribute scarce resources, government was forced to monitor every aspect of Irish life. 'Total war' in combatant countries necessitated the mobilisation of all sections of the community in the service of the war effort. Although neutral, Ireland faced similar difficulties. The government managed issues of supply and demand, as well as exceptional circumstances such as typhus outbreaks, with Emergency Powers legislation. The Emergency Power (Number 46) Order was retained after the war in section 38 of the Health Act 1947.[151]

The 1947 Health Act was a massive statute, covering infectious disease, institutional development, food safety and the infamous Mother and Child scheme.[152] Although originally introduced in 1945, the bill did not become law until 1947. The powers of detention and isolation for carriers of infectious disease caused some comment among Dáil deputies wary of coercive measures. Compulsory examination of schoolchildren was decried by the opposition because it would end parental discretion over their children's medical treatment.[153] The minister proposed to punish those with an infectious disease who did not take steps to prevent its spread to others.[154] Infectious diseases ranged from typhus and venereal disease to whooping cough, scabies and mumps.[155] The 1945 bill emphasised compulsion, a feature that distinguished it, according to J. H. Whyte, from comparable international legislation.[156] That people could be isolated at the discretion of county medical officers was described by Richard Mulcahy as 'an unprecedented attack on personal liberty'.[157] Other deputies worried about the image of Ireland abroad, since the bill's enforcement of minimum hygiene standards clearly implied that the average citizen was less than spotless.[158] Patrick McGilligan questioned that an exceptional circumstance could justify the general application of a power:

> Is a wandering collection of tramps and tinkers, who caused trouble from the West up to Donegal, responsible for this? Are we really building up the public

health provisions for this country in the future in a permanent way upon the
vagaries of some group of tinkers operating in the most curious times of the last
few years?[159]

The parliamentary secretary to the minister, Dr Conn Ward, attempted to
quell criticism by stating that compulsory powers in relation to infectious
diseases were not a statutory innovation. Sections 148 and 149 of the Public
Health (Ireland) Act, 1878 empowered the Minister for Local Government
and Public health to make regulations for the treatment of persons affected
with an infectious disease.[160] Mulcahy then asked why, if typhus was
attributed to Travellers, all citizens were targeted in the legislation.[161] Ward
addressed the fears of deputies that powers would be applied generally

> This section is being debated as if it was going to be uniformly applied to every-
> body who contracted an infectious disease. I do not deny that it could be, and, if
> anybody says it could be, there is no use arguing with him because undoubtedly it
> could. But it is as clear as noonday that unless you take statutory powers to cope
> with exceptionally difficult circumstances you cannot cope with the exceptionally
> difficult circumstances when they present themselves.[162]

As Ward mentioned the non-co-operation by Travellers in Donegal, he
seemed to imply that the application of detention powers would be restricted
to the exceptional case posed by Travellers. However, the extensive parliamentary debates on this statute were no guide to its eventual application.
Despite this legislation, the administration seemed to consider Travellers a
minor problem. Disease was not blamed on a reservoir of infection located in
Traveller camps, for the department was aware that 'the incidence of the
principal infectious diseases in a country may fairly be taken as an index of the
sanitary circumstances of that country'.[163] In the context of sanitary deficiencies
and poor living conditions, the public health threat posed by Travellers was
insignificant. Dr James Deeny recognised that a typhus epidemic was most
likely in poor 'villages and the isolated houses on the more remote part of the
Atlantic seaboard';[164] the 1940 Donegal outbreak adhered to this pattern.
Moreover, if Travellers spread typhus, why were outbreaks not more common
and extensive? Some regional officials attributed endemic typhus infection to
Travellers but prevailing official opinion was that sanitary improvements
would eradicate the disease. The coercive 1940 Order and succeeding section
38 of the Health Act 1947 were formulated in response to Traveller non-
compliance but were applicable to any citizen of the state. Yet the powers of
detention were used only once in the period 1947–57.[165] Available records from
the Department of Health suggest that women with venereal disease rather

than Travellers were detained under section 38.[166] Once again the target of the public official's interventionist zeal shifted to more vulnerable and accessible members of the settled community. By 1960, the Department of Health did not consider infectious diseases spread by Travellers to be sufficiently problematic to merit sustained attention.[167]

CONCLUSION

Before the 1960s, voluntary organisations perceived Travellers to be worthy recipients of aid while government agencies both ignored and excluded them. Indeed, Travellers' success or failure in accessing welfare benefits depended upon a number of factors. Powerful officials could intercede on their behalf, but hostile local representatives could also prevent Travellers securing minimal welfare benefits. The community defined by welfare agencies did not include Travellers – geographically mobile individuals without a valid claim to local funding. It was voluntary organisations that provided education and often mediated on Travellers' behalf with the structures of church and state. The St Vincent de Paul Society and the Legion of Mary represented a consistent source of assistance for families in need. Neither the Legion of Mary nor the society forced Travellers to abandon nomadism and even facilitated travelling by helping to purchase horses and wagons for needy families. Voluntary organisations provided an alternative welfare service; for those neglected or excluded by welfare agencies they offered the only assistance available. The reformatory and missionary possibilities of work with Travellers also attracted these organisations, who played an important role in the settlement programme described in chapter 6. But as for official welfare initiatives, voluntary charity was local in character.

In general, Traveller access to public services was uneven and dependent on interested individuals. Thus, when politicians and officials wished to coerce individuals into education or health care, Travellers were correspondingly vulnerable. The very real protection afforded by the constitution prevented the imposition of compulsory education on Travellers that would have destroyed family units. Even when the 1947 Health Act targeted Travellers, the consequences were not serious, as recourse to the law was never sought. As a group Travellers were never subject to sustained legislative control because central government had difficulty categorising individuals who presented problems under many headings. The Department of Education was responsible for administering school attendance; the Department of Local Government and Public Health, and later the Department of Health were responsible for the possible sanitary implications of unauthorised campsites and infectious diseases; the Department of Local Government was responsible for determining land-use policies and promoting town planning; Bord Fáilte and the Department of Local Government defined the landscape.

In the context of administrative divisions of responsibility, Travellers were not exclusively part of any departmental remit. The nature of Traveller nomadism, accommodation patterns and lifestyle could be affected by many departments but, paradoxically, this ensured that no department was willing to tackle them as a specific group. Even as the Department of Local Government and Public Health extended its compulsive powers over citizens, ostensibly including nomads, Travellers were ignored. Travellers successfully evaded government attention because various parts of the system, from district justices to department officials, were unwilling or unable to view their existence as an urgent problem. Their escape from government intervention was perhaps unique when the institutionalisation of other 'problem' groups such as unmarried mothers and destitute children is considered. How and when Travellers were finally categorised as the 'itinerant problem' will be outlined in the next chapter, which will discuss the response of central government to the minority. Once the government applied a label to unauthorised camping, wandering horses and poor school attendance, the creation of a policy to deal with Travellers as a group was not far behind.

FIVE

SOME PRACTICAL SUGGESTIONS

THE GOVERNMENT RESPONSE, 1949–63

—

While various welfare aspects of the 'itinerant problem' had been considered by government departments, none felt compelled to address the issue. Aside from the difficulties of categorisation already outlined, there was a reluctance to make major changes to the legal system in order to target Travellers as a group. The government believed the legal implications for the whole population of anti-Traveller measures were not worth enduring. Public representatives who, in the 1950s, represented suburban residents rather than farmers, raised the 'itinerant problem' in parliament. When the government refused to tackle conflict between Travellers and settled people, local communities and authorities took extra-legal or indirect action to move Travellers on. Only when Dublin representatives persistently complained about Traveller camps did the government begin to consider the issue. The official response to complaints about Travellers hardly varied until the Commission on Itinerancy was appointed in June 1960 by the Taoiseach, Seán Lemass. The responsibility for the Commission lay with the Department of Justice and its ambitious Parliamentary Secretary, Charles Haughey.

This chapter will analyse why the government finally appointed a commission to report on the position of Travellers in Irish society. The comprehensive report contains valuable information on the relationship between Travellers and settled people, as it devoted much consideration to the attitudes of the communities towards each other. It was especially useful for analysing settled people's beliefs about Travellers, in official and popular terms. Of particular importance was the role envisaged for voluntary agencies, who were to guide Travellers through the machinery of the state. In keeping with their reformatory missions, charitable organisations were allocated a primary role in the settlement policy advocated by the Commission. Directed by the government to find methods of assimilating Travellers, the Commission did not challenge its remit. Although judged harshly by contemporary activists the report's recommendations were, at times, surprisingly nuanced and restrained, and repay further analysis.[1] Latter-day government policy on Travellers cannot be understood without a careful study of the first government report on the community.

THE POLITICAL DEBATE, 1949–60

From as early as 1931, Dáil deputies asked the government to 'do something' about vagrancy, trespass by animals and the public health risks posed by Traveller campsites. If public representatives were vocal for so long, why was a report not commissioned until 1960? The complaints by public representatives and government responses to them explains administrative inaction. From 1925 to 1963, 31 parliamentary questions concerning Travellers were posed to different ministers. Only five of these questions preceded 1949, indeed the majority of references covered the period 1949–60. Many allusions to Travellers shared one feature from 1925 to 1960: most deputies addressed their complaints to the Minister for Justice, demanding that his department draft legislation for dealing with wandering and trespassing animals, campsites, begging, public disorder and the generalised, almost indiscriminate, wrong-doing of which Travellers were accused.[2] While the Department of Justice supervised the police force and the judiciary, it was not the only department that drafted legislation criminalising behaviour, as the analysis of educational and environmental statutes in previous chapters has shown. Parliamentary members occasionally placed their concerns before the Ministers for Local Government or Agriculture but appealed most persistently to the minister associated with law and order, in spite of the fact that the control of camping clearly lay with the Department of Local Government rather than with Justice.

The Minister for Justice rarely responded to deputies' complaints made during the estimates debates, catch-all annual debates that could cover a vast range of topics depending upon the fixations of the deputies who contributed. Parliamentary questions were more useful for extracting information from the minister although they were rigidly scripted and supplementary questions were restricted. When questioned about the problems created by Travellers, various ministers undertook to ask the gardaí to deal with the matter.[3] Only in 1950 did the Fine Gael Minister for Justice, General Seán Mac Eoin, explain his department's policy. Neither the minister nor his civil servants had introduced legislation because they believed no 'satisfactory solution' existed.[4] Mac Eoin even pointed out to the House that there were '6,000 of these persons whose people have been on the roads for centuries and that they have a prescriptive right to be on the roads'. The failure of the Northern Ireland parliament to pass the Gypsy Bill in 1950 had been noted in Dublin and they were not anxious to repeat the mistake of their Stormont counterparts.[5] In 1951, the Fianna Fáil Minister for Justice, Gerry Boland, again told deputies that his department would not introduce legislation to control 'vagrants': 'The problem has been examined on a number of occasions with a view to the introduction of legislation, but, owing to the practical difficulties of enforcement, the proposal has had to be abandoned.'[6] In 1956, an apparent increase in RUC activity targeting Northern Travellers worried Dáil deputies, who believed that the nomadic population south of the border was growing. Deputy Michael J. Kennedy told the House that 'Itinerants were more or less banished out of the Six Counties and they all came in here', complaining, 'They have been unloaded onto us'.[7]

In 1958, the Minister for Justice, Oscar Traynor, explained to the Dáil that he had seriously considered the matter, which was, in the opinion of officials from the Departments of Justice, Health and Local Government, 'insoluble'. Traynor presented to his officials a scheme 'suggesting that every county should provide a certain acreage on the edge of towns of some importance and that the itinerants would be allowed to park only within the precincts of these enclosed areas'. To his surprise, he was told that this 'was an old remedy, that it had been suggested on a number of occasions, that there was nothing new about it'. There was even support within the department for 'the right of itinerants to operate as they have been operating in the country'. The Minister believed that Travellers were 'a decent class of people' despite the 'considerable amount of dislocation' they caused on the roadsides of Ireland.[8] But deputies were not silenced; in 1959, Traynor once again addressed the House on 'the old annual complaint about tinkers'. He outlined the practical difficulties facing legislators and law enforcement agencies who sought to restrict camping by Travellers.

> If we prohibit camping on the roads, we force them to camp on private property. If we restrict them to sites approved by the local authority – and can enforce such a restriction – we create, in the selected areas, permanent 'colonies' of tinkers. What about the residents in the neighbourhood who will find themselves pestered day in, day out, and whose property will depreciate in value?[9]

Interestingly, publicly funded camping sites had been considered by government but the potential unpopularity of the proposal had deterred legislators and politicians. On the question of trespass, the Minister asked deputies to consider the only enforceable legal option – making trespass a crime.

> How can we deal with trespass, which is a civil wrong only, when the owner of the trespassing animals is not a mark for damages? [*sic*] We could, of course, make trespass a criminal offence but this would be a major change in our law and would certainly have serious repercussions on the relations between neighbours in rural Ireland particularly. I cannot see any Minister proposing such a step and I cannot see the Oireachtas accepting it.[10]

Clearly, the disadvantages of changing the trespass law outweighed the advantages of solving the 'itinerant problem'. The general repercussions of laws intended to restrict Travellers alone had been considered and finally dismissed by government departments. Restricting the numbers of horses owned by Travellers would deprive them of 'one of their honest means of livelihood'. School attendance could be enforced only if children were removed from their parents. Traynor asked the house, 'Will any Deputy advocate that we do that, even if the Constitution would permit it?',[11] perhaps forgetting that legislation outlining that course of action had already been put forward by his colleague, Thomas Derrig, in 1942. Once again, the Minister explained that he had considered the problem. He had suggested compelling Travellers to camp in local authority campsites which would function as 'types of stations through which the tinkers would pass on their journeys through the country'.[12]

> That was turned down as not being possible, because, first of all, I was told no county council or local authority would pay the money which would be involved and, secondly, the people contiguous to the fields to which I refer, would be very far from thankful for having these people as their neighbours as they would probably be the first to be robbed. . . . These are the sort of problems we are up against.[13]

In Traynor's opinion, the political risks of dealing with settled people's complaints in a manner that did not infringe constitutional rights or disproportionately penalise Travellers were not worth taking. Officials and politicians refused to implement a solution founded on coercive legislation that pursued Travellers. Also, politicians and local authority administrators were sensitive to the political unpopularity of the only legal solution: publicly funded campsites. After surveying the various options, Traynor concluded that there was 'no solution' to conflict between settled and Travelling people over land usage and animals. He urged those deputies who complained to offer a workable remedy, since his personal opinion was that 'The only hope is that they will move along, and keep moving, and not stay too long anywhere'.[14]

An important aspect of the political debate was the increasing volume of complaints from urban representatives in the 1950s, particularly Dublin-based TDs. Significantly, the 1956 census of Travellers included the county boroughs for the first time. Helleiner noted that after the election of the majority Fianna Fáil government in 1957, 'deputies representing urban areas took up the Traveller issue with unprecedented intensity'.[15] The increasing visibility of Traveller camps on the fringes of the capital city probably pushed central government to tackle the issue seriously. Although Travellers had camped in Dublin County Borough from as early as 1932, by the 1960s camps in Dublin city and county were much larger than in other parts of the country.[16] Both

Seán Lemass and Charles Haughey represented Dublin constituencies while civil servants resided in the suburbs of the city. A previously rural preoccupation with wandering horses and campsites was now uncomfortably close to home. The excessive centralisation of the Irish state – centred on Dublin city and its hinterland – has been noted elsewhere.[17] If the perspective of government has been 'subtly distorted'[18] by the growth of Dublin city, the political concern of administrators with the Traveller issue may have been determined by their personal interest in the capital.

During the 1950s the government had decided that no action was preferable to the options they could foresee. Once central government refused to draft a policy to solve illegal sites and animal trespass, local authorities were left to cope as best they could. Thus Travellers were at the mercy of different local government bodies who used their powers according to the level of public complaint about encampments. Dáil deputies continued to raise the issue with ministers, especially the Minister for Justice while *ad hoc*, temporary solutions were adopted by local government. A local authority that wished to provide camping facilities did not have the legal power to do so. Under the Local Government (Sanitary Services) Act 1948, local authorities could grant licences to landowners who wished to develop facilities for campers,[19] but no private landowner provided sites for Travellers. By washing its hands of the matter, central government left the dispute firmly in the hands of local bodies who attempted to satisfy complaining ratepayers by eradicating Traveller encampments. As outlined in chapter 3, some authorities enacted the prohibitions against camping in the 1948 Act. However, not all local authorities acted within the Act and their actions against Travellers were of dubious legal standing.[20] Yet the persistent complaints at national level about Traveller encampments suggest that the 1948 Act was not a panacea for local politicians or police.

Gardaí responded to complaints by moving Travellers on, often without recourse to legal niceties. Travellers camping on road verges were not committing a crime, but their presence was crime enough for some residents. As an article in *Iris an Gharda* explained to members of the police force:

> Parking byelaws are in force in the main centres of population throughout the country and unless caravans are parked contrary to the provisions of these byelaws, or in a manner which obstructs or is calculated to prevent or interrupt the free passage of any person or carriage, there is no offence committed.[21]

In most cases, camping Travellers were not breaking any law. The persistent complaints from politicians illustrate that there was no legislation under which camping Travellers could be prosecuted. Since official policy had no answer to complaints about Travellers, unofficial, illegal action was taken by communities, gardaí and local government to rid themselves of the 'itinerant problem'. Deputy Tadgh Linehan freely admitted to the Dáil how he helped break up encampments: 'Time and again people have come to my office and asked me could I get in touch with the local superintendent and get him to authorise the local sergeant to send out four or five Guards to shift them out of a particular place'.[22] Nationally, the policy was to move Travellers on when settled people complained. This was, as Traynor understood, no solution. The widening social and cultural disparity between Travellers and poorer settled people, in addition to greater restrictions on informal land usage, meant that conflict between the two communities would only increase. The government finally addressed the issue in 1960, with the appointment of a commission to study the 'itinerant problem'.

THE COMMISSION ON ITINERANCY

The Commission on Itinerancy was appointed in 1960 for a number of reasons. The volume of complaints from public representatives was increasing, in spite of compulsory purchase, enclosure and legal prohibition. Most significantly, the boundaries of the social welfare system were being extended. Many social issues since independence had been tackled in an *ad hoc* fashion; benefits were extended piecemeal to various categories of entitlement such as school-going children, widows, unemployed men. Those outside such definitional categories of need were effectively ignored until the 1960s, when government expanded its social remit even further. Reports were commissioned in 1960 and 1967 on those suffering from mental handicap and illness,[23] while health and education policy was also reassessed.[24] Central government grew in size and complexity in the 1960s.[25] In addition to a shift in government, the reforming impulses of younger politicians like Charles Haughey provoked a re-examination of the Traveller issue specifically. Haughey's energy was channelled into Traveller-settled relations by the Taoiseach Seán Lemass, who asked him to tackle the subject. It is unclear exactly what prompted Lemass to ask the Department of Justice about the Traveller issue. Perhaps a representation from a constituent or a newspaper article drew his attention to the matter. With characteristic efficiency, the Taoiseach ensured that the question of Traveller campsites and wandering horses was finally considered seriously by central government.

Lemass first proposed a Commission to the Minister for Justice, Oscar Traynor, in March 1960. Receiving no reply from Traynor, Lemass suggested that the Parliamentary Secretary, Charles Haughey, assume responsibility for the Commission. Traynor's department was a reluctant sponsor of the Commission and reminded the Taoiseach that 'the primary problems of itinerancy were rehabilitation, health and education'.[26] Haughey surveyed the problem and submitted a memorandum to government on 25 May 1960. The cabinet approved the appointment of a commission, 'to be appointed by the Taoiseach, in view of the differences of opinion as to ministerial responsibility and to avoid creating the impression that law-and-order was the paramount aspect'.[27] The members were to represent a number of backgrounds and interest groups. The government recommended a former judge to the chair, with a sociologist, two people with local government experience, an educational official, a police officer, a clergyman and 'a person with a wide knowledge of farming' among the members.[28] These categories would represent the various branches of the administration that dealt with Travellers, or complaints relating to their conduct. Strangely, no representative from the Department of Social Welfare was suggested. In contrast to the 1927 report on the poor law, no charitable organisations were represented. Presumably, the clergyman was expected to articulate the importance of Christian charity and spiritual education, perhaps indicating that Travellers were perceived as God's poor. Justice Brian Walsh, whose later judgements were landmark cases involving human rights,[29] chaired a Commission comprising:

> George Claxton, National Farmers' Association
> Fr Thomas Fehily, Director of the Dublin Institute of Catholic Sociology
> Chief Superintendent Thomas Mc Donagh
> Proinsias Ó Tighearnigh, former Chief Inspector Department of Education
> Matthew Macken, County Manager for Carlow and Kildare[30]
> Dr Maurice Mc Parland, County Medical Officer of Health for County Donegal
> Dr John O'Regan, Chief Medical Officer, Dublin Health Authority
> Cornelius Meaney, Chairman of General Council of the Committees on Agriculture
> Dr Angela Russell (affiliation unknown)

The rationale behind the choice of particular individuals is largely unclear. Fr Fehily became associated with the Traveller issue after his defence of the travelling way of life at a meeting of public health inspectors in 1959; a motion to ban itinerancy had been tabled against which nobody, save Fr Fehily, was willing to speak.[31] This meeting was judged to have 'foreshadowed' the Commission's report.[32] He also combined the role of clergyman and sociologist. Other members clearly represented the categories suggested by Haughey to the cabinet; as individuals they may also have had a personal interest in Travellers.

Although ostensibly appointed by the Taoiseach, Charles Haughey was *de facto* responsible for the Commission.[33] His association with the issue of itinerancy was such that James Dillon styled him the 'Parliamentary Secretary for tinkers'.[34] Addressing the Commission members, Haughey described the 'itinerant problem' as one which was present for a 'very long time and about which a great deal has been written and spoken'. The Commission was appointed because various departments, local authorities and the gardaí had failed to put forward 'any practical suggestions as to what might be done to improve the position generally'. Government departments had analysed the issue from their own particular viewpoints and Haughey was anxious that the Commission 'examine the problem as a whole in all its aspects'.[35] The terms of reference, drafted in the Department of Justice, were

1   to enquire into the problems arising from the presence in the country of itinerants in considerable numbers;
2   to examine the economic, education, health and social problems inherent in their way of life;
3   to consider what steps might be taken
    a) to provide opportunities for a better way of life for itinerants
    b) to promote their absorption into the general community
    c) pending such absorption, to reduce to a minimum the disadvantages to themselves and to the community resulting from their itinerant habits and
    d) to improve the position generally; and
4   to make recommendations[36]

Before the Commission began its work, it was told to advocate absorption and assimilation. Given the lack of reliable information on the issue, this direction was certainly pre-emptive. Thus, an important part of the Commission's work was fact finding. To collect up-to-date information, the Commission directly contacted those bodies or individuals 'whose functions or activities in any way impinged upon the itinerants and their way of life'. Press and radio advertisements invited those with an interest in the matter to submit memoranda of evidence to the Commission. Government departments were asked to furnish statistics and observations to the Commission. The Department of Justice contacted garda superintendents to ascertain the extent of the itinerant problem in their respective areas. Every local authority in Ireland was requested to indicate:

1   their experience of applications of housing from itinerants;
2   whether they found it necessary to take action against itinerants under the Sanitary Services Acts;

3   Whether itinerants in their respective areas were provided with health and welfare assistance.[37]

All of the religious congregations in Ireland were contacted and invited to submit memoranda or observations to the Commission. The response to the Commission's request was enthusiastic, although not everyone who publicly expressed an opinion on Travellers contacted the Commission.[38] Arguably, the Commission had a surfeit of information with which to assess Traveller–settled relations nationwide. The Departments of Agriculture, Education, Health, Justice and Local Government submitted evidence. Every county and county borough council, and Urban District Council (UDC) in the country provided information on their respective areas.[39] Many representative groups, charitable societies and semi-state bodies also contacted the Commission. The variety of organisations which contacted the Commission was extraordinary: the Scrap Metal Merchants Association of Ireland; Bord na Móna; the Society of St Vincent de Paul; Ardagh Diocesan Branch of the Christus Rex Society and the Irish Medical Association to name but a few. Evidence came from as far afield as two individuals living in Georgia and California respectively.[40] International nomadic populations were also carefully considered by the Commission, who asked Irish representatives abroad to report on the experiences of various governments.[41] Information from Northern Ireland and Britain was obtained directly from local and national authorities.[42]

Apart from near universal prohibitive and restrictive measures, it was discovered that the Netherlands was the only country where state-funded accomodation provision had been made for nomads. Six Commission members decided to visit the country to gather first-hand evidence: Justice Brian Walsh, Fr Fehily, Dr Mc Parland, Mr Macken, Mr Ó Tighearnigh and the Secretary, Mr Aidan McDonald, spent 17–24 September 1961 in the Netherlands. They met central government officials, local authority members and toured encampments in different parts of the country. Members of itinerant groups were interviewed with the aid of interpreters.[43] Dutch nomads, the Woonwagenbewoners, are a nomadic group who do not identify themselves as Romanies, while the settled population views them as descendants of house dwellers who took to the road in the nineteenth century.[44] The parallels with Irish Travellers were obvious. The Commission members were impressed at the efforts of local and central government in the Netherlands. The visit undoubtedly influenced their deliberations, especially as the delegation felt that the Dutch situation was 'in many respects similar to that in Ireland'. They were particularly impressed by the attitude of the authorities, who were 'imbued with a sense of social justice and charity in their general approach to the problem rather than a desire to eradicate a nuisance to the

settled community'.[45] The Dutch experience in education and campsite provision provided a model for some of the Commission's recommendations,
which are detailed later.

Unfortunately, the records of the Commission did not survive in either the
files of the Departments of Justice or Local Government. It seems likely that
administrative divisions of responsibility over the settlement programme,
explained in chapter 6, led to careless handling of archival material. If the
records of the Commission had survived, they would provide a wealth of
information about settled people's reaction to Travellers. But no matter how
broad the source base of the Commission, the thrust of its inquiries were
determined by its definition of an itinerant and the assumption that settlement was the only solution to conflict between Travellers and settled people.
The Commission's definition of 'itinerant' was 'a person who had no fixed
place of abode and habitually wandered from place to place, but excluding
travelling show-people and travelling entertainers.[46] Although the terms of
reference illustrated the shortcomings of government information about
Travellers, this ignorance of the problem did not prevent Haughey from
advocating a solution – absorption and assimilation. The possible findings of
the Commission were inevitably restricted by this solution yet its members
did not challenge the settlement concept. Indeed, they wholeheartedly agreed
that it was the long-term solution both to poverty among Travellers and
conflict with the settled community.

The second term of reference in particular – 'to examine the economic,
education, health and social problems inherent in their way of life' – asserted
the government's belief that Travellers, as a distinctive nomadic group, were a
problem to be solved. Difficulties between Travellers and settled people were
created by Travellers following traditional routes and practices. The only
solution to the conflict was absorption into the settled community, where
Travellers would adopt the values and lifestyle of the majority population.
The Commission accepted the principle of settlement without dissent. It did
not view Travellers as a separate ethnic group, although it acknowledged that
the settled population were inclined to view them as 'a single homogenous
group, tribe or community within the nation'.[47] For contemporary representative organisations promoting Traveller ethnicity, this denial invalidates
the Commission's report. Also, its assimilationist goals, now ostensibly abandoned, have tarnished the 1963 report for many activists and social scientists.
While Travellers now rightly criticise a report which portrays their community
simply as a problem, the report and government intentions were not entirely
mercenary. Haughey told the Commission members:

One over-riding consideration which dominates the entire background of this problem and is of paramount importance in relation to it is the simple fact that the humblest itinerant is entitled to a place in the sun and to a share in the benefits of our society. His fundamental rights as an individual and his religious beliefs are sacred and inalienable.[48]

Contemporary scholars, in particular sociologists, would argue that the *Report of the Commission on Itinerancy* is an ethnocentric justification of an absorption policy predicated on the eradication of cultural difference.[49] A sociological 'reading' of the Report contrasts considerably with an analysis of the historical context in which the document was written. A few points must be made in favour of the Report. It did not advocate that settlement be enforced by law and it outlined facilities to be provided for nomadic Travellers. A whole range of accommodation provision was presented in the Report, from long-term campsites (admittedly for families adjusting to settlement) to halting sites for transient, fully nomadic Travellers. If the balance between site provision and housing since the publication of the Report was poor, it cannot overshadow what was a finely balanced and subtle analysis of Travellers' position in Irish society. It contained some statements that are now considered objectionable but, in the context of the time, it was progressive.[50] It would be ahistorical to expect 1960s administrators to approach the issue as an ethnic one, especially since 'ethnicity' was a relatively recent concept – the term was first defined by the *Oxford English Dictionary* in 1953.[51] The zeal for a settlement policy was clearly founded on a sincere belief that many Travellers living in poverty should be allowed the same opportunities as economically deprived settled people. That Travellers would chose their apparently unstable and difficult way of life over the advantages of settled living simply did not occur to the Commission members. Arguably, the settlement policy – its successes and failures – was the catalyst for the development of cultural politics among Travellers that gathered pace in the late 1960s and early 1970s. Just as slum dwellers were politicised by the status granted to them as public-authority tenants, so Travellers being 'resettled' began to articulate their accommodation preferences.

The Commission's report was a unique document, presenting considerable detail on Irish Travellers in the early 1960s. A total of 166 pages long, with 56 pages of appendices, it was a comprehensive consideration of Traveller–settled relations in twentieth-century Ireland. However, the greatest criticism levelled at the report was that no Traveller was a member of the Commission. Even *Dublin Opinion* noted this deficiency.

A poem. Personnel of Itinerants Commission
I have looked at each name.
It's a cause for shame
That should never be forgot.
Someone's ears should tingle;
There isn't a single
Itinerant in the lot.[52]

Given the formidable literacy barrier facing Travellers, their participation would have been surprising.[53] Similar problems were encountered by the Northern Ireland Committee on Gypsies and like Itinerants, when the Chair, Professor E. Estyn Evans, suggested a Traveller be asked to sit on the committee.[54] However, Travellers were not completely excluded from the Commission on Itinerancy. While members realised that Travellers were unlikely to approach the Commission directly, they believed that discussions with Travellers themselves were vital to the success of their study. Consequently, the Commission visited campsites in counties Carlow, Clare, Cork, Donegal, Galway, Kerry, Kildare, Kilkenny, Laois, Leitrim, Limerick, Mayo, Roscommon, Sligo, Tipperary, Waterford, and Wexford.[55] Individual members also interviewed Travellers as they encountered them in their daily work. Approximately 300 families were contacted to ascertain their opinions on travelling, occupations and settlement. In general, it was felt that these visits would be more valuable if they were unannounced and unplanned. In Dublin city, an official whose duty it was to evict Travellers from Corporation property took Commission members to visit campsites. In spite of his job, Mr William Reynolds had apparently won the confidence of many families. Outside Dublin, gardaí helped the Commission to locate campsites, but did not attend the interviews with Travellers.[56] Only one meeting with Travellers camped in Ballyfermot, Dublin, was prearranged at which a spokesman, Mr Joseph O'Donoghue, addressed the Commission. However, this method of gathering evidence was not repeated 'as it was felt that the formality of the occasion tended to make them ill at ease and to leave most of their discussion to . . . their spokesman'.[57]

Interviews and meetings were supplemented by two censuses taken by the gardaí on December 1960 and June 1961. These censuses elicited basic information from those questioned such as family abode, birthplace and literacy levels. But the thirty-three questions also sought detailed information about employment and unemployment, access to health care and whether the person had suffered from TB or a skin disease. Travellers were carefully questioned about travel and accommodation patterns, specifically whether they wished to settle permanently.

30 Would head of family prefer to settle in one place if means of livelihood available? If 'Yes' state County

31 Would mother of family unit prefer to settle in one place if means of livelihood available? If 'Yes' state County

32 Was a Council house or flat ever applied for?

33 If so, where?[58]

Questions 30 and 31 were clearly designed to discern Travellers' attitude to permanent settlement. In keeping with the terms of reference, the Commission was attempting to find a method of promoting the absorption of Travellers. Since nomadism separated them from the majority community and provoked hostile reactions from settled people, an end to travelling seemed the best way to solve problems attributed to Travellers. But before permanent settlement could be recommended, Traveller opinion had to be sought. The responses to questions 30 and 31 in the census were overwhelmingly positive. In the 1960 census, approximately 78 per cent of men and women questioned indicated a desire to settle if a means of livelihood were available. Commission members also posed the same question to those Travellers they interviewed personally. After collecting this oral evidence, the members were satisfied that 'a very substantial number of families, particularly those with young children, would settle down in houses if given the opportunity'. The evidence of Travellers applying for public authority housing or becoming private home owners further supported this conclusion.[59] It was a fortunate coincidence that the evidence collected coincided perfectly with terms of reference advocating the assimilation of Travellers. That Travellers understood 'settled' differently was not acknowledged, even though census takers did discover that 'settled' parents claimed by some interviewees 'were, in fact, itinerants themselves who owned houses in which they lived for a substantial part of the year when not travelling'.[60] Perhaps those respondents who expressed a preference for settlement were not indicating a desire to abandon the road, but seeking a permanent base for the winter months.

There were other weaknesses in the Commission's methodology: conscious of the danger of unreliability in answers provided to the police, the Commission asked each enumerator to comment on the information provided. Thus Traveller's responses were weighted and possibly filtered by gardaí. The usefulness of the appendixes included in the report are somewhat compromised by the knowledge that the Commission allowed for a 'probable degree of unreliability' in assessing the census results.[61] Unfortunately, the instructions for enumerators are not reproduced as an appendix. Nevertheless, it is clear that the Commission was careful to contact Travellers directly before finally reaching its conclusions. Owing to the paucity of sources on Travellers, the information in the Commission's report, whatever its flaws, remains valuable.

FINDINGS OF THE COMMISSION ON ITINERANCY

The Commission established a number of important facts about Irish Travellers and their relationship with the majority population. Firstly, the numbers of Travellers and their distribution across the counties had be established. Chapter 1 has already outlined how small the nomadic population was. On average, only 6,000 people were counted as Travellers. Indeed, the recorded number of Travellers never totalled one per cent of the population. As table 5.1 shows, Travellers were also widely distributed in every county in Ireland. These figures showed considerable variation across counties and over time.

Table 5.1   Traveller population by county, 1944–61

County	1944	1952	1956	1960	1961
Carlow	188	151	122	123	139
Cavan	194	152	151	215	100
Clare	201	344	150	171	255
Cork	315	604	430	574	477
Donegal	78	228	221	175	206
Dublin	38	158	340	418	258
Galway	485	855	966	822	814
Kerry	363	238	376	247	283
Kildare	—	216	260	107	206
Kilkenny	193	109	132	233	128
Laois	127	214	183	113	167
Leitrim	148	156	146	143	145
Limerick	211	309	426	397	265
Longford	179	134	131	144	143
Louth	172	150	216	146	132
Mayo	251	323	407	478	329
Meath	165	122	178	161	136
Monaghan	82	138	222	120	134
Offaly	169	141	414	219	180
Roscommon	257	356	325	288	164
Sligo	103	104	155	162	238
Tipperary	385	447	460	400	450
Waterford	180	69	165	75	31
Westmeath	247	179	180	279	131
Wexford	304	281	279	277	255
Wicklow	120	133	113	104	112

1 The figures for 1944 and 1952 do not include County Boroughs
2 No separate figures for Carlow and Kildare, which comprise a single garda division, are available for 1944. The figures shown for Carlow for 1944 include those for Kildare.
3 The exact dates of the taking of each census are as follows: 6 September 1944, 30 April 1952 (except for Carlow and Kildare which was taken on 2 May 1952), 10 September 1956, 1 December 1960, 1 June 1961.
Source: *Report of the Commission on Itinerancy 1963*, Appendix ii.

It is difficult to discern a pattern, but more Travellers were counted in County Galway than anywhere else. Other counties with large numbers were Cork, Mayo, Tipperary and Dublin. However, the rise or fall in numbers from census to census, even within a county boundary, show little consistency. The object of scrutiny for the Commission on Itinerancy was numerically insignificant and unevenly distributed across the country. Arguably, never had a Commission investigated such a small group. The reluctance of successive governments to address an issue which provoked heated discussion but pertained to so few people is perhaps understandable. TDs described large convoys of caravans, hordes of animals and persistently complained about growing numbers of Travellers[62] but the reality was less menacing. In Galway, a county with a population of 149,887 in 1961, the 814 Travellers enumerated there represented 0.5 per cent of the county's population.[63] For more populous counties with fewer Travellers, the proportions were even smaller. This did not prevent deputies from making sweeping, impressionistic statements. Mr Donogh O'Malley, representing Limerick, described the county as 'a happy hunting ground for tinkers' since Limerick Corporation had lost its case in the High Court (see chapter 4).[64] Even if all the 426 Travellers in the county in 1956 were concentrated in Limerick city, their numbers would hardly be noticed in an urban area of 50,886 people.[65] The stark contrast between the rhetoric of threat and menace and the reality of tiny numbers merely serves to illustrate the hostility provoked by a statistically insignificant, but highly visible group of people. Indeed, the numbers were so small that it is tempting to wonder whether many settled people had *any* regular contact with Travellers. However, the Commission did not limit its investigations to numbers, being equally concerned with the nature of Traveller society.

STRUCTURE OF TRAVELLER SOCIETY

Despite occasional methodological shortcomings, the report gives a valuable insight into the structure of Traveller society. Travel patterns, trades and wealth differed among Travellers, and the Commission classified the economic circumstances of four distinct sub-groups. A small minority, numbering approximately 40 to 60 families, lived in motor trailers and travelled extensively to deal in linoleum, household goods, scrap and rags on a large scale. Their living conditions were good, their incomes high. The Commission found that these Travellers owned valuable cars, vans and caravans and were 'never short of the necessities of life and have many of the comforts'. Even though well off, a number of families begged for food and milk.[66] Many also owned houses where women and children stayed during the winter months. Their conspicuous economic success proved that nomadism was not necessarily impoverishing. Indeed, their trading income depended on nomadism. The Commission judged this group to be clean and comfortably dressed, with modern and well-kept caravans. Significantly, this group regarded themselves as 'superior to other classes of itinerants' and did not associate with poorer families.[67]

A second group of Travellers also travelled widely though they were less economically successful. This group numbered 300 to 400 families who lived in horse-drawn caravans. They traded horses and other animals and undertook contract labouring work such as beet or potato picking. Their living conditions were not as comfortable as their trailer counterparts, with tents supplementing the caravans. Nevertheless, their incomes were judged 'more than adequate for their needs'. The members of this group begged extensively, obtaining most of their food in this way. A third group only travelled in a small area and was further divided into families owning horse-drawn caravans and those who possessed only tents for shelter. These families travelled a regular route over a small area, remaining as long as they were able in each place. Caravan dwellers were better off than tent dwellers, trading on a small scale in scrap and horse hair. Many claimed to be tinsmiths, chimney sweeps or makers of artificial flowers. They also migrated for seasonal farm labour opportunities. Without the proceeds from begging, the Commission believed that the 350 to 450 caravan-dwelling families would starve. However, they were wealthier than the 300 to 400 families who lived in tents alone. Their incomes were estimated to be 'extremely low, below subsistence level and derived almost entirely from begging'.[68] The Commission described this group as 'largely unemployed and unemployable'.[69] Those Travellers who covered a limited area were 'not the same nuisance to the farmers because they are too well known in their particular areas'.[70] Apart from the motor trailer group, Travellers usually regarded 'all other itinerants fraternally as part of the community of travellers'.[71]

Thus potent class divisions existed in the Traveller community as well as among the settled. Michael MacDonagh has briefly outlined the class divisions in Irish Traveller society. One group of Travellers 'have a long nomadic tradition and are very confident about their identity as Travelling People'.

Other Travellers had close ties with the settled community, often inter-marrying. MacDonagh admits that in the 1930s, marriage to the latter was frowned on by the former. These distinctions are now less significant but were 'a lot clearer and more pronounced in the past'.[72] While MacDonagh emphasises contact with settled people as the dividing line in Traveller society, economic circumstances were also significant. Possibly, economically successful families who could sustain extensive nomadism drew a line between them-selves and less mobile, less well-off Travellers. Travellers themselves were not 'antagonistic' towards the settled population but they held themselves 'aloof' from the majority population and showed 'no discernable inferiority complex'. As contact with settled people was confined to buying, selling and begging, Travellers rarely presented their real personality to members of the settled community.[73]

Although the Commission found Travellers were religious in sentiment, their Church attendance was poor. Catholic parents were careful to ensure their children received the sacraments of Baptism, Penance, Holy Communion and Confirmation. The gardaí often allowed families to remain in one place to secure religious education.[74] Travellers were even more scrupulous about sexual morality and fidelity within marriage. Parents of young couples insisted upon marriage once courtship commenced and were unwilling to allow their children to emigrate before marriage.[75] Sexual morality was central to Traveller society and allegations of adultery were the cause of 'some of the most savage family feuds'.[76] It was feared these high standards would be 'imperilled' during absorption and the Commission hoped that Travellers would not be affected by 'the less desirable incidents of life in the settled community'.[77] Understandably, the social and economic circumstances of the settled com-munity were not examined by the Commission. Only when analysis touched on the extent of social distance between the two communities did the Commission refer to settled Irish society. The settlement programme was urgent precisely because of the continuing rise in living standards in the general population. The gap between Travellers and the settled was 'constantly widening'. Such 'an evergrowing disparity in relative social standards' would only provoke increasing hostility from settled people struggling to make 'the mental adjustment' necessary to tolerate Travellers.[78] The Commission evidently believed that the cultural gap between Travellers and settled society was a reflection of these differing living standards; the culture of poverty distin-guished the minority from the majority.

ATTITUDES TO TRAVELLERS IN THE SETTLED POPULATION

The Commission did not devote much attention to the reasons for hostility towards Travellers, accepting that experiences of trespass, begging, theft and drunkenness were the foundation of a certain amount of justifiable resentment among the settled population. No data on the extent of Traveller criminality was produced, but many of the recommendations were aimed at protecting the general population from these transgressions. Yet the Commission was unafraid to state the extent of prejudice that existed among the settled population. Employers refused work to Travellers and publicans refused to serve them, preferring to sell them off-licence alcohol. In the absence of effective legal redress for trespass, some farmers resorted to violent retaliation, including assaulting and attacking Travellers or their animals.[79] Horses were wounded or disfigured by slashing or cutting of tails and manes, and driven long distances.[80] While these were a minority of cases, the gardaí recognised that retaliation was significantly under reported.[81] The Commission felt that any attempt to settle Travellers in rural areas would fail if the law did not provide adequate protection for farmers.[82] Next to trespass, begging was 'probably the greatest single cause of hostility on the part of the settled population'. The Commission considered it a 'source of considerable annoyance and irritation' and especially injurious to the tourist industry as visitors were 'more persistently importuned'.[83]

Apart from commercial transactions or hostile encounters, the majority of the settled population avoided contact with Travellers. Even those who regarded them 'kindly as "God's poor" would not care to have them living permanently in their own district'.[84] Public brawling fuelled by excessive drinking further added to settled people's fear of Travellers. The Commission acknowledged that 'the reputation of itinerants in this respect will be one of the major difficulties in making progress with any scheme of absorption'.[85] Feuding was felt to be the result of a dearth of pastimes and illiteracy, historically comparable to features of rural Irish life before the Famine.[86] However, physical violence among Travellers rarely affected the settled community, unless they intervened in a fight.[87]

Yet not all Travellers provoked hostility. Those who moved in a comparatively small circuit were 'better known in the area and incur less dislike that their more travelled brethren'. 'Local itinerants' were often regarded as 'decent inoffensive people'. Since these families were relatively poor, owning few if any animals, the lower levels of hostility were unsurprising.[88] Personal acquaintance also helped promote mutual understanding. The Commission was optimistic that closer contact would facilitate improved relations between Travellers and settled people. But the plight of poor Travellers was a serious problem 'which has not troubled the public conscience to any degree'. People hoped that the nuisance to the settled community would be solved, without worrying about 'the lot of families living a primitive and harsh existence'.

> There is so far little apparent desire on the part of the general public to act collectively for the betterment of the itinerants as they do in many ways for other poor sections of the community. In general, little serious consideration has been given either to the futility or the grave social injustice of a policy of just moving them on.[89]

The Commission rejected the popular belief that Travellers could settle down if they wished, pointing out that 'virtually insuperable difficulties' faced families who left the road. Even families who had settled were known scornfully as 'tinkers'.[90] Since local authorities refused to house Travellers[91] and public housing tenants revolted at their presence, the obstacles to settlement were almost impossible to overcome. Despite the deep and long-standing hostility felt by settled people, most submissions to the Commission advocated absorption as the only real solution to the problem. Astutely, the Commission noted that 'it is quite clear that many of the settled population will be very slow to accept this, particularly if it is to take place in their areas'.[92] The paradox of demanding settlement but refusing to countenance living near Travellers illustrated that many settled people advocating the eradication of cultural difference did not truly believe it could be achieved.

The Commission on Itinerancy investigated the relationship between two separate and distinct communities in Irish society. The findings of the Commission detail the structure and value system of Traveller society in the early 1960s. Although the Commission denied that Travellers were culturally separate, their findings undermine that assertion. The Commission rightly identified a deep antipathy towards Travellers among the settled population, a hatred it believed could be ameliorated. Part of the solution lay in improving the behaviour of Travellers, whose apparent disregard for the law had to be seen to be eradicated. By proving to the settled community that Travellers were culpable for their actions, vigorous law enforcement would reassure the majority while simultaneously educating Travellers about social conventions and responsibilities. In addition, a spirit of Christian charity and goodwill was to be the basis of co-operation from settled people. The practical methods for fostering this spirit are outlined in full in the next section.

REPORT AND RECOMMENDATIONS

The Commission made a large number of recommendations, from more vigorous law enforcement to the provision of housing and halting sites for Travellers. All policies aiming to help Travellers or deal with problems they caused 'should always have as their aim the eventual absorption of the itinerants into the general community'. The Commission believed absorption could not be based on compulsion: 'It is not considered that any worth-while progress could be made by a policy of compulsory settlement, even if it were legally possible'.[93] Some of the most significant proposals envisaged close co-operation between voluntary organisations and the welfare system. As with the homeless and other difficult cases requiring reform or rehabilitation, the voluntary sector would act as a mediator between Travellers and the state. In many respects, this formal co-operation was a new departure for both charitable organisations and the state. Voluntary groups no longer feared the contagion of bureaucracy, while the state was now willing to address in a social problem outside the limited remit of income support. From accommodation to employment, the charitable sector was to play a key role in bringing Travellers into contact with the established structures of the state.

ACCOMMODATION

The Commission believed that 'The first major step towards a solution of many of the problems arising from the itinerant way of life will be taken when the itinerant family can be settled or permitted to settle in a house or on a camping site where they can stay indefinitely if they so desire.' Given earlier government refusals to build campsites it was surprising to see the Commission propose temporary and permanent sites. Approved camping sites would be established when there was difficulty providing houses immediately for large numbers of Travellers or for families who did not want to live in a house. The Commission suggested a design template for public authority campsites, including sanitation, facilities for keeping horses and storage areas for scrap collection.[94] It was stressed that sites be 'convenient to the urban area, to churches, schools and shopping centres to overcome any danger of isolation and the creation of a separate community'.[95] Similar to public housing schemes, central government subsidies were advocated to help local authorities fund campsites. Camping in the radius of an official site was to be prohibited.[96] Thus settlement would be encouraged with a carrot and stick policy. If local authorities took the time and trouble to provide facilities for some Travellers, they would earn additional punitive powers over the remainder. Sites were 'only the first step of stabilisation in a policy aimed at eventual housing of the families using the sites. The sites might also serve as clearing stations for the housing of itinerants where the overall demand for houses necessitates a waiting list.'[97] Campsites were not intended to offer permanent residency for Travellers, as the eventual aim of the absorption programme was settlement in houses.

However, authorised halting places were recommended for short stays by families who continued to be nomadic: 'The main purpose of the halts is to provide itinerant families depending upon horse-drawn vehicles with a camping place upon which they will be allowed to park without fear of ejection'.[98] By recommending halting sites, the Commission acknowledged that not all Travellers were able or willing to relinquish nomadism. These recommendations were founded on a belief that nomadism would last longest among the poorest families, despite its own findings on the relationship between extensive travel and wealth in the Travelling community. Travellers, as defined by public policy, were poor. If the 'itinerant problem' was interpreted as a matter of raising living standards among poor Travellers, this approach was understandable. But since the Commission was also hoping to end tension over illegal encampments between Travellers and settled people, ignoring the commercial success of the most mobile Travellers was a serious error. Families who travelled widely were among the wealthiest in Traveller society and owned large numbers of animals, whose grazing alienated the settled population. If the greatest hostility was provoked by the lifestyle of well-off families with no economic incentive to settle, limiting the solution to poorer Travellers was short sighted.

Campsites were not seen as the permanent solution to Traveller accommodation: 'The immediate objective should be to provide dwellings as soon as possible for all itinerant families who desire to settle.' The Commission made a number of recommendations on how local authorities should approach Traveller settlement. Applications for housing from families living in tents and caravans were to be given priority, while local authorities were urged not to house Travellers in isolated settlements apart from the rest of the community. On the other hand, group housing was discouraged: 'Itinerant families . . . should be free from any feeling that they are being placed on a reservation. At the same time the other tenants should not feel that they cannot cope with the number of itinerants settled among them or feel oppressed by their numbers.' The Commission understood that the settlement programme would pose difficulties but it asked local authorities not to be

easily discouraged by the difficulties they will certainly experience in the early years. The problems that local authorities will have to face in this task should not be insuperably greater than those so successfully faced by many local authorities in slum clearance.[99]

The Commission considered, but rejected, a suggestion that substandard dwellings should be provided for Travellers for a probationary period: 'Singly or collectively, the deliberate provision of substandard dwellings for itinerants would stigmatise those persons as inferior beings.' Such sensitivity sat uneasily next to another recommendation that advised tenancy agreements between local authorities and 'itinerant tenants' include a provision 'giving the local authority a right of entry to abate all nuisances'. [100] As the aim of settlement was to eradicate difference between Travellers and settled people, any programme would have to treat Travellers as ordinary citizens. Special measures acknowledging their unequal access to housing could be taken, but policies that penalised Travellers as a group were rejected. Yet the Commission also recommended measures that would have stigmatised Traveller tenants, illustrating the fundamental contradiction at the heart of the Report. However much it was denied, Travellers, and their relationship with the institutions of the state, were different. That was especially true in the case of education. The special needs of nomadic children with no experience of permanent schooling and the Netherlands example determined the Commission's recommendations.

EDUCATION

The education of Traveller children was deemed urgent. Children settled in houses could attend mainstream schools, but older children would require individual attention. If there were large numbers of children requiring special tuition, a qualified teacher could be recruited solely for the purpose of teaching them.[101] Camp schools would be established if there were large numbers of children living on a halting site. The Commission recommended the adoption of the system of education established in the Netherlands. That programme attempted to preserve continuity of education for children moving from camp to camp. If more than twelve children attended a mainstream school, a separate class would be established. The curriculum proposed for Traveller children was to be substantially different from that taught in national schools. If necessary, teaching in reading, writing and arithmetic could be curtailed to facilitate manual training. Boys would learn woodwork and elementary metalwork, while girls would be taught knitting, needlework, simple cookery and domestic training.[102] Interestingly, given the sacrosanct status of the Irish language, it was recommended that teaching of Irish be 'restricted to half an hour each day, and confined to oral work'.

The Commission was aware that remaining in one place in order to secure education for children was, for most families, 'economically impossible'. Nomadic families were not to be punished for evading school: 'compulsory school attendance should only be enforced when their economic condition has been ameliorated to the extent that there remains no sufficient excuse for their not remaining in one area in which suitable education is available for them.' Institutional care for all Traveller children was suggested to the Commission. This suggestion was not made with a view to better education, but based on the belief that the break up of Traveller families would end their nomadic lifestyle and that 'in one generation the itinerants as a class would disappear'. The Commission rejected this policy because the 'evil social consequences' and 'suffering' caused by it 'would far outweigh the 'advantages' of an education imposed in such conditions with its lasting legacy of bitterness'.[103] Although the Commission outlined detailed plans for the education of Traveller children, it believed that little could be done about adult illiteracy, hoping that local voluntary organisations would organise vocational classes for adults.[104] Sidelining the issue of adult literacy reduced the likelihood that Travellers would be able to 'adapt themselves to the employment patterns of the ordinary population'.[105]

EMPLOYMENT

The integration of Travellers into the labour market was considered a matter of 'the utmost importance if absorption into the general community' is to succeed'.[106] Once again, local voluntary organisations were expected to play a key role in informing Travellers about employment opportunities.[107] To facilitate self-employment by families dependent upon scrap metal collection, the Commission suggested legislation to regulate the trade. This regulation would, it was hoped, improve conditions for some families, while giving them an incentive to settle in one area. The collection and purchase of scrap metal would be licensed and each licence would permit collection only in a clearly defined area. Travellers were to be preferred when licences were issued.[108] All the Commission recommendations on employment were directed at absorption. Thus opportunities open to settled people, such as employment on schemes for the relief of unemployment, were to be extended to Travellers.[109] A similar attempt to widen Traveller access to freely available services motivated the recommendations on welfare benefits. However, the Commission's belief that Travellers as a group suffered from certain distinct social ills influenced their recommendations.

WELFARE BENEFITS

One of the most important recommendations made by the Commission concerned Travellers' access to welfare benefits. Travellers rarely made use of unemployment benefits, since 'signing on' at the dole office was not compatible with nomadism. Children's allowances and pensions were almost universally applied for, as the cheques could be picked up at prearranged locations along a route. Consequently, the welfare state had not replaced charity in the subsistence economy of the majority of Travellers. The Commission advised that assistance be available for Travellers who would lose the income derived from begging. It believed that it was 'essential that any special difficulties . . . in the way of itinerant families obtaining any of the State or local authority allowances for which they are eligible should be eliminated'. This recommendation signalled formal acceptance of Travellers as part of the welfare community, although it was primarily motivated by the settlement programme. Better benefits would encourage settlement 'by providing them with means of livelihood pending their adaptation to the employment patterns of settled life and in particular by replacing . . . the substantial part of their income which will be cut off . . . by a successful effort to curtail or eliminate begging'.[110] But Travellers would not receive the same treatment as the rest of the population. More frequent registration for unemployment benefit was advocated for persons of no fixed abode, while the Commission recommended that Travellers who were not housed or living on an approved camping site receive welfare benefits in voucher form, 'so as to overcome abuse by dissipation on intoxicating liquor'. The key liaison between Travellers and the labyrinthine bureaucracy of benefit provision would be local voluntary organisations.[111] Charitably inclined settled people would aid illiterate Travellers unfamiliar with the benefits system to apply successfully for income support. Organisations such as the St Vincent de Paul, who in the early years of the state were reluctant to become formally involved in the welfare system, were now envisaged as playing an important role in the distribution of benefits. The role of the most important sponsor of voluntary charity, the Roman Catholic Church, was not ignored. The Hierarchy was asked to consider the appointment of a national chaplain for the spiritual care of Travellers, as was done in France and the Netherlands.[112] While half of the report advocated (and occasionally qualified) tolerance, consideration and understanding, an equal portion was devoted to changes in the criminal law aimed at Travellers.

Improved law enforcement was considered to be crucial to the success of the settlement and absorption policy. The Commission believed that if Travellers were more diligently pursued by the police, they would understand and respect the social norms practised by the rest of the community. Settled people would also feel more secure if they felt that Travellers could not evade the law. It seems that Travellers often escaped the attention of police, or were deliberately ignored by parts of the legal system. Gardaí were unwilling to serve warrants on Travellers because of the likelihood that they would not be executed, thereby reflecting badly on the force's apparent ability to solve crime.[113] The Commission instructed that 'Considerations of cost should not determine whether to proceed with the investigation of, or to follow up, criminal offences by itinerants.' It also hoped that 'Excessive tolerance and leniency by the Courts should be discouraged.' To ensure compliance, persons of no fixed abode convicted of an offence would have to pay fines immediately.[114]

Some radical changes were recommended to the trespass law to prevent Travellers evading the legal consequences of camping on private land or grazing their animals in farmers' fields. The Commission felt that any attempt to settle Travellers in rural areas would be frustrated if the law did not provide adequate protection for farmers.[115] It therefore recommended that the law be amended to heavily penalise 'a person of no fixed abode' who camped, placed any animals on or interfered with the fences of another's land without his permission. The Commission was suggesting that trespass be a criminal offence, but only if committed by a person of no fixed abode. Such an individual would have to prove that he had permission to camp on another's land; he would be 'deemed to have trespassed unless the contrary could be proved'.[116] In addition, any member of the Garda Síochána could seize an animal wandering the public highway if he had 'reasonable grounds' for believing it to be in the custody of a person of no fixed abode.[117] Trespass would be a criminal, rather than a civil, matter only if committed by persons of no fixed abode, therefore surmounting the problems of general application that Traynor anticipated in 1959. The recommendation was not accepted, perhaps because the judiciary and the Department of Justice maintained their resistance to punitive selective legislation.

The Commission's recommendations on begging did not similarly target persons of no fixed abode because, by the 1960s, begging was rare outside Traveller society. Rising welfare benefits and a better standard of living among the poorest had ended the need for begging by settled people. Begging would be discouraged 'if the settled community were less indiscriminate in their almsgiving', implying that despite resentment of the practice, refusal was rare. Various amendments to existing legislation were proposed by the Commission, which also recommended more vigorous enforcement of laws prohibiting begging. A significant change was proposed to the Children Act 1908, which would make it easier to convict the parents of children found begging (see appendix). The amendment would force parents to prove they did not send their children to beg, rather than the authorities proving the children were asked to beg by their parents. Another suggested amendment to the criminal law would further shift the burden of proof from the police to the individual charged with the offence. The Commission proposed the creation of a new offence by which a person previously convicted of begging would, if charged with loitering or importuning, be deemed guilty 'unless the contrary is proved'.[118] Where a member of the Garda Síochána observed an alleged offence, he could arrest the alleged offender without a warrant.[119] Such radical amendments to criminal law and process could have had significant implications for all citizens, although their clear purpose was to target Travellers. These proposals were not accepted by the Department of Justice.

However restrictive some of its proposals were, the Commission spurned a number of draconian suggestions. Identity cards were mentioned, but rejected as undesirable since cards would single out Travellers for 'special treatment for police purposes'. (However, other proposals on law enforcement were directed specifically at Travellers.) Such a system would have 'damaging effects on any process of absorption' as well as being an administrative nightmare and open to abuse. It was also suggested that Peace Commissioners, rather than District Justices, be authorised to deal with certain offences such as vagrancy and drunkenness. That would solve problems of remand, bail and non-appearance at court. However, that was considered to conflict with the constitution and was thus rejected.[120] A similar proposal emanating from the 1956 Report of the Committee on Gypsies and like Itinerants in Northern Ireland was made law, illustrating that Ireland's written constitution, which protected its citizens' right to trial in court, afforded valuable protection to unpopular minorities like Travellers.[121]

ATTITUDE OF THE SETTLED POPULATION

Arguably, the hostility of the settled community that had plagued previous efforts to house Travellers was the most intractable problem. Devising measures to address that prejudice was the most challenging aspect of the Commission's remit. Most of the Commission's recommendations indirectly addressed the attitude of the settled population. The very concept of absorption and assimilation was a response to members of the settled community who wished that Travellers, as a recognisable group, would simply vanish. Legislation to prevent begging and provide redress for trespass were attempts to address 'the legitimate grievances of the settled population'. While 'preventing or restraining the more injurious activities of the itinerants' underpinned the Commission's approach, 'a positive policy of social reclamation' would complement the punitive legal measures. Public opinion would play an essential role in this social policy.

> Steps should be taken to inform the minds of the settled population on the whole problem of itinerancy and to educate them to the fact that not only do the dictates of charity and common humanity require that steps should be taken to rescue the itinerant population from its present plight but that the material and social interests of the settled population itself will be advanced by a just solution of the itinerant problem.[122]

Thus welfare and charity were to be extended to Travellers not only on the basis of their material needs, but because the population as a whole would benefit. Travellers would be part of the welfare community, a community from which they had previously been excluded. The Commission believed that 'Christian charity and brotherly love'[123] would form the basis for public co-operation in the absorption programme. Educating the general population about the need to extend charity and material resources to Travellers would be a difficult task since fostering brotherly love was not a government responsibility. The Commission foresaw a significant role for voluntary organisation. Indeed, the complementary strengths of voluntary charity and state welfare would be the key to the success of the rehabilitation and settlement policy.

IMPLEMENTATION: CO-ORDINATION OF EFFORT

The Commission recommended the establishment of an unpaid central body whose members would represent all concerned government departments and 'the principal voluntary social and charitable organisations in the country'.[124] The central body would promote the rehabilitation and absorption of Travellers. This body would be appointed by the minister given overall responsibility for all issues relating to Travellers. This centralisation of power was necessary because responsibilities for education, campsites, housing and law enforcement lay with a number of government departments. The central body would make use of all existing government machinery and foster 'all local voluntary effort directed towards the absorption of itinerants'. It would be an important advocate, endeavouring to 'create a favourable public opinion in support of the policy of absorption and encourage the active co-operation of members of the public in that policy'.[125] Local voluntary groups would be central to the success of policy implementation, bridging the gap between Travellers and the settled community. Committees interested in Traveller settlement would be formed from branches of existing charitable organisations – the Legion of Mary or the St Vincent de Paul – or from parish committees including representatives of the Irish Countrywomen's Association, farmers' organisations and trade unions. Committee members would visit newly settled families to encourage them to persist with the experiment. Such visitation would help overcome problems encountered by Travellers adapting to unfamiliar surroundings and habits. As these committees would minister to Travellers as charity cases, their participation was not envisaged. Local groups would also take on a more onerous task: promoting good relations between Travellers and settled people. The Commission acknowledged that this work would not be easy and would depend upon 'dedicated personnel and sustained effort'. It was hoped that these voluntary organisations would be supported by 'trained welfare officers whose services would be made available to them by the Minister or the local authority'.[126] Thus the Commission recommended voluntary committees working between the two communities, helping Travellers to negotiate the bureaucracy and social mores of settled society, while countering hostility from settled people.

CONCLUSION

Rehabilitation and the importance of Christian charity were emphasised in the Commission's report. A 'spirit of Christian charity and goodwill' was seen to be the solution to opposition from settled people.[127] Reassuring settled people by making Travellers amenable to the law would also encourage new attitudes. The Commission held a belief that was widespread until recently about the innate lack of prejudice among Irish people.

> Hostility to a class or group as now exists in relation to the itinerants is uncharacteristic of our people and its existence is indicative of the extremity to which the settled community or a large portion of it feels it has been driven. The normal kindly feelings of the people ... will once again predominate when the immediate pressure of the itinerant's wrongdoings has been relieved or, at least, substantially reduced.[128]

Once Travellers ceased to trouble settled people, hostility would vanish. Little did the optimistic Commission realise that, settled or nomadic, the existence of Travellers would continue to bother many settled people. Changing attitudes to marginal land among the settled community, facilitated by the Derelict Sites Act 1961 did not augur well for the settlement programme (see appendix). Grants were made available by the Department of Local Government to improve derelict sites in 1961. Private individuals were a majority of applicants in the first year; 607 compared to 62 applications from local authorities. Local development associations could also take up these grants to reclaim unsightly or hazardous sites in their area.[129] Grants for works of public amenity were also introduced in 1961. Local authorities and local development organisations were eligible for grants covering 50 per cent of works which cost less than £100.[130] From 1962–3, 137 applications were made to the Department.[131] As definitions of appropriate land usage and appearance were codified in Irish society, the Commission's report recommended tolerance towards a group whose land usage patterns were at odds with the majority community. It was not an auspicious context for a successful accommodation programme.

The Report of the Commission on Itinerancy sought to understand the values of Traveller and settled societies, and how they could be harmonised. Ultimately, only Travellers were expected to make substantive changes. Travellers were asked to surrender nomadism, family economy, self-employment, flexible work patterns, horses and their own homes for the dubious pleasures of public housing, full-time school attendance, subsistence on welfare benefits and organised charity. In return, they would gain better living conditions, a secure income, access to wage employment and a more regulated existence. Many working-class families had already traded under-employment, privately rented accommodation and family economies for the comforts of public housing and the stability of the dole. There was no reason to believe that Travellers would refuse the opportunity to improve their living standards. Yet the Commission was astute enough to note that few Travellers were unhappy with their lifestyle: 'One of the greatest problems is the fact that most itinerants are neither sufficiently conscious of nor sufficiently dissatisfied with their present way of life and its standards to do anything about it.'[132] That did not bode well for a settlement programme that could not succeed without the co-operation of Travellers.

Whatever its flaws, the Commission's report provides a comprehensive and balanced exposition of the relationship between Travellers and settled people, as well as providing considerable detail on Traveller economy and society in the early 1960s. The Commission on Itinerancy marked the first government effort to document the 'itinerant problem'. Many of the Commission's proposals depended heavily on the contribution of local voluntary organisations. Catholic teaching had long encouraged governments to leave social work to charitable organisations that would not interfere in the family. The government's influence was thought to be dangerous, pernicious and potentially communistic in the limitations it placed upon individuals. Welfare benefits that provided income security 'at the expense of personal independence and initiative' were opposed by the Catholic Church.[133] Scholars believe that the powerful influence of Irish Catholic social thought stunted the ideological development of welfarism.[134] However, the Commission's report marks a new approach to voluntary organisations and state welfare support. Two previously distinct approaches, with different aims and methods, were drawn together. The Traveller settlement policy would marry the flexibility and humanity of charity with the funding resources and legal machinery of the state. How this arrangement worked will be discussed in the following chapter that will outline the implementation of the Commission's recommendations.

SIX

ASSIMILATION AND ABSORPTION

—

The Report of the Commission on Itinerancy was well received by local and national government because it foresaw an end to unauthorised encampments and – if settlement led to assimilation – the disappearance of Travellers as a distinctive, nomadic community. The principle of settlement was accepted wholeheartedly by the public and politicians alike, though the provision of Traveller accommodation was as politically fraught as various ministers had predicted. How a national policy was received locally will be analysed here. Cork city provides a useful study of the implementation of the Commission's recommendations by one local authority. The prospect of Traveller accommodation provoked outrage in the Cork city's middle- and working-class suburbs, preventing the local authority from implementing its plans. That public outcry was repeated across the country and appeared to be insurmountable.[1] Faced with political and administrative paralysis, charitable organisations and interested individuals provided basic facilities for Traveller families without even the right to live in one place. Embryonic Traveller politicisation was mobilised by Grattan Puxon, an English activist. The role of the settlement committees in persuading local residents to accept Traveller accommodation will be assessed. Of crucial importance in countering objections was the constant use of the word 'resettlement', which implied that Travellers were merely temporarily displaced rather than truly nomadic. What this chapter reveals is that agreement on settlement did not imply an acceptance of accommodation in settled people's local areas. The delay in central government on instructing local authorities perhaps suggests that the Commission's recommendations were disputed, although there was no clear evidence of that.

THE REACTION OF CENTRAL AND LOCAL GOVERNMENT

Justice Brian Walsh met the Taoiseach, Seán Lemass, in early August 1963 to present the Commission's finished report.[2] The Commission's key recommendation on settlement and housing for Travellers was accepted apparently without question by the government. Unusually for a report outlining a radical change in policy, very few of the Commission's suggestions were dismissed outright.[3] Lemass lost no time in presenting the Cabinet with the most important governmental aspect of the report: the allocation of departmental responsibility.

The implementation of the Commission's recommendations could not proceed without an end to the confusion over which department was responsible for Travellers as a group. As chapter 4 demonstrated, Travellers avoided governmental scrutiny partly because the problems they posed the settled community did not fall within the remit of any one department. A central recommendation of the Commission – that one minister be given overall responsibility for Travellers as a group – had to be addressed before the settlement policy could be adopted. Lemass informed the cabinet that the department nominated would have complete responsibility for Travellers. Other departments would furnish their observations on the report and a draft White Paper embodying the government's response would be prepared. The co-ordinating department would also supervise the implementation of the policy outlined in the White Paper. When the Commission's recommendations were assigned to the relevant departments, Justice was responsible for six, compared to three each for Local Government and Social Welfare, and two for the Departments of Health and Education.[4]

The Department of Health maintained that Travellers could access the health services available to the rest of the population, and that low life expectancy could be attributed to their living conditions rather than availability of health care. As the responsibility for improving living standards lay with the Department of Local Government, the Department of Health could claim it had fulfilled its duties to Travellers.[5] The Department of Education believed that the education of Traveller children was 'one case where *ad hoc* arrangements will just have to be made to suit local circumstances'.[6] This suited the nature of the National School system, in which schools were managed by the churches, but paid for by the state. The delicate balance of the educational partnership between the churches and the state precluded grander gestures. One special school was built in Ballyfermot, Dublin to educate Traveller children.[7] However, in 1970 the Department of Education decided that no more special schools would be provided since it hindered the absorption of Traveller children into mainstream classes.[8] The Department of Social Welfare acted in 1967 to make access to unemployment assistance by Travellers easier. The Social Welfare (Miscellaneous Provisions) Act 1967 removed the provision that had, since 1940, restricted the payment of unemployment assistance to people moving from rural to urban areas unless they could satisfy a special residence or employment test. Section 14 of the act abolished the residency and employment test to remove any obstacles faced by Travellers living in urban areas (see appendix).[9] However, the overwhelming importance of settlement dictated that the department responsible for housing should lead the government response to Travellers. Accordingly, the Department of Local Government was assigned co-ordinating responsibility in August 1963.[10]

The Department of Local Government pondered the implications of the Commission's report for a year. During this time, deputies in Dáil Éireann continued to raise the issue of Traveller encampments with the minister, Neil Blaney. Blaney repeatedly told deputies that his department was considering the report and that a solution to unauthorised encampments would have to wait until a policy decision had been made.[11] While the department reflected on how best to implement the Commission's recommendations on housing and campsites, local authorities continued to break up Traveller encampments. The remedies used were similar to earlier decades: compulsory purchase, redevelopment or landscaping and court orders. In Cork, campsites adjoining corporation property on the north side of the city were cleared by court order. To prevent Travellers returning, the corporation erected concrete posts on the edges of the footpath. This did not prove effective and a number of caravans returned. The City Engineer proposed developing the open spaces in the area under a scheme intended to provide employment for men receiving unemployment benefit. The redevelopment was a steel rail around each area to prevent trespass by Travellers and dumping by others. This was intended to be a short-term solution; a compulsory purchase order to bring private land under the corporation's control was to be drafted. In order to completely eradicate camping, the corporation hoped to 'erect houses where trespass by itinerants occurs'. One councillor asked whether the manager could consider the provision of a designated campsite with water and sanitation facilities for Travellers. The Lord Mayor (Gus Healy of Fianna Fáil) replied that the corporation had 'no such area available'.[12] The open spaces about to be purchased by the authority in order to end illegal camping would have been the obvious choice, but the corporation refused to take any positive action. Cork Corporation's actions were not unusual; in Dublin, the corporation refused to provide campsites until told by the Department of Local Government to do so. A large camp on Dublin Corporation property on the Ring Road in Ballyfermot was targeted in December 1963. Dr Noel Browne asked the minister whether any accommodation would be provided for families displaced by Dublin Corporation, but there were no plans to provide a permanent campsite for Travellers as the corporation had 'no express statutory authority to do so at the present time'.[13] The question of conferring such powers was under consideration by the department. Publicly no truce was declared, but privately the department was worried about the tactics of

Dublin Corporation. This concern was due in part to the activities of Grattan Puxon, an Englishman who was to the forefront of a movement called the Itinerant Action Campaign.

A pacifist and peace campaigner, Puxon had fled to Ireland in 1960 to avoid being drafted by the British army that was then engaged in Cyprus.[14] He bought and lived in a barrel-topped caravan and soon began to protest over the conditions Travellers lived in as well as the constant round of evictions they endured. In 1963, a group of Travellers led by John MacDonald, Kevin Keenan and Grattan Puxon marched from Ballyfermot, where many were camped, to Dublin City Hall, carrying banners saying 'No more Eviction' and 'Education for our Children'.[15] Sinn Féin were attracted by Puxon's radical politics and participated in a protest march to Lansdowne Park. An IRA 'flying column' on bicycles rode ahead of the wagons to demolish concrete bollards blocking a gate. Those allies were not necessarily advantageous as Special Branch officers subsequently kept Puxon and other prominent figures under surveillance.[16] In February 1964, Grattan Puxon was arrested on a charge of possessing explosives. Fr Thomas Fehily believed that Puxon had encouraged Travellers to smuggle weapons across the border[17] while Acton explains the arrest thus:

> Some extremist Republican bodies had been amongst the supporters of the
> Travellers' movement, and demanded reciprocal help; when Grattan Puxon refused
> to support some of their activities, they probably informed the police of explosives
> which had been hidden in the back garden of a house still under Puxon's ownership.[18]

Puxon was given bail but the charges were not dropped for 16 months.

The numbers camping at the Ballyfermot site had increased since 1960, when the Commission on Itinerancy had interviewed some of its residents.[19] In December 1963, Travellers established a camp school, Naomh Cristóir (St Christopher, the patron saint of travellers), that was opened by the grand old man of Irish radical politics, Peadar O'Donnell. To applause from gathered families, O'Donnell said, 'This building is a pathetic gesture by the poor to help the children of the poor'.[20] As Dublin Corporation intended to clear the campsite in early January, the school was a gesture of defiance. Puxon was making skilful use of the politics of passive resistance and succeeded in raising public interest in the issue. The Department of Local Government tried to persuade Dublin Corporation to leave the campsite undisturbed until St Patrick's Day, when it was believed that Travellers would move of their own volition.

> The Local Government view is that the itinerants will move of their own accord
> and that stern measures by the Corporation, in addition to being unnecessary in

the long run, will undoubtedly give rise to publicity and to allegation of inhuman behaviour, especially as the papers and TV appear to be poised for any story emerging from the situation.[21]

Despite the intervention of central government, the corporation evicted approximately 150 Travellers on 7 January 1964. A cavalcade of caravans and carts left peacefully and settled on another site a few miles away. Joseph Donohue told the gathered reporters 'We will not resist but we will camp on one site after another until the Government do something about the Itinerant's Commission'.[22] That the corporation intended to use the Ballyfermot site for housing purposes further increased the poignancy of the eviction.[23] Dublin Corporation officials pointed out that they possessed no power to allocate land for Traveller campsites. The corporation 'could not make this move until the report of the commission on itinerancy had been adopted by the Dáil and Order had been made by the Minister for Local Government authorising local councils to set up camping sites for itinerants'.[24] The attitude of the Department of Local Government suggested that major statutory changes were needed before sanitary authorities could provide campsites for Travellers. Yet, as Noel Browne pointed out, campsites could be built using public funds when Dublin slum dwellers needed emergency accommodation. Browne asked the House and the government to examine their conscience.

> How is it that we can take these views that are extraordinarily partisan, and at the time closely related to the racism and the evil of apartheid? The difference between us and them is they do not need the amenities we need. Their children do not need education or the old people do not need care when they grow old.[25]

When the minister made his long-awaited announcement on the implementation of the Commission's report, he recommended no statutory changes. There was no White Paper issued, merely a circular sent to all local authorities in November 1964.

The Commission's recommendation on an unpaid advisory committee 'to promote the rehabilitation and absorption of itinerants' was accepted by the Department of Local Government. Any local voluntary committees established to 'help in the resettlement of itinerant families' would receive financial assistance from the government. On the question of settlement, the circular departed somewhat from the Commission's report. The department advised that 'Pending the solution of the difficulties associated with the housing of itinerants, local authorities will be advised to provide fully serviced camping sites for the accommodation of itinerants.' The Commission had advocated housing as the primary objective, but the department seemed more concerned with site provision. Also, there was no instruction to give Travellers priority in housing allocation, as the Commission had recommended. However, the department did ask local authorities to ensure that Travellers received every health and welfare benefit to which they were entitled.[26]

The campsites were to be established under the Local Government (Planning and Development) Act, which had been on the statute books since 7 August 1963, the month the Commission submitted its report. Local authorities were reminded that Section 77 (2) of the 1963 Act gave them powers to establish campsites. Section 16 of the Act provided the basis for combined action for local authorities. The management of the sites would be a matter for each responsible authority but the memorandum suggested the recommendations of the Commission on Itinerancy be followed as far as possible. There had been no need to draft new legislation enabling local authorities to develop campsites. Since 1963, publicly funded facilities for camping Travellers were legally possible. Yet while the government considered its response to the Commission's report, local authorities refused to provide facilities for Travellers, claiming they were not empowered to do so. The Department of Local Government never contradicted this, and indeed, the minister expressly supported this claim. That legislation enabling local authorities to provide campsites had been available – but not used – suggests a reluctance in the co-ordinating department to accept wholeheartedly the Commission's recommendations on accommodation. Their long consideration of the report and the damp squib that was the implementation policy did not augur well. Despite the Taoiseach's ready acceptance of the Commission's report in 1963, the Department of Local Government had allowed the settlement issue to recede. Local authorities were even more reluctant than central government to tackle the issue, as the response of the General Council of County Councils (GCCC) demonstrated.

The opinions expressed by the GCCC, a local authority representative body, indicated the nationwide political response. After the circulation of the above recommendations, the GCCC wrote to the Taoiseach. Its members believed that the 'problem of itinerancy is not one for the Department of Local Government and the Local Authorities alone, but that other Government Departments are also involved, particularly, Health, Justice and Education'. Clearly anxious to evade responsibility for decisions that were unpopular, local authorities considered 'itinerancy a national rather than a local problem'. The Minister for Local Government reassured the GCCC that Travellers were not the sole responsibility of the local authorities. He reiterated the importance of voluntary organisations to the process of rehabilitation. On the issue of the co-ordination of effort, the minister pointed out the importance of the Advisory Committee on Itinerancy, which held its first meeting in May 1965.[27]

The Commission had proposed the appointment of an advisory committee to liaise between all the departments concerned with aspects of Traveller life. The Committee would also enable communication between voluntary groups helping Travellers and all branches of government. Its members were appointed to advise on the implementation of policy and 'to assist in gaining the support of the public generally for rehabilitation measures'.[28] Justice Brian Walsh, the chair of the Commission, chaired a committee comprising:

> Fr Thomas Fehily, Member of the Commission on Itinerancy
> Mr Jeremiah Buttimer, County Cork
> Dr Anthony Eustace, County Medical Officer, County Meath
> Dr Patrick J. Fleming, Dublin
> Mrs G. O. Simms, Dublin
> Mrs Desmond Foley, Carlow
> Mr Dermot P. Honan, Ennis, County Clare
> Mr Thomas King, County Galway
> Mr Thomas Mc Donagh, County Louth
> Mr Thomas J. McManus, City Manager, County Sligo
> Miss Mary O'Connor, Department of Local Government
> Miss Eileen McArdle, Department of Local Government.[29]

Those members whose affiliation is not listed represented voluntary organisations and local authorities. The groups represented were the Legion of Mary, the Society of St Vincent de Paul, Muintir na Tíre and the Irish Countrywomen's Association. The Departments of Health, Social Welfare, Justice and Education appointed liaison officers to the committee.[30] It was stressed that Travellers would not be compelled to abandon the travelling way of life. Authorised campsites would enable Traveller children to attend school while remedying 'to some extent the features of the itinerants' way of life which was a real cause of irritation and annoyance to the settled population'.[31] There were no Traveller representatives on the Committee but it did make contact with Grattan Puxon and the Dublin Committee of the Itinerant Action Campaign.

TRAVELLERS' VOICES

These contacts had given important legitimacy to Puxon's campaign as the publicity surrounding this Traveller-led committee had made it impossible to ignore. According to Puxon, those charged with solving the 'itinerant problem' believed this agitation was damaging and sought to end it by means of a 'frank bargain'.

> In exchange for giving us an interview at the next session of the Advisory Committee to hear our plan for organising Itinerants' Committees and possibly following this with close cooperation in which we would arrange direct meetings between the Itinerants' Committee and the Advisory Committee, they ask us to stop our propaganda both in Ireland and in other countries.[32]

Puxon was not enthusiastic about the bargain but concluded 'if we are to penetrate the Establishment and make the travellers' voice heard we must make this bargain'.[33] With advice from international bodies such as the International Evangelical Gypsy Mission and the Communauté Mondiale Gitane (CMG – World Gypsy Community), Puxon and his associates sought to turn their '*ad hoc* attack on Dublin Corporation into a national campaign and organisation'.[34] Puxon felt that as a non-Catholic Englishman and a pacifist, he was particularly unpopular with the government and Church.

> But my disclosure of the appalling conditions and plight of the Travelling people, while making me almost 'Enemy Number One' has caused the Establishment to tackle the problem and do something substantial to assist the families, and in effect, grant them their rights.[35]

Here, Puxon was crediting himself with forcing the government to tackle the issue of Traveller accommodation when the Commission had been appointed before he established the Itinerant Action Campaign. His activities had kept the issue in the public eye, but he was not solely responsible for drawing official attention to the plight of Travellers. In July 1965, Puxon campaigned in the West of Ireland with Lawrence Ward,[36] 'last of the bare fist pugilists to carry the title King of the Tinkers'.[37] Puxon hoped to camouflage his activities, conducting the First National Convention of the Irish Travellers' Community in secret. It was to be held at the Ballinasloe Horse Fair, an annual event that attracted Travellers from all over Ireland and Britain. There, 'responsible and leading' Traveller men (but not women) from all over Ireland would meet with Lawrence Ward and John Connors, the Dublin Chairman, to discuss a plan of action. They would meet Vanko Rouda, a prominent Romany activist who would outline 'how the fight for rights is progressing in other countries'.[38] Puxon hoped those attending the meeting would become trained leaders in each region in Ireland, reporting to the Dublin Committee that would then liaise with the government Advisory Committee. In addition, the same men would become members of the official Itinerants' Committee which he hoped would be established by the Advisory Committee. Puxon's strategy is best explained with an extended quotation:

> In this way, without announcing that we have set up the Irish Travellers' Community and thus, at this delicate stage upsetting the Establishment, we gain effective control . . . we will be only one step away from establishing an officially recognised Irish Travellers' Committee instead of the present 'rebel Irish Travellers' Community' which is not recognised.
>
> The value of having official recognition is that the Travellers' own suggestions about the solving of their problems will be heard and probably largely accepted, instead of a bureaucratic 'solution' being imposed from above as an act of charity. Also if the Government and Church plans come to a stop, we can re-open our attack with far more strength and get them moving again.[39]

Puxon had ambitious international aims for Traveller action. He was anxious to formalise ties between Romany and Traveller activists. The presence of Vanko Raudo would demonstrate that Irish Travellers were affiliated with the international Romany community and capable of mobilising effective support from other countries.[40] Since this contact could not be formally announced, the union between Romany and Traveller would be symbolically expressed in the adoption by Raudo of two of Ward's grandchildren.

The Advisory Committee opposed the holding of the meeting but finally agreed to send Fr Fehily as a representative.[41] The Ballinasloe convention was not a harmonious event, bringing about a 'permanent personal estrangement' between Fr Fehily and Grattan Puxon.[42] The adoption ceremony did not proceed after Fr Fehily warned the Wards that participation in a Romany ritual would break Roman Catholic baptismal vows.[43] A militant 'Travellers' Committee' was set up after the Ballinasloe convention but it could not implement Puxon's ambitious programme. Acton's analysis places the blame with the 'Establishment' which frustrated action 'partly by a policy of judicious co-option of a very few selected Travellers and well-wishers onto Government-sponsored bodies, and partly by harassment of individual agitators like Puxon and Connors'.[44] Some Travellers co-operated with officialdom but they were not the individuals favoured by Puxon and his group. The extent to which Puxon represented all Travellers is difficult to discern, but his Dublin base would have distanced him from a significant portion of the community. The failure of the Itinerant Action Campaign to spread beyond Dublin could be reflective of the limits of his political agenda. Even within Dublin, Joseph Donohue in the Cherry Orchard camp disputed Puxon's right to speak on behalf of Travellers saying 'You can't have people speaking for the tinkers who aren't tinkers. They don't know what kind of a

life it is.'[45] Disregarding the importance of Roman Catholicism and the
respect in which priests were held by Travellers was almost certainly a fatal
mistake. Puxon was told that 'he personally, was the major obstacle to fruitful
co-operation between the Government, the Church and the Travellers'.[46] In
early 1966, he left Ireland to pursue his policy of Romany activism in Britain.
Joseph Donohue and John Connors also emigrated to Britain. Puxon
remembers it thus

> Charity, albeit on a scale unseen before was still the Tinker's portion. They would
> remain politically impoverished for a decade to come . . . In some vital respects I
> had failed, defeated by the outdated paternalism of the Catholic Church.[47]

This short-lived episode of political mobilisation in Traveller society is
not mentioned by Irish scholars, who have ignored Acton's and Puxon's
writings. Since both men have worked together in Romany organisations in
Britain, they obviously present a partial and biased version of events.[48]
Nevertheless, the significance of Traveller activism in the Itinerant Action
Campaign should not be dismissed. Though it foundered after the leading
figures left Ireland, other politicised Travellers later took their place.

After the dissolution of the embryonic Traveller's rights movement, the
government and voluntary organisations implemented a settlement policy
without any official input from the Travelling community. The following
section will outline the response of local authorities and groups to the Report
of the Commission on Itinerancy. Exactly what settlement meant divided
those concerned as some believed in housing immediately, and others in
halting sites as a step towards final settlement in houses. Initially, I shall
outline the response of a specific council, Cork Corporation. According to the
Commission report, an unusually small number of Travellers camped in and
around Cork city and, unlike Limerick, the numbers did not increase markedly during the winter months.[49] The failure of the corporation to accommodate even a proportionately small number of Traveller is instructive. Local
authorities with smaller budgets and larger numbers faced a more difficult task.

CORK CITY: THE IMPLEMENTATION OF
THE SETTLEMENT POLICY

Once Cork Corporation received the circular detailing the recommendations of the Commission on Itinerancy, the manager was asked to report on
measures to implement the proposals.[50] The City Architect, Town Planning
Officer and City Engineer submitted reports in February 1965, outlining plans

for a campsite in Churchfield, a public-housing suburb on the north side of the city, whose residents immediately appealed against the location of the campsite.[51] When the Housing Committee considered the proposed campsite, they rejected it, asking that 'the officers examine the matter again and make suggestions for the provision of a suitable alternative site in the city or within 5 miles of its perimeter'.[52] The planning officers had been overruled by local tenants and their public representatives. As the Commission had anticipated, opposition from residents to Traveller accommodation was fierce. This was hardly surprising given the experience of local authorities who had attempted to house Travellers before the settlement programme was adopted. On one occasion, settled people on a waiting list refused to accept tenancies because Travellers were accommodated in the estate.[53]

The Department of Local Government circulated local authorities in June 1965 about the Advisory Committee on Itinerants. The Cork Borough Council voted unanimously that the City Manager forward an analysis of the situation in the city to the committee. The memorandum sparked a discussion about Travellers among council members. Councillor Mrs Dowdall asked whether any facilities for Travellers were included in the development plan for the Cork area.[54] This pertinent question was sidestepped by the Chairman, who informed the council that the planning officers were examining suitable sites.[55] The manager, Walter McEvilly, informed the members that the officers of the corporation and Cork County Council would discuss the situation in their respective areas.[56] The tone of this council discussion on Travellers was quite moderate. Councillor T. P. Leahy felt that 'it was desirable to take action on the rehabilitation and incorporation into the community of itinerants and [the] education of their children'.[57] His contribution illustrates the extent to which the language of absorption promulgated by the Commission on Itinerancy had entered the political arena.

In the summer of 1965, Cork Corporation and County Council discussed the provision of accommodation for Travellers. The County and City Managers agreed to submit suggestions on 'sites for consideration for both authorities'.[58] The report on their discussions was placed before the Housing Committee in November. There was agreement among local authorities and the Cork Health Authority that 'a policy of re-settling itinerants in permanent homes over a period of years should be adopted'. The County Council had experience of housing Travellers, who were 'gradually being integrated into the community'. The City Manager asked the Borough Council to 'agree in principle to grant tenancies of its houses to itinerants who are regarded as suitable for housing'. That agreement was not strictly necessary, since people living in poor conditions, Traveller or settled, were already eligible for public housing. Interestingly, McEvilly sought agreement 'in principle' suggesting that the council would be asked to agree to each individual tenancy. That would have been a significant deviation from normal practice, since tenancies were allocated by housing officials rather than elected representatives. Before houses were allocated to Traveller families, they would need interim accommodation. The manager recommended the provision of a fully serviced campsite and suggested three locations: Old Whitechurch Road, Killeens Road and Ballyvolane Road. Those sites were on the northern side of the city, close to public housing developments. It was further recommended that the corporation 'confine itself to the problem as it now exists and should be careful not to take any action which might attract itinerants to the area'.[59] The corporation was determined not to provide for more than the 36 families camped in and around the city, approximately 38 per cent of the average number of Traveller families counted in Cork county in 1960 and 1961. Since Cork city held 35 per cent of the county's population, this did not represent a disproportionate burden.[60] The Housing Committee deferred a decision on the report until its members had inspected the proposed sites personally. Once again, the elected representatives were unusually involved in the ostensibly apolitical task of locating a public facility. In Ireland, the management system of local government was designed to remove patronage from the hands of apparently venial elected representatives. Thus the Chief Medical Officer assessed the suitability of dwellings for human habitation, while the manager and his officials chose appropriate sites for suburban public housing estates. Yet on the issue of Traveller accommodation, the manager was actively seeking the involvement of the council.

The powerlessness of the corporation to prevent illegal camping was further highlighted at this meeting of the Housing Committee when members discussed 'the annoyance caused to residents' in the Knockpogue Avenue–Closes Road area by Traveller encampments. The manager explained that 'the remedies open to the corporation were no ultimate solution to the problem'.[61] Moving Travellers on from the area had already cost £300 to £400. Breaking up encampments was perhaps the one area of local government where money was no object. However, McEvilly believed that the acquisition and development of a suitable campsite could take at least 18 months. The committee did agree to recommend the manager's report to the council.[62] When the council considered the report, the class implications of the sites chosen were highlighted by the contribution of Alderman Allen. He suggested that campsites be located in the Blackrock and Model Farm Road areas, well-heeled Cork middle-class suburbs, but the council did not agree with this amendment and approved the locations proposed by the manager.[63]

Yet when the matter was again raised in January 1966, council members contested the manager's policy. Alderman Allen believed he had not agreed to a settlement policy and stated 'Preference for rehousing should not be given to itinerants over citizens who had been waiting rehousing for a considerable time'. The four families considered suitable for immediate housing could hardly be described as a threat to the chances of people on the waiting list. While Councillor Healy called for a camp 'to screen, over a period of time, those itinerants who wish to settle down', Councillor O'Donovan pointed out the difficulties of building such a camp. He believed that 'every rate payer in the vicinity of such a camp would justifiably object as the value of property in the vicinity would be seriously affected'. Councillor Barrett suggested that any camp be located at least three miles away from a built-up area, an isolation policy the Commission report specifically advised against. As the discussion concluded the Lord Mayor (Con Desmond, Labour Party) struck an unco-operative attitude. He believed that 'the Corporation could not be expected to solve the problem on its own. He thought that the Minister for Local Government should take up the rehousing of itinerants with all local authorities and the corporation would then know how many it would be responsible for'. It was an odd request since the minister had already asked authorities to draft housing policies for Travellers. Determining the numbers of houses or sites needed was, of necessity, a local concern. Central government did not assess the demand for public housing because it was not responsible for housing provision. The Lord Mayor was hoping to avoid the corporation's responsibilities or at least to delay their acceptance. After an extended discussion, the council reaffirmed the decision taken on December 1965. It also asked the manager, in consultation with voluntary bodies, to take a census of Travellers camped in or near the city.[64] Members of the St Vincent de Paul met with corporation officials in late 1966, but the outcome was not reported to the council.[65]

Traveller accommodation was again before the Housing Committee in January 1967 when members were asked to approve the allocation of tenancies to five families. The inhabitants of the areas concerned protested at the allocation of tenancies to Travellers. Residents of Adelaide Street and Frenches Quay asked that the decision be rescinded.[66] The North Main Street Traders' Association also concerned itself with the allocation of houses in Adelaide Street to Travellers. After (unminuted) discussion, it was agreed to house two families, one on Frenches Quay and one on Adelaide Street. The other two families listed would be housed 'by the Corporation in the ordinary way'[67] and no other Travellers were to be housed in Adelaide Street. Presumably, the members intended that two families would be housed from the waiting list rather than under separate circumstances. That decision was contrary to a recommendation from the Commission that asked authorities to give Travellers priority in housing.[68] When that intention was placed before the council, Councillors Barrett and Allen proposed an amendment to the decision. Barrett believed

> that the housing of itinerants in the Frenches Quay and Adelaide Street area was unfair to both the residents and to the itinerants themselves as hostility and bad relations between the two parties were inevitable. The itinerant problem should be tackled on a national basis. Itinerants should be put into a community together and only when they have proved themselves as ready for integration with the citizens generally should they be rehoused.[69]

The amendment was comprehensively defeated, 3 votes to 11. The members agreed that the housing allocation was the 'first genuine attempt' to integrate Travellers into the settled community.[70] However, absorption would make slow progress if only a handful of families could be housed. Campsite provision was no less contentious.

Plans to build three halting sites in Cork city ran into considerable middle-class opposition in 1968. The Department of Local Government held a sworn inquiry into the compulsory purchase orders made by the corporation for land in Ballyvolane and Bishopstown. The corporation intended to develop a third site on land it already owned in the Blackrock area. McEvilly told the inquiry that the corporation had turned to compulsory purchase orders because it had concluded that sites for Traveller accommodation could not be obtained by agreement. The halting sites would form part of the city's plan for accommodating Travellers; by May 1968, it had already housed 13 families.[71] Though residents from both parts of the city objected, Bishopstown householders were the only group to hire a solicitor. Mr Charles Hennessy represented the Melbourne Estate Residents Association and the 300 members of the Bishopstown Development Association. Mr Hennessy asked the manager to agree that the value of property in an area with a halting site would be lowered. McEvilly insisted 'that to imagine this was to suppose that the camp would be a nuisance', whereas it would be under control and well supervised. He told the inquiry that Travellers on sites were eventually destined for public housing, as the Commission on Itinerancy had envisaged. McEvilly further stated that there was no corporation housing in Bishopstown and there were no plans to develop public housing in the area. The line of questioning then taken by Mr Hennessy revealed, in a frank and forthright manner, the deep class consciousness engendered by public and private housing schemes. He suggested that 'it might be a much better proposition to place the camp nearer the corporation housing estates for which they [Travellers] were eventually destined'. When the manager replied that it made no difference, Mr Hennessy pointed out that Bishopstown was 'the greatest scheme of middle-class housing in Cork: there were 20 separate estates with over 2,000 houses'. He suggested that 'more consideration must be given to the man who owned his house, buying it on a loan, than to a corporation tenant with no commitment other than paying his rent every week'. Since this was a public inquiry, those tenants objecting to the halting site in Ballyvolane were undoubtedly present to hear this. McEvilly did not agree with Hennessy, arguing it was not right to suggest that corporation tenants deserved less consideration. Mr Hennessy then made the astonishing statement, 'Everyone deserves well, but who deserves most?' He proposed that halting sites be built adjacent to public housing rather than near people who owned their homes 'and might in six months time have to sell them'. Furthermore, Travellers would eventually live in public housing, so it was more appropriate to place caravan sites in 'those areas'. When McEvilly protested that 'a clear distinction was being made in a way he did not like', Hennessy replied 'I don't like it either but those are my instructions'.[72] Mr Hennessy was articulating solid middle-class opinion which equated the spatial organisation of the city with its class boundaries.[73] For Bishopstown residents, placing a halting site in Ballyvolane was the natural choice because it would be on the north side of the city and adjacent to housing estates built to accommodate slum dwellers. South-side home owners could not be expected to live near Travellers who were allocated the lowest rung on the social ladder. No halting site was built in Bishopstown; out of the three proposed sites, only one was built by 1970.[74] Bishopstown remained overwhelmingly middle class until the corporation built large-scale public housing schemes there in the 1970s.[75]

The implementation of the settlement programme by Cork Corporation was poor; by 1970, just six families lived on a halting site.[76] Cork city was not unique in failing to provide facilities for Travellers; by 1978 Meath County Council had not even built a halting site.[77] The figures in table 6.1 illustrate the poor record of site provision nationwide. Site provision was more politically controversial than housing, which progressed at a faster rate. Between January 1962 and July 1969, 229 families were housed by 49 local authorities.[78] Although Cork Corporation had an unusually small number of families to accommodate, it is clear that public, political and bureaucratic reluctance to countenance Travellers' rights to basic facilities slowed the provision of accommodation. The fault lines of class loyalties were exposed by the corporation's attempt to accommodate Travellers. Middle-class residents forced the corporation to hold a public inquiry, yet the residents who complained most about Travellers lived in public housing on the north side of the city. Corporation tenants could also force the abandonment of halting site plans, as Churchfield residents did in 1965. Opposition to Traveller settlement crossed class boundaries but it is important to note that not all settled people

Table 6.1 Numbers of sites provided and families accommodated, 1966–9

	1966	1967	1968	1969
Kildare County Council	1 (4 families)			
Limerick County Council	1 (14 families)			
Dublin Corporation	(40 families)	1		1 (20 families)
Cork Corporation			1 (6 families)	
Athlone Urban District Council			1 (1 family)	
Galway County Council				1 (8 families)
Galway Corporation				4 (18 families)
Clare County Council				2 (4 families)
Kerry County Council				13 (16 families)
No. of families provided for	18	40	10	66

Source: *Dáil Éireann Debates*, vol. 244, cols 297–8 (5 Feb. 1970).

opposed Traveller accommodation. Indeed, the failure of local authorities to face down opposition to Traveller settlement led to the growth of the Itinerant Settlement Movement.

ITINERANT SETTLEMENT COMMITTEES

Following the establishment of the Advisory Committee in 1965, the government also encouraged the foundation of local voluntary committees, whose objectives would be 'to help in the resettlement of itinerant families and to encourage the employment of professional social workers by local authorities'.[79] In 1969, the Irish Council for Itinerant Settlement, an executive committee and supervisory body, was established to co-ordinate the work of local committees.[80]

The first Itinerant Settlement Committee (ISC) was founded in Dublin by Victor Bewley,[81] Lady Wicklow[82] and Fr Thomas Fehily.[83] Archbishop

John Charles McQuaid agreed to be patron of the Committee. His name persauded the clergy and religious organisations to believe that, at least, there was little point in opposing the settlement policy.[84] When the committee met with Dublin County Council officials in 1965, they were informed that 12 sites had been proposed, but that all had been abandoned owing to public opposition.[85] Fr Fehily then realised that voluntary work was the only way to circumvent official intransigence.[86] Bewley and Fehily travelled the country establishing settlement committees and publicising the idea of Traveller settlement. Their visits were not always welcomed; in one parish the Vicar General (one rank below the Bishop) warned parishioners that he was 'an evil man'. Until at least 1974, an annual 'Itinerant Week' was held to promote the ideals of the settlement movement.[87] A bi-monthly newsletter called *Settlement News* was also produced.[88] Although it was never intended as an aid body, the committee began to receive donations that it spent on providing caravans for tent-dwelling families. The nationwide character of the movement is worth stressing: after 1967 there was at least one committee in 16 counties. In Tipperary, three town sub-committees reported to a county committee.[89] However, these committees were not unanimous on the most appropriate way to settle Travellers. Gmelch and Gmelch reported a division within the settlement movement over the appropriate accommodation for Travellers. The Irish Council and 75 per cent of local committees believed in placing families on serviced campsites before offering them housing. The site was therefore 'an indispensable first step on the way to conventional housing'. By 1974, over 300 families were settled on 70 sites across the country.[90] A quarter of settlement committees favoured housing over sites, believing that the physical isolation of sites prevented Travellers integrating with the settled community. Between 1965 and 1974, 150 families were housed. Housing was easier to provide in areas outside Dublin city, which suffered from a public housing shortage during the 1960s. Committees favouring direct housing over site provision were based outside the major urban centres.[91] Despite this difference of opinion, the ISCs achieved significant results: between 1965 and 1974, ISCs created or found accommodation for over one third of the Traveller population.[92]

The membership of these committees was dominated by members of the St Vincent de Paul. Given the organisation's history in helping Travellers, it is likely that members of the Legion of Mary also joined in large numbers. In 1966, the St Vincent de Paul assessed its 'modest contribution to the itinerancy problem'. It was estimated that it provided housing for 50 families, while co-operating with other organisations in the provision of education for Traveller children. Several conferences were devoted exclusively to such work.[93] In 1968, a new conference was established in Longford to work solely with

Travellers.[94] Thus, in addition to settlement committees linked to Fr Fehily's Dublin committee, there were dedicated conferences of the St Vincent de Paul working to settle Travellers. In 1969, a survey revealed the extent of the Society's participation in the settlement movement.

> In a number of areas, Itinerant Settlement Committees were entirely composed of its [SSVP] members and in most places Society was strongly represented on these Committees. The members bore the brunt of local opposition to settlement proposals, but it was encouraging to learn that they stood up and were counted in the cause of justice for a suffering and unpopular group of people.[95]

Puxon may have scorned the charitable basis of government policy in the 1960s, but the importance of mobilising vocal support for Travellers among the settled community was central to Fehily's idea of the settlement committees. Voluntary organisations provided unpaid social workers and supporters of Traveller accommodation. Gmelch and Gmelch noted, 'Some ISCs spend as much time selling settlement to the Irish community as they do working with Travellers'.[96] That work was an essential part of their success and probably reduced the opposition to local authority plans. As sites began to be established across the country, the extent of co-operation between voluntary agencies and the administration became clear. The Minister for Local Government informed the Dáil that sites offered temporary accommodation, essentially a preliminary stage in the settlement of Traveller families. The sites also provided a base from where 'voluntary helpers and official agencies can co-operate to set in motion a comprehensive programme of rehabilitation, with special emphasis on education and employment'.[97] The importance of social work in the settlement programme was clear, although no professional social workers funded by public money were appointed until 1969. A subsidy of 50 per cent was contributed by central government to the salaries and expenses of social workers employed by local authorities to work exclusively with Travellers.[98] In 1969, just four social workers were employed on this basis.[99] With so few professionals in the area, voluntary work remained significant.

Fr Fehily believes that settlement committees became pioneers by accident, making decisions because government bodies would not take the initial steps.[100] Although local and national government generally failed to address the politically controversial issue of Traveller accommodation, a politician interested in the issue could make a significant contribution. When Kevin Boland was appointed Minister for Local Government in 1966, his determination to provide facilities for Travellers made an impact upon reluctant local authorities. In the late 1960s, with some success, he pressured local government bodies to provide sites and accommodation for Travellers.[101] In a

1969 letter to the Taoiseach, Fr Fehily praised the 'interest and hard work' of the minister, describing him as 'a tower of strength'.[102] Had Boland not resigned in 1970, Dr Michael Flynn felt that he would have implemented the recommendations of the Commission more thoroughly than his predecessor or many of his successors.[103] Because of government inertia, voluntary groups worked hardest to provide facilities for Travellers. Sites could be selected, purchased and developed by settlement committees, but they still required planning permission from local authorities. Victor Bewley's attempts to develop a halting site on land owned by the Bewley firm ran up against this obstacle.[104] In addition to housing and site provision, ISCs helped organise educational facilities for Traveller children. Nationwide, from 1965 to 1974, ISCs organised 17 special classes and six special schools. Some committees purchased buses to transport children from scattered roadside camps to school. Those small-scale efforts could hardly hope to address the problems of adult illiteracy and irregular schooling that continued to distinguish Travellers from settled people.[105]

A major flaw in the Itinerant Settlement Movement was the lack of official consultation with Travellers themselves. A few ISCs included Travellers in their work, but these were exceptional.[106] According to Gmelch and Gmelch, some officials in the Movement 'openly discouraged' the participation of Travellers.[107] Nevertheless, the National Council for Travelling People (NCTP) was established in 1969, a body in which settled people and Travellers worked together. Essentially, the council was a continuation of the Itinerant Settlement Movement, but with a different emphasis on the extent of Traveller participation. It remained publicly associated with Bewley, Fehily and Sister Colette Dwyer, another prominent pro-Traveller activist. Yet internal divisions and disagreements led to a 'very bitter break-up' of the NCTP in 1990.[108] The council's place was taken by the Irish Traveller Movement (ITM), an organisation with more significant input from Travellers themselves.[109] The history of these organisations is outside the scope of this book, but Travellers' developing political awareness can be clearly seen in the establishment and dissolution of various bodies. This study concludes before Travellers were officially part of the decision-making process on issues affecting their community. Contemporary Traveller representatives, whose work has influenced government decision making and media commentary, have been labelled an 'ethnic intelligentsia'.[110] Arguably, the settlement policy, and the large-scale intervention in Traveller society that it required, politicised members of the community.

CONCLUSION

The implementation of the settlement policy depended upon voluntary organisations, who were willing to fight the opposition of other settled people and local politicians. The class affiliations of ISC members can only be guessed at but, drawn heavily as they were from the St Vincent de Paul and the Legion of Mary, most ISCs were probably middle class.[111] Galway ISC members fighting for facilities for Travellers believed it 'represented a necessary, and long overdue, national duty consistent with the goals of a modernising Catholic city and country'.[112] Few seemed to share this view; plans for halting sites and housing faced determined opposition from a middle class anxious to preserve the spatial segregation between public tenants and homeowners, and a working class bent on improving their lot. A working class that had experienced considerable upheaval with the growth of public housing was not willing to sacrifice its newly acquired petit bourgeois status to facilitate the accommodation of Travellers. Living in suburban housing estates with large gardens and commuting to the city centre, former slum dwellers had ostensibly become middle class. As government intervention had often forcibly changed the economic and social structure of the working class, public-housing tenants had responded by becoming politically aware and articulating their rights. The local authorities that had housed them now faced the additional responsibility of heeding their tenant's concerns.

Given determined opposition from residents, local authorities left the task of accommodating Travellers to the voluntary sector. In a long-standing tradition of the Irish welfare system, religious orders, the Church and religiously motivated voluntary groups accepted the challenge of caring for an unpopular minority that had proved too difficult for the administration to handle. Just as the St Vincent de Paul and the Legion had taken on the task of rehabilitating the homeless and ex-prisoners in the 1920s and 1930s, so they accepted responsibility for helping nomads to adjust to permanent settlement in the 1960s. State welfare still restricted itself to providing subsistence benefits, leaving more complex social work to the Catholic voluntary sector. This arrangement may have benefited Travellers since bureaucracy often cannot respond appropriately to poverty and exclusion when the people it seeks to help are illiterate and do not have a fixed abode. Charities are more flexible in dispensing aid and present a more human face than officialdom. But in the case of Travellers, who lacked shelter and security of tenure, the state refused to honour even the narrowest definition of welfare support. Classed as a charity case, Travellers were not given their welfare entitlements as citizens of the state.

SEVEN

CONCLUSION

—

This study has analysed the historical relationship between Travellers and settled people. That relationship deteriorated markedly after the Second World War when Travellers were defined by the majority community as a public problem. Scattered references to their presence in the 1920s and 1930s were far from complimentary, but hostility towards Travellers increased in volume and intensity in the 1950s. Why should unauthorised encampments, animal trespass and begging suddenly become a problem when, by virtue of nomadism and economic structure, Travellers had always infringed upon the norms of settled society? Smith has pointed out that 'not all social problems become concerns in the public domain' and that it is difficult to predict what will be defined as a public problem.[1] George Gmelch's explanation – that Travellers in the post-war period moved from rural to urban areas – has become a popular truism. Progress or modernisation displaced Travellers and, it seems, they have never recovered. Judith Okely's nuanced study of English Traveller-Gypsies has comprehensively refuted the argument that nomads were dependent upon now obsolete craft skills for their economic survival, and the adaptive nature of the Traveller economy is slowly being understood. Gmelch also assumed that Travellers belonged to the countryside, yet they were perceived as outsiders by the small farmers studied by Arensberg and Kimball. Travellers were neither urban nor rural, for nomadism, which esteems travelling rather than the origin or destination, makes a nonsense of such a binary opposition.

However, the modernisation model posited by Gmelch should not be completely disregarded. The processes of change loosely termed modernisation played a role in determining the social and economic contexts of minority–majority relations in twentieth-century Ireland. Undoubtedly one of the most important developments to affect Travellers was the decline of fairs and markets. Their presence was an essential part of every fair and they may have symbolised the holiday atmosphere surrounding these occasions. Once fairs vanished, settled people saw no purpose to Travellers' visits and perhaps resented their appearance. For Travellers themselves, the fairs were opportunities to earn money, and meet family and friends normally scattered throughout the country. The end of fairs impoverished Travellers both socially and economically. Fairs faded away because of a complex interplay of market forces, social change and commercial developments best summed up in the word 'modernisation'.

Yet the most important changes which affected Traveller–settled relations did not result from an inexorable modernisation process. Greater control over street trading instituted in 1926 illustrated the desire by government and police to regulate the economic and social lives of the urban poor. With the provision of public housing in the 1930s, the planning of urban areas revolutionised the position of the Irish working class. The standard of living among the poorest in Irish society dramatically improved but their independence was greatly circumscribed. Trades and crafts practised in tenement basements or yards could not continue in public-housing estates because of strict planning regulations differentiating residential and industrial areas. With their opportunities for self-employment limited, many working-class families became more dependent on social welfare payments. In response to this increased demand, welfare payments were increased in 1938 though they could hardly be described as generous.

Those Travellers who did not live in local authority housing were relatively untouched by these changes. However, those anxious to settle permanently or temporarily found the supply of cheap rented property now controlled by local government. The application process discriminated against illiterate people while some local authorities deliberately refused housing to Traveller families. In general, however, the effect upon Travellers was more indirect; the transformations in social and economic organisation profoundly affected their position in Irish society. When the whole family economy was abolished by compulsory school attendance and the informal labour habits of the working class criminalised, some central values of Traveller society were deemed unacceptable. The gap between Travellers and poor settled people was widening. As local authorities acquired land for housing, compulsory purchase orders had the consequence, unlooked for or not, of eradicating Traveller encampments. When former slum dwellers became responsible members of local residents' associations, they began to lobby the local authority to remove Travellers who reminded them of their uncomfortably recent past. The language of planning and tourist amenity further legitimised complaints about Travellers. Public housing and town planning evolved in tandem, arguably because the former created the need for the latter. The Department of Local Government and Public Health believed in 1934 that neat, well-maintained public space was a corollary of rising living standards made possible by preventative medicine and slum clearance. Creating a tourist-friendly landscape justified the improvement of derelict sites and space was tailored for public consumption. Tourist income did not necessarily originate from foreign visitors, though no study has yet documented the importance in domestic tourism in independent Ireland.

In addition to this politicisation of space, the importance of welfare and charity must be considered. In the first half of the twentieth century, Travellers were not alone on the roads. The wandering poor and insane subsisted on charity, joined by a number of individuals who functioned as news bearers in a pre-literate society. As welfare benefits increased, begging by settled people declined. Travellers were then distinguished from the majority population by this practice. By virtue of their nomadism and illiteracy, they were less likely to avail themselves of benefit while many local authorities were reluctant to help. But as state-funded assistance was known to provide the basic necessities of life, resentment over begging may have gradually developed. Also, when subsistence production on farmsteads was replaced by food bought in a grocery store, householders may have become less inclined to dispense charity. Catholic charitable organisations long recognised that Travellers were unable to secure welfare benefits. Typically, St Vincent de Paul and the Legion of Mary ministered to the material and spiritual needs of those neglected or forgotten by the state and Travellers were no exception. A well-established pattern in welfare provision was followed: voluntary organisations took on difficult social work such as caring for the homeless while local and national government provided basic subsistence allowances.

The extent to which Travellers were ignored by government was perhaps unparalleled in the history of Irish welfare provision. Even the coercive measures designed to target Travellers after an outbreak of typhus in 1940 were later applied only to women with venereal disease. Despite their lack of schooling and unconventional upbringing, Traveller children evaded institutional care because the legal and governmental systems were unwilling to commit them. The same local government officials that denied Travellers housing also refused to pay the industrial school fees for nomadic children. When government stirred itself to take action against Travellers in the Education Bill 1942, it was barred by the constitution. But the most significant factor protecting Travellers, a politically powerless minority, from government surveillance was the administrative division of responsibility in which no department was concerned with Travellers as a group. If Travellers caused settled society problems, these issues were allocated to various arms of government. Therefore, no one department was ever unduly worried by their presence and complaints from voters and local representatives could be passed endlessly between departments. The ending of this administrative vacuum was one of the recommendations contained in the *Report of the Commission on Itinerancy*. Set up in response to increasing complaints from urban residents, the Commission gathered evidence and deliberated on the 'itinerant problem' from 1960–3. The Commission produced a thoughtful and comprehensive report that advocated settlement and absorption as the solution to Traveller poverty and the problem of illegal campsites. Its proposals for sites and housing were detailed and humane, with advice about providing accommodation adjacent to schools and shops. Although the Commission knew the settled population would object to living near Travellers, it recommended the implementation of the settlement programme in the strongest terms. This was the first official examination of Travellers by the Irish state. Yet during the Commission's deliberation, the passing of the Derelict Sites Act in 1961 further politicised the use of marginal land. As private and public landowners reclaimed derelict land, definitions of conventional land use hardened. The political implications of Traveller accommodation were heightened by the increased value given to previously neglected sites.

When the Commission's report was accepted by the cabinet in 1963, the Department of Local Government was given overall responsibility for Travellers as a group. While the department formulated policy, local authorities continued to break up Traveller campsites on public property. A nascent Traveller political organisation, based in Dublin, was headed by Grattan Puxon. The Itinerant Action Campaign protested about the constant round of evictions suffered by Dublin Travellers; central government was embarrassed, but Dublin Corporation was not deterred. Puxon returned to England in 1965 and many of the group's Traveller leaders followed him. Without an organised representative body, Travellers as a community had little influence over the settlement programme. The voluntary Itinerant Settlement Committees (ISCs) were mainly responsible for driving settlement forward when local government was paralysed by vociferous opposition to housing and campsites from residents. Given the society's pioneering role in providing welfare services for Travellers in the 1930s, it was appropriate that many ISCs were dominated by members of the St Vincent de Paul Society. In co-operation with local authorities, ISCs liaised between both communities, attempting to convince Travellers and settled people that settlement was a viable proposal. ISCs also ensured that Travellers could take up any welfare benefits to which they were entitled. Government welfare was still restricted to providing basic subsistence, leaving more complex social work to the Catholic voluntary sector. Yet local and national government reneged upon their responsibilities to Travellers as citizens by not providing them with basic sanitation and housing. At a time when the government was promoting the benefits of universal sanitation to sceptical farmers,[2] this was an indictment of their claims to treat Travellers simply as poor citizens in need of assistance. While welfare programmes had long been undertaken for the disadvantaged by society as a whole, prejudice against Travellers placed them outside the welfare community. Collective responsibility for their situation was denied. Although the Commission was careful to deny the ethnic status of Travellers, the behaviour of settled people towards them was clearly determined by an unshakable belief in their irreconcilable cultural difference.

RESETTLEMENT AND RESISTANCE SINCE 1970

—

The period after 1970 is considerably easier to survey because material is available that directly addresses the relationship between Travellers and settled people. The government engagement with the 'itinerant problem' that followed the publication of the Commission on Itinerancy produced reports and survey data that did not exist before 1970. The importance of the Commission has often overshadowed the social developments that heralded its establishment, but the significance of later decades is amply demonstrated by other scholars.[1] Nonetheless, a brief survey of the later period follows.

Given the refusal of settled people to countenance Traveller camps, houses or sites in their neighbourhood, one theme has continued to dominate the public discussion: where will 'they' live? Property and its uses remain as vexed a question as it did when the 'Irish land question' dominated public debate in the nineteenth and early twentieth centuries. Most Travellers remain outside the land ownership system though the ostentatious property consumption by some Rathkeale families illustrates the difficulties of generalising about a population when regional and social differences are often elided by the collective noun, 'Traveller'.[2] The use of the term 'Traveller', which gradually replaced 'itinerant' and 'tinker', was due to the rise of an 'ethnic intelligentsia' in the Traveller community.[3] The increasing participation of Travellers themselves in the public and political debate about their community marks the decades after 1970 as wholly distinct from those that preceeded it, where Travellers' voices were heavily censored.[4] The settled population has not responded generously to Traveller politicisation and reactionary voices continue to go unchallenged. However, the introduction of equality legislation has considerably strengthened the position of Travellers who have been arbitrarily excluded from public houses or places of business. Finally, the economic boom has changed the society beyond all expectations, as migrants from all over the world seek to live and work in Ireland. It is striking that in spite of such sudden change, the daily relationship between Travellers and settled people remains unaffected by wider debates about cultural difference and tolerance. While Travellers now have a political voice, settled people have become more adamant in their refusal to contenance their rights as citizens.

As the final chapter detailed, voluntary organisations were more important than local government in providing accommodation for Travellers. After 1970, Travellers themselves began to be more closely involved in organisations lobbying on their behalf. This was facilitated by some settled activists, such as Joyce Sholdice, who bravely confessed to her past shortcomings. In 1980, Sholdice admitted

> We expected too much in the past, were paternalistic and possessive about them. Talk of 'our families, our children' is suspect – they are not ours, they belong to themselves. We perhaps lacked respect or intruded on their privacy, or wanted them to love us: this created false dependency on us in some, and resistance to us in others. . . . We must examine ourselves very carefully to see that our work is for the sake of the Travellers and not to fill our own needs.[5]

The Irish Settlement Committee, discussed in chapter 6, was renamed and reorganised as the National Council for Travelling People, an organisation that formally admitted Travellers. However, the transition from paternalism to participation was gradual until the Irish Traveller Movement (founded in 1990) replaced the NCTP.[6] The new umbrella organisation represented local groups where Travellers and settled people worked together rather than settlement-minded 'country people' deciding unilaterally how and where to accommodate Travellers. Those who worked with Travellers continued to come from charitable organisations such as the St Vincent de Paul or the Simon Community, as Seán Ó Riain's account of his work shows.[7] In a similar way to the pioneers in the settlement committees, those individuals believed that moving Travellers on when there was no alternative accommodation available was a short-sighted and unjust policy. However, the minority who worked with, and on behalf of, Travellers faced determined opposition from those who felt profoundly threatened by the minority's presence. Seán Ó Riain endured threatening behaviour and phone calls when he identified himself with local Travellers' struggle for accommodation.[8] In the 1980s, Travellers began to organise themselves without the involvement of settled people; the first organisation to pioneer grassroots activism was Minceir Misli, led by Michael McCann. This group became the Dublin Travellers' Education and Development Group, and later Pavee Point, the most significant Traveller representative organisation in Ireland today.[9] The politicisation of Travellers was partly a reaction to crude and insensitive 'reform' efforts: for example, Traveller women were given coats and encouraged to discard the traditional shawl.[10]

Increasingly strident demands for Traveller entitlements provoked a mostly ugly response from the settled community. In 1988, the chair of NCTP observed that attitudes to Travellers had hardened as the previously silent minority became more vocal and organised.[11] In light of the levels of personal animosity revealed in Mícheál Mac Gréil's study of prejudice in Dublin in 1972–3, a time when the integrationist settlement campaign was at its height, this reaction to Travellers unwilling to abandon their identity was deeply worrying.[12] Unfortunately, the fears of activists were well founded: Mac Gréil's later survey of attitudes in 1988–9 revealed a deterioration in the levels of toler- ance afforded to Travellers by the settled community. Whereas Mac Gréil had shown how Travellers were allocated 'lower caste' status in the 1970s, he now described their situation as 'Ireland's apartheid'.[13] Some 10 per cent of those surveyed advocated denying citizenship to Travellers, a disturbing indication of the depth of feeling against a tiny minority.[14] However, attitudes to other individuals had also significantly deteriorated, leading Mac Gréil to conclude that prejudice in Dublin had grown since his last survey.[15]

As the hostility towards Travellers became more entrenched, their numbers rose although they remained a tiny proportion of the population. The government continued to count Travellers as families rather than individuals, since those people remained an administrative 'problem' that could be solved with housing units. In 1974, 1,690 Traveller families were enumerated by the Department of Local Government. By 1980, the numbers had risen to 2,490 families.[16] In 1990, 3,705 families were counted by government.[17] The increase in the population was partly due to improved health and social welfare services, as well as the fluctuating travel and migration patterns between Britain and Ireland.[18]

The flaws in such family counts were the same as for earlier decades dis- cussed in chapter 1: opaque definitions of who was a Traveller and Traveller status being ascribed by officials rather than the individuals surveyed. That those counted continued to be those in need of accommodation showed the definition of 'Traveller' that prevailed in the official mind related exclusively to poverty and want, not cultural distinctiveness. Since family counts mea- sured housing needs, those who were already accommodated could be ignored, meaning that the figures did not accurately reflect the size of the Traveller population. Seeing Travellers in housing as no longer worthy of inclusion in statistics on the community was a failure to recognise the com- plexity of identity in Traveller society. This should have been recognised earlier, when Travellers settled in the 1930s by local authorities in Tralee and Athlone did not stay in the houses allocated to them for significant periods of time (see chapter 4). By excluding housed families, the family counts refused to acknowledge that Travellers would ever travel again, in spite of ample local-authority experience that housing did not guarantee permanency of residence.[19] Although the rhetoric of assimilation, which dominated the 1960s, 1970s and 1980s, had receded by the 1990s the government still believed housing was the solution to the Traveller 'problem'. Reliable figures on the size of the minority population were not deemed important until 2002, when Travellers could describe themselves in the census, producing a figure of 23,700 people, just 0.6 per cent of the total Irish population.[20] That formal enumeration, the first since 1956, should be seen in the context of a government and society grappling with the idea of equality, as the 2002 census also included a question on disabled people and their carers.[21] The interaction of government with groups that have represented a 'problem' such as Travellers and the disabled has been long and complex, with the 1960s marking the beginning of that process. The rhetoric of inclusiveness and rights is now officially sanctioned, however imperfectly. Yet the provision of facilities for Travellers remains challenging.

Although housing and assimilation were universally accepted solutions to unauthorised campsites in the 1960s, the initial attempts by local authorities to provide sites or houses for Travellers were thwarted by the objections of homeowners and local authority tenants alike, as chapter 6 demonstrated. The Itinerant Settlement Committees and voluntary organisations strove to secure accommodation for families whose plight did not trouble many settled people. Between 1960 and 1980, private efforts secured accommodation for 350 families.[22] Private charity also worked with local authorities to develop sites and select families for public housing, a contribution that is difficult to enumerate. However, the charitably inclined could not persuade most settled people to tolerate Travellers as neighbours. Since some people even refused to offer the peace to Travellers at Mass, it was no surprise that they were physically attacked by those opposed to their presence.[23]

A word that came to encapsulate violent hostility directed at Travellers originated from Rahoon, a suburb of Galway city. In the late 1960s, as a result of attacks and protests by local authority tenants, 'Rahoonery' became national shorthand for opposition to Traveller accommodation.[24] Such intimidation and aggression were shocking demonstrations of blatant prejudice and bigotry. The term was still in use as late as 1999, when Dick Roche TD used it in the Dáil chamber.[25] However, one suburb should not be exclusively associated with belligerence directed against Travellers, as Bryan Fanning's study of Ennis, County Clare demonstrated.[26] The failure of many local authority initiatives can be ascribed to NIMBY (Not In My Back Yard), a phenomenon that thrived long before wealth apparently eroded community ties in Celtic Tiger Ireland.[27] In 1983, the Travelling People Review Body noted that residents opposed 'shelters and hostels proposed for battered wives, deprived children, the mentally handicapped, convalescent psychiatric patients, the down-and-outs cared for by the Simon Community and accommodation for slum dwellers.' However, compromises were often reached that ensured the success of such projects, whereas Traveller accommodation initiatives invariably failed.[28] Clearly, the prejudice against Travellers was exceptionally severe. In general, 'implementation was geared to what was feasible, or politically possible, rather than what was required'.[29] Nevertheless, some local authorities did provide accommodation for Travellers.

The pattern of accommodation provision since the publication of the Commission on Itinerancy is surprisingly complex, as Michelle Norris and Nessa Winston have argued. Their analysis reveals that even though assimilation was the stated aim until the 1990s, a significant proportion of 'Traveller specific accommodation' – halting sites and group housing – was built after 1970. Ironically, since the 1995 *Report of the Task Force on the Travelling Community* advocated respect for Traveller culture, most of the new units built have been standard houses rather than Traveller-specific facilities. Norris explains that the divergence between policy and implementation arose partly as a result of planning laws.[30] Indeed, the role played by legislation and the legal system in Traveller–settled relations has been considerable since 1970. The High Court adjudication between Limerick Corporation and Mrs Mary Sheridan in 1952 can therefore be seen as an early example of the judiciary mediating between government and the marginalised (see chapter 3). Gerry Whyte has examined the role played by judicial interpretations of various statutes in defining Travellers' rights. Travellers have successfully sought protection from certain local authority decisions in the higher courts, but residents opposing halting sites have also won important cases. Indeed, the strength of resident's opposition remains a significant obstacle in the provision of Traveller accommodation. Although the courts have upheld the right to a halting site, 'securing the implementation of those rights in practice is an entirely different matter'.[31]

The recourse to the courts by both Travellers and settled people reflected the growing importance of legislation. Statutes did not mention Travellers specifically in the decades before 1970, but this changed after the first explicit mention of Travellers in the Housing Act 1988. Under that statute, local authorities were empowered to provide halting sites. However, the more punitive Housing (Miscellaneous Provisions) Act of 1992 gave local authorities the power to remove caravans parked within five miles of such a site, proving that legislation was no panacea to Travellers' problems. Further progress was made with the Housing (Traveller Accommodation) Act 1998, when consultation between Travellers and local authorities on accommodation was established. Unfortunately, was a chasm between the spirit of the legislation and its implementation, as the history of the County Clare Traveller

Accommodation Advisory Committee revealed. It was the first time that Travellers were consulted about accommodation for their community, but initially only one representative was allowed to join the committee. Its report was accepted in principle by the County Council, who subsequently ignored its recommendations when sites were planned and built.[32] National government promulgated legislation that was inclusive and progressive but imposed no penalties on local authorities that flouted the principles enshrined in the statute book.

Arguably, the most valuable legislative initiative affecting Travellers was the Prohibition of Incitement to Hatred Act 1989. The explicit inclusion of Travellers and homosexuals in the Act was a victory for those who wished to strengthen the protection offered to vulnerable minorities. However, no one has yet been prosecuted for inciting hatred towards Travellers under that statute.[33] The legislation was weak, but it marked the beginning of an equality discourse in Irish society that went beyond gender. An Equality Authority, which had been sought by the Task Force on the Travelling Community, was established by the Equal Status Act in 2000. Individuals who experienced discrimination finally had recourse to a complaints procedure outside the criminal justice system. Travellers energetically pursued cases against publicans who had refused to serve them, challenging the segregation of public houses that even the Commission on Itinerancy had noted. Complaints from Travellers against licensed premises dominated claims made under the Equal Status Act in 2002 and 2003.[34] Since cases were resolved more often in favour of the complainants than the defendants, the vintners' organisations were unhappy with the Equality Authority. Representatives of the drink trade claimed that Travellers asserting 'their "rights"' were increasingly violent and maintained that publicans 'should have the right to refuse without giving a reason'.[35] Reflecting how Irish politics is driven by the successful lobby group, the vintners ensured that the provisions of the Equal Status Act were undermined by the Intoxicating Liquor Bill 2003, which removed cases concerning licensed premises from the Equality Authority, returning them to the criminal justice system. The Equality Coalition, an organisation made of groups representing Travellers, the disabled, the elderly, women and homosexuals who opposed the change, failed to sway the government.[36] The vintners triumphed over other advocacy organisations and the bill became law. Legal avenues are exploited by many groups in Irish society, including powerful interests with a history of treating Travellers unfairly. The modification of the Equal Status Act and the successful actions taken by residents opposed to Traveller accommodation demonstrate that legislation and the courts must represent all interests in society, and cannot impose goodness or fairness on members of that society. Nevertheless, the courts should be fundamental to understanding Irish society, where a public debate on crime and deviance has evolved since the 1960s.

The incidence of crime, its victims and perpetrators as well as the perceptions of criminality are notoriously complex issues. While the courts are the arbiters of criminal and social justice, popular attitudes to crime are rarely dictated by statute or legal argument. Historically, the public has been fascinated by the lurid details of crime, an appetite accordingly fed by the media.[37] However, as Anthony Keating has illustrated, the Irish print media were restricted in the early years of the state from reporting sex offences, the most sensational of crimes.[38] Court reports may have dominated the regional newspapers, but the prosaic presentation and absence of banner headlines indicated that scandal was not consciously exploited by editors. While censorship ensured that crime coverage was low key, the attitudes of Irish society to violence were not especially censorious. An incident where a garda was beaten unconscious during a street brawl involving Travellers and settled people was not covered in the local newspaper, and was sparsely reported outside the county.[39] Would such an incident be received with indifference by the contemporary media? As demonstrated elsewhere, the media portrayal of Travellers as violent and criminal was not a feature of newspaper coverage in the 1960s. However, using tenuous evidence in 1996 *The Irish Times* was willing to identify Travellers as the perpetrators of serious crime against the elderly in rural Ireland.[40] Fears about crime committed by Travellers re-emerged in 2005 with the conviction of farmer Padraig Nally for the manslaughter of John Ward, a Traveller.[41] Nally believed that Ward was guilty of a number of thefts from his property. The coverage of Nally's trial deserves close examination but the connection between violent crime in rural areas and Travellers had been established in the print media at least a decade previously. Yet a regional study by Nora Casey suggests that newspapers are not acknowledged as a influence on attitudes to Travellers. Instead, what people heard from their neighbours and acquaintances determined their perceptions.[42] Clearly, the much-lamented 'community' with its informal methods of transmitting knowledge plays an important role in shaping beliefs about a minority that few people encounter in their daily lives.

That mutual distance is central to understanding Traveller–settled relations. Traveller representative bodies reflect the welcome politicisation of that community, but the parallel strengthening of organised settled opposition demonstrates the elusiveness of a solution to community conflict. For without pro-Traveller initiatives from organisations made up wholly or predominantly of settled people, there can be little progress in building relationships between the communities.[43] Representative bodies and lobby groups are a fundamental part of Irish politics as Niamh Hardiman has argued.[44] Yet interest group politics has served some in Irish society better than others; for Travellers it has meant opportunities for the politically active to speak out and contribute to debates about housing, horses, equality, discrimination and the shape of multicultural Ireland. Those who wish to exclude Travellers have benefited from the same process and used the same instruments: lobbying politicians and taking court actions. By virtue of their numerical weakness and marginality in most areas of public life and business, Travellers remain, broadly, on the losing side. If public opinion has remained as profoundly antagonistic as previous surveys have suggested (and there is little reason to believe it has improved), Irish society must reconcile the rhetoric of inclusiveness with the unpalatable truth that many people refuse to see the individual men, women and children behind the collective noun 'Traveller'.

Appendix

Legal Glossary

—

DUBLIN POLICE ACT 1842 (5 VICT., C. 24)

This legislation was used to prosecute street traders in Dublin city but proved inadequate, as proving individuals caused an 'obstruction' was difficult

SUMMARY JURISDICTION (IRELAND) ACT 1851 (14 & 15 VICT., C. 92)

An Act to consolidate and amend the Acts relating to certain Offences and other Matters as to which Justices of the Peace exercise Summary Jurisdiction in Ireland.

This statute was used for a variety of purposes. In Dublin, Gardaí applied it in conjunction with the Dublin Police Act 1842 to control street trading. In Northern Ireland, the RUC applied the act's on provisions road offences to control Travellers. These included turning animals loose (section 10 (1)), leaving carts etc. on the roads (10, (3)), making fires on or near the road (10, (8)) and a driver leaving his vehicle (12, (4)). Section 20 allowed a farmer or property owner to seize and detain animals causing damage until compensated by the animal owner. Amendments made to it by the Northern Irish government in 1958 (outlined below) were further designed to restrict Traveller's movements.

PEDLARS ACTS 1871 (34 & 35 VICT. c. 96) AND 1881 (44 & 45 VICT. c. 45); HAWKERS ACT 1888 (51 & 52 VICT. c. 33)

Under these statutes, licences were available for pedlars, defined as travelling merchants without a beast of burden, and hawkers, those with transportation. In March 1924, 186 licences had been issued under the Hawkers Act.[1] The Commission on Sick and Destitute Poor reported that 348 individuals (148 men, 122 children) were 'Bona fide hawkers, pedlars etc' in November 1925.

PUBLIC HEALTH (IRELAND) ACT 1878 (41 & 42 VICT. C. 52)

Sections 148 and 149 empowered the Minister for Local Government and Public Health to make regulations for containment of an infectious disease. Although Dr Ward maintained it allowed for the detention of infected persons, section 149 was not as specific as its replacement, section 38 of the Health Act 1947, which was based on an Order drafted to detain and isolate Travellers resisting treatment for typhus.
Section 149 read

> Whenever any part of Ireland appears to be threatened with or is affected by any formidable epidemic, endemic or infectious disease, the Local Government Board may make, and from time to time alter and revoke, regulations for all or any of the following purposes; (namely)
>
> (1) For the speedy internment of the dead; and
>
> (2) For house to house visitation
>
> (3) For the provision of medical aid and hospital accommodation; and
>
> (4) For the promotion of cleansing, ventilation, and disinfection, and for guarding against the spread of disease.

Promotion and prevention did not necessarily imply detention and compulsion.

EMPLOYMENT OF CHILDREN ACT 1903 (3 EDW. VII, C. 45)

The Act gave any local authority the power to make byelaws regulating, for all children or for girls and boys separately, the types of occupation and hours of employment allowed.

CHILDREN'S ACT 1908 (8 EDW. VII, C. 67)

'An Act to consolidate and amend the Law relating to the Protection of Children and Young Persons, Reformatory and Industrial Schools and Juvenile Offenders, and otherwise to amend the Law with respect to Children and Young Persons.' Section 14 covered begging, sections 57-70 dealt with committal to an industrial school, reformatory or the care of another person.

EDUCATION (PROVISION OF MEALS) (IRELAND) ACTS 1914
(4 & 5 GEO. V C. 35) ; 1917 (7 & 8 GEO. V C. 53)

Meals could be provided to schoolchildren, funded jointly by local authorities
and central government.

LOCAL GOVERNMENT ACT 1925 (5/1925)

This act abolished Rural District Councils and transferred functions of road
maintenance to county councils and the sanitary duties to county councils.
Section 20 was formulated to deal with Travellers encampments.

> 20 (1) A tent, van, shed or similar structure used for human habitation, or a barge,
> lighter, boat or other vessel on any river, canal or inland water (in this section
> referred to as a 'barge') used for human habitation, which is in such a state as to
> be a nuisance or injurious to health, or which is so overcrowded as to be
> injurious to the health of the inmates (whether or not they are members of the
> same family), shall be deemed a nuisance within the meaning of section 107 of
> the Public Health (Ireland) Act, 1878, and the provisions of that act shall apply
> accordingly.
>
> (2) A sanitary authority may make byelaws for promoting cleanliness in, and
> the habitable condition of tents, vans, sheds and similar structures used for
> human habitation, or of barges used for human habitation, and for preventing
> the spread of infectious disease by persons inhabiting the same, and generally
> for the prevention of nuisances in connection with same.

STREET TRADING ACT 1926 (15/1926)

Designed specifically for Dublin city, section 14 of the Act extended the
power to enact byelaws to local authorities governing populations of 1,500 or
more. Byelaws could prohibit stall trading in any street and prescribe the
times and types of trading allowed. Local authorities could also enforce
standards for cleanliness of items on sale and prohibit the handling of goods
without wrapping. A street trader's certificate and a street trader's stall-licence
were required to trade legally in permitted areas.

SCHOOL ATTENDANCE ACT 1926 (17/1926)

This act amended the compulsory attendance clauses of the Education Act (Ireland) 1892 (55 & 56 Vict. c. 42). In Cork, Dublin, Limerick, Waterford and the Urban Districts of Blackrock, Dún Laoghaire, Rathmines, Rathgar and Pembroke the act was to be administered by School Attendance Committees. The committees in the rest of the country were abolished, their duties taken over by the gardaí. Children from 6 to 14 years old were covered by the Act. Under Section 4 a 'reasonable excuse' for missing school was allowed, including 'light agricultural work' for 10 days between 1 April and 15 May, and 1 August and 15 October each year. Under section 17 (4), upon a second or more offence by the same child, 'the child can be sent to a certified industrial school or committed to the care of a relative of other fit persons named'.

CHILDREN'S ACT 1929 (24/1929)

Amended section 58 (1) of 1908 Act. Amendment outlined in detail the rights of parents, the mothers of illegitimate children and the minister over children committed to institutional care.

CORK CITY MANAGEMENT ACT 1929 (1/1929)

This act established the division of policy and executive powers between elected councillors and local officials, a concept inspired by city management in the United States. Philip Monahan, who had run Cork city as Commissioner since the suspension of the Corporation in 1924, became the state's first City Manager. City management was extended to Dublin in 1930, Limerick in 1934 and Waterford in 1939.

ROAD TRAFFIC ACT 1933 (11/1933)

An Act to amend and consolidate the law relating to mechanically propelled vehicles, the regulation and control of road traffic, and the use of mechanically propelled vehicles, the regulation and control of road traffic, and the use of mechanically propelled vehicles for the carriage of passengers, to make provision for compulsory insurance against liabilities arising from negligent driving of mechanically propelled vehicles, and to make provision for other matters connected with the matter aforesaid.

Under this act (sections 147–160), the Commissioner of the Garda Síochána was given powers to regulate road traffic. Although local authorities retained some control when fairs or markets took place, the Garda's general power was outlined in section 160.

> 160 Nothing in this Act shall prejudice or derogate from the general power and duty of the Commissioner and other members of the Garda Síochána to preserve order in public places and to regulate and control traffic therein.

This statute was repealed and replaced by the Road Traffic Act 1961 (24/1961).

UNEMPLOYMENT ASSISTANCE ACT 1933 (46/1933)

The first comprehensive and dedicated piece of legislation on unemployment assistance, it contained an important residency test to prevent the rural poor joining the ranks of the urban unemployed. Section 15 (1) (e) meant an applicant had to prove he was 'that either he has been ordinarily resident in such urban area for at least one year before his latest application for unemployment assistance or has had at least three months' employment in such urban area within one year before such latest application'.

HOUSING (MISCELLANEOUS PROVISIONS) ACT 1931 (50/1931)

This Act introduced measures for 'the clearance of unhealthy areas and the repair and demolition of insanitary houses'. Under this legislation and its 1932 amending successor, local authorities received generous subventions if they demolished slums and housed former slum dwellers in newly built public housing. Under section 2 (1) an 'unhealthy area' meant

> an area the dwelling houses in which are by reason of disrepair or sanitary defects unfit for human habitation or are by reason of their bad arrangement or the narrowness or bad arrangement of the streets, dangerous or injurious to the health of the inhabitants of the area and in which the other buildings, if any, are for a like reason dangerous or injurious to the health of such inhabitants.

UNEMPLOYMENT ASSISTANCE (AMENDMENT) ACT 1938 (2/1938)

Section 4 increased rates of assistance.

SHOPS (HOURS OF TRADING) 1938 (3/1938)

'An Act to make further and better provision for regulating the hours during which shops may remain open for the serving of customers.' Traders without shops – stallholders and door-to-door salespeople – were also regulated.

TOWN AND REGIONAL PLANNING ACTS 1934 (22/1934) AND (AMENDMENT) ACT 1939 (11/1939)

The 1934 act was 'to make provision for the orderly and progressive development of cities, towns, and other areas, whether urban or rural, and to preserve and improve the amenities thereof'. Those statutes were the first attempt to introduce planned development but failed because they proved cumbersome and expensive for local authorities to implement. Nevertheless, the acts successfully introduced the concept of planning permission.

ACQUISITION OF DERELICT SITES ACT 1940 (29/1940)

A derelict site was defined as

any land –

a) which is unoccupied or is not being put to any bona fide use by the occupier thereof and,

b) on which either all the buildings re ruinous or in disrepair or there have, for a period of at least two years, been no buildings, and

c) which is or is likely to become injurious to health or the amenities of the neighbourhood by reason of its objectionable or neglected condition or by reason of the deposit or collection thereon of débris, rubbish or insanitary material, and

d) which is not held or occupied by a local authority or nay body corporate for the purposes of any railway, tramway, dock, canal, water, gas, electricity, or other public undertaking.

This act had significant implications for Travellers' use of marginal land.

HEALTH ACT 1947 (28/1947)

Section 38 allowed for the detention and isolation of individuals infected with those diseases deemed 'infectious' by the government.

> 38 (1) Where a chief medical officer is of opinion . . . that such person is a probable source of infection with an infectious disease and that his isolation is necessary as a safeguard against the spread of infection, and that such person cannot be effectively isolated in his home, such medical officer may order in writing the detention and isolation of such person in a specified hospital or other place until such medical officer gives a certificate (for which no charge shall be made) that such person is no longer a probable source of infection.

Anyone who resisted detention or attempted to escape could be punished with a fine not exceeding £50 and/or three months imprisonment. (38 (6))

LOCAL GOVERNMENT (SANITARY SERVICES) ACT 1948 (3/1948)

Although intended to eradicate unauthorised camping at beach resorts, this statute was applied by many local authorities to ban Traveller encampments. Section 30 and 31 were the most significant.

> 30 (1) A sanitary authority may make bye-laws regulating the use of temporary dwellings in their sanitary district and the bye-laws may, in particular, provide for all or any of the matters mentioned in the second schedule of this Act.
>
> 31 (1) A sanitary authority may by order prohibit the erection or retention of temporary dwellings on any land or water in their sanitary district if they are of the opinion that such erection or retention would be prejudicial to public health or the amenities of the locality or would interfere to an unreasonably extent with traffic on any road.
>
> (2) A prohibition under this section may relate either to specified land or water or all land or water of a specified class and, in particular, may relate to all land or water within a specified distance of the centre line of any road or specified road.

Common law rights were protected under section 34 (12)

> 34 (12) Nothing in this section shall prohibit or restrict the use of land for camping–
>
> a) if the land is agricultural land and the camping is carried on during the same seasons in each year by persons engaged in farming operations on the land or

b) if the land is occupied in connection with a permanent dwelling situate on or in the vicinity of such land, and the camping is carried on by no persons other than the occupier of the permanent dwelling and members of his household.

SMALL DWELLINGS ACQUISITION ACTS 1957 (11/1957)

The act amended statutes going back to 1899 that enabled tenants to purchase public housing, but the application of such schemes varied according to the age of the dwelling and the legislation under which it was built. The role played by government in extending home ownership in Ireland has not yet been studied.

DERELICT SITES ACT 1961 (3/1961)

This replaced the 1940 statute which had proved too cumbersome and difficult to use. Local authorities now had better powers of acquisition, increasing their control over marginal land used for camping by Travellers.

LOCAL GOVERNMENT (PLANNING AND DEVELOPMENT) ACT 1963 (28/1963)

An Act to make provision, in the interests of the common good, for the proper planning and development of cities, towns and other areas, whether urban or rural (including the preservation and improvement of the amenities thereof), to make certain provisions with respect to acquisition of land and to repeal the Town and Regional Planning Acts 1934 and 1939 . . .

Under Section 77 (2) (b), local authorities could provide caravan sites.

77 (2) A local authority may provide –

(b) factory buildings, office premises, shop premises, dwellings, amusement parks and structures for the purpose of entertainment, caravan parks, buildings for the purpose of provisional accommodation, meals and refreshments, buildings for provisional trade and professional services and advertisement structures

This was the statutory instrument under which the first halting sites in Ireland were provided.

SOCIAL WELFARE (MISCELLANEOUS PROVISIONS) ACT 1967
(18/1967)

Section 14 abolished the residency tests that were contained in the 1933 Act.

Northern Ireland

CHILDREN AND YOUNG PERSONS ACT (NORTHERN IRELAND)
1950 (14 GEO. VI, C. 5)

Section 20 targeted nomadic parents who did not send their children to school

20 (1) If a person habitually wanders from place to place and takes with him –

   a) any child who has attained the age of five; or

   b) any young person who has not attained the upper limit of compulsory school age

he shall unless he proves that the child or young person is not, by being so taken with him, prevented from receiving efficient full time education suitable to his age, ability and aptitude, be liable on summary conviction to a fine not exceeding two pounds.

(2) Any constable who finds a person wandering from place to place and taking a child or young person with him, may, if he has reasonable ground for believing that the person is guilty of an offence under this section, apprehend him without a warrant, and may take the child or young person to a place of safety in accordance with the provisions of this Act.

Section 20 (1–2) was remarkably similar to the powers contained in the Education Bill 1942, found unconstitutional by the Irish courts.

SUMMARY JURISDICTION AND CRIMINAL JUSTICE ACT
(NORTHERN IRELAND) 1958 (6 & 7 ELIZ. II, C.9)

Under this act, justices of the peace could hear cases of offences committed under the Vagrancy Acts. Section 5 (1–3) made a number of amendments to the 1851 Summary Jurisdiction Act.

Notes

—

1   *Report of the Commission on Itinerancy* (Dublin, 1963), p. 13.

2   *Report of the Travelling People Review Body* (Dublin, 1983), p. 6.

3   All three government reports were surveyed by Sinéad Ní Shúinéir, 'Solving Itinerancy: thirty-five years of Irish government commissions' (Unpublished conference paper, New Directions in Romani Studies Conference, Greenwich, 11 June 1998).

4   Aoife Bhreatnach, 'The "itinerant problem": the attitude of Dublin and Stormont governments to Irish Travellers, 1922–60', *Irish Historical Studies* (forthcoming).

5   See for example, Sinéad Ní Nualláin, and Mary Forde, *Changing Needs of Irish Travellers: Health, Education and Social Issues* (Galway, 1992); Ronnie Fay, 'Health and racism: a Traveller perspective' in Fintan Farrell and Philip Watt (eds), *Responding to Racism in Ireland* (Dublin, 2001), pp. 99–114; Irish Travellers Movement, *Travellers' Health and Accommodation Status* (Dublin, 1995); Northside Travellers Support Group, *Traveller Accommodation and the Law: Action for Change through the Courts* (Dublin, 1995).

6   Bryan Fanning, *Racism and Social Change in Ireland* (Manchester, 2002); Steve Garner, *Racism in the Irish Experience* (London, Dublin, Sterling Virginia, 2004); Ronit Lentin and Robbie McVeigh (eds), *Racism and Anti-Racism in Ireland* (Belfast, 2002).

7   Mícheál Mac Gréil, *Prejudice and Tolerance in Ireland Revisited* (Maynooth, 1996), p. 341.

8   *Romani Studies*, continuing the *Journal of the Gypsy Lore Society*, publishes articles on any aspect of the cultures of nomadic groups. Fields covered include anthropology, art, folklore, linguistics, literature, political science and sociology.

9   David Mayall, *Gypsy-Travellers in Nineteenth-Century Society* (Cambridge, 1988); *Gypsy Identities 1500–2000: From Moon-Men to the Ethnic Romany* (London, 2003).

10   Robert Humphreys, *No Fixed Abode: A History of Responses to the Roofless and the Rootless in Britain* (London and New York, 1999); Lionel Rose, *Rogues and Vagabonds: Vagrant Underworld in Britain 1815–1985* (London and New York, 1988); Lynn Hollen Lees, *The Solidarities of Strangers: The English Poor Law and the People 1700–1948* (New York and Cambridge, 1998).

11   The innovative work of early modern Irish historians is in stark contrast to the conventional political history overwhelmingly practised by modernists. See, for example, Toby Barnard, *Making the Grand Figure: Lives and Possessions in Ireland, 1641–1770* (London and New Haven, 2004); Clodagh Tait, *Death, Burial and Commemoration in Ireland, 1550–1650* (Basingstoke, 2002).

12   Jacinta Prunty, *Dublin Slums 1800–1925 A Study in Urban Geography* (Dublin, 1998); Ruth McManus, *Dublin, 1910–1940: Shaping the City and Suburbs* (Dublin, 2002).

13 Seamus Ó Cinnéide, *A Law for the Poor: A Study of Home Assistance in Ireland* (Dublin, 1970); Mel Cousins, *The Birth of Social Welfare in Ireland* (Dublin, 2003); Marilyn Silverman's recent work, *An Irish Working Class: Explorations in Political Economy and Hegemony 1800–1950* (Toronto, 2001) concentrates on a small town in County Kilkenny.

14 Christopher J. Smith, *Public Problems: The Management of Urban Distress* (New York and London, 1988), p. 3.

15 George Gmelch, *The Irish Tinkers: The Urbanization of an Itinerant People* (California, 1977).

16 Addendum, *Report of the Task Force on the Travelling Community* (Dublin, 1995), pp. 289–90.

17 David Sibley, *Outsiders in Urban Societies* (Oxford, 1981), pp. 77–88.

18 Ibid., pp. 31–9.

ONE: 'GIPSIES' AND 'TINKERS'

1 Patrick J. O'Connor, *All Ireland is in and about Rathkeale* (Newcastlewest, 1996), pp. 142–5; Mary O'Malley, 'Emigration of Irish Travellers', in Mary Clancy (ed.), *The Emigrant Experience* (Galway, 1991), pp. 102–110; George Gmelch and Sharon Bohn Gmelch, 'The Cross-Channel migration of Irish Travellers', *Economic and Social Review* 16, 4 (1985), pp. 287–96.

2 Sinéad Ní Shúinéir, 'From apocrypha to canon: inventing Traveller history', *History Ireland* 12, 4 (2004), pp. 15–19; Ní Shúinéir 'Travellers or the travelling people' in Brian Lalor (ed.), *The Encyclopedia of Ireland* (Dublin, 2003), pp. 1071–3.

3 *Report of the Commission on Itinerancy* (Dublin, 1963), p. 34.

4 Thomas Acton, *Gypsy Politics and Social Change: the Development of Ethnic Ideology and Pressure Politics among British Gypsies from Victorian Reformism to Romany Nationalism* (London and Boston, 1974), p. 206.

5 *Irish Daily Independent*, 1 July 1910, Scott Macfie Gypsy Collection (SMGC) K4 542–3 p. 153, Sidney Jones Library, University of Liverpool (SJL).

6 *Irish Times*, 20 May 1911, SMGC K5 p. 103 SJL.

7 Pádraig Mac Gréine, 'Irish Tinkers or "Travellers": some notes on their manners and customs, and their secret language or "cant"', *Béaloideas* 3 (1931), p. 170.

8 David Mayall, *Gypsy-Travellers in Nineteenth-Century Society* (Cambridge, 1988), pp. 79–93.

9 Jane Helleiner, 'Gypsies, celts and tinkers: colonial antecedents of anti-traveller racism in Ireland', *Ethnic and Racial Studies* 18, 3 (1995), pp. 532–54.

10 Rúnaí Aire Department of Education to Rúnaí Príobháideach Department of Taoiseach, 28 Oct. 1958, DT S12337, National Archives Ireland (NAI).

11 *Dáil Éireann Debates*, vol. 94, col. 1528 (19 Sept. 1944).

12 *Dáil Éireann Debates*, vol. 161, col. 765 (7 May 1957).

13 *Report of the Travelling People Review Body* (Dublin 1983), p. 7.

14 *Kerryman* (Cork edn), 17 July 1948.

15 The large shawl was 'either a large black woven shawl with a fringe along the outer edge, or a heavy multicoloured shawl reminiscent of a blanket or a rug'. Anne O'Dowd, *Common Clothes and Clothing 1860–1930* (Dublin, 1990), p. 8.

16 Michael Verdon, *Shawlies, Echo Boys, the Marsh and the Lanes, Old Cork Remembered* (Dublin, 1993), p. 69.

17 *Commission on Itinerancy*, p. 45; See also *Kerryman*, 13 Aug. 1960; Patrick Logan, *Fair Day: The Story of Irish Fairs and Markets* (Belfast, 1986), p. 113; Michael Houlihan, *Puck Fair: History and Traditions* (Limerick, 1999), p. 50. Photographic evidence of Traveller dress and appearance in the 1970s can be found in Sharon Gmelch, *Tinkers and Travellers* (Dublin, 1975) and Janine Wiedel, *Irish Tinkers* (London, 1976).

18 Houlihan, *Puck Fair*, p. 50.

19 Sigerson Clifford used red hair as a distinguishing characteristic in both 'The Ballad of the Tinker's Daughter' and 'The Ballad of the Tinker's Son', *Travelling Tinkers* (Dublin, 1951). Newspaper reports also featured red-haired tinkers, *Kerryman* (Cork edn), 23 July 1953; *Kerryman* (Cork edn), 9 July 1960; *Kerryman*, 13 Aug. 1960; *Kerryman* (Cork edn), 15 July 1961.

20 *Kerryman* (Cork edn), 8 July 1950. The 'canabhan' is an anglicisation of *Ceann bhán*, 'Bog Cotton', a common plant in bogland areas.

21 Logan, *Fair Day*, p. 113.

22 *Kerryman* (Cork edn), 14 July 1956.

23 I am grateful to the Head of School, UCD Irish, Celtic Studies, Irish Folklore and Linguistics, for permission to reproduce extracts from the Irish Folklore Collection. [IFC = Main Manuscript Collection] IFC 1255, p. 77.

24 Jean Pierre Liegeois cited in David Mayall, *Gypsy Identities 1500–2000: From Moon-Men to the Ethnic Romany* (London, 2003), p. 16.

25 Sharon Gmelch, *Nan: The Life of an Irish Travelling Woman* (London, 1986), p. 128.

26 IFC 1255, p. 87, UCD.

27 *Irish Press*, 3 Mar. 1934, SMGC K12 p28 no.1, SJL; *T.P.'s Weekly*, 15 Oct. 1909, SMGC K3 p. 209 no.783, SJL.

28 Mac Gréine, 'Irish Tinkers or "Travellers"', p. 171.

29 Ibid., p. 172.

30 Nan Joyce and Anna Farmer, *Traveller: An Autobiography* (Dublin, 1986), p. 12.

31 Author's interview with Nioclás Breatnach, 29 Dec. 2001.

32 *Irish Press*, 3 Mar. 1934, SMGC K12 p. 28 no.1, SJL.

33 Logan, *Fair Day*, p. 117.

34 Older boys slept in a tent when a second caravan was unavailable, *Commission on Itinerancy*, p. 41.

35 *Commission on Itinerancy*, p. 40 and Appendix XXXII, p. 145.

36 *Commission on Itinerancy*, Appendix XXXII, p. 145.

37 Justice Brian Walsh's address as Chairman of the Itinerant Advisory Committee to General Council of County Councils, 5 Aug. 1965, General Council of County Councils file (GCCC).

38 Joyce and Farmer, *Traveller*, p. 12.

39 Mícheál Mac Éinrí, '"Ceant" agus Saoghal na dTincéirí', *Béaloideas* 9, 2 (1939), p. 229.

40 *Dáil Éireann Debates*, vol. 167, col. 158 (15 Apr. 1958).

41 *T.P.'s Weekly*, 15 Oct. 1909, SMGC K3 p. 209 no.783, SJL; IFC 1255, p. 139, UCD.

42 IFC 1255 p. 108, UCD.

43 Gmelch, *Nan*, pp. 31–2; Nan Joyce's grandparents lived in a house for six months of the year, Joyce and Farmer, *Traveller*, p. 22; *Commission on Itinerancy*, p. 58.

44 Sean Maher, *The Road to God Knows Where: A Memoir of a Travelling Boyhood* (Dublin, 1998), p. 10; Gmelch, *Nan*, p. 77, p. 86; Logan, *Fair Day*, p. 114.

45 IFC 1255, p. 69, UCD.

46 Ibid., p. 87.

47 [IFC S = Irish Folklore Collection, Schools Manuscript Collection] IFC S 351 pp. 77–8, UCD.

48 O'Connor, *Rathkeale*, pp. 128–76.

49 Joyce and Farmer, *Traveller*, p. 27.

50 Ibid., p. 39.

51 Gmelch, *Nan*, p. 31.

52 Ó Nualláin to Taoiseach, 1 Jan. 1964, DT s 17506 A/63, NAI.

53 IFC 1255 p. 67, UCD; *Connacht Tribune* (1st edn), 26 May 1945.

54 *Sunday Press*, 18 May 1952.

55 Maher, *Road to God Knows Where*, p. 17.

56 Ibid., p. 140.

57 *Irish Independent*, 29 Dec. 1933, SMGC K12 p. 26 no. 1, SJL.

58 Author's interview with Nioclás Breatnach, 29 Dec. 2001. Breatnach collected Romany from a member of the Oliver family who passed through County Limerick in 1934.

59 Gypsy Photos Ireland F-I. Ireland 1–8, SMGC, SJL.

60 See also *T.P.'s Weekly*, 15 Oct. 1909, SMGC K3 p. 209 no.783, SJL; *Irish Press*, 3 Mar. 1934, SMGC K12 p. 28 no.1, SJL.

61 *Irish Press*, 20 Jan. 1936, SMGC K13 p. 167, SJL.

62 *Irish Independent*, 20 Mar. 1935, SMGC K13 p. 75, SJL.

63 *Irish Times*, 10 Jan. 1936, SMGC K13 p. 170, SJL.

64 Mac Gréine, 'Irish Tinkers or "Travellers"', p. 175.

65 Gmelch, *Nan*, p. 119; Nan Joyce describes her Romany aunt as 'great sport', Joyce and Farmar, *Traveller*, p. 61.

66 Acton, *Gypsy Politics and Social Change*, p. 207. The close ties between English Gypsy and Irish Traveller society are exemplified in the autobiography by Bartley Gorman with Peter Walsh, *King of the Gypsies* (Reading, 2002).

67 *Report of the Council of Ireland 1932*, p. 115, Society of St Vincent de Paul (SSVP).

68 *Irish Press*, 20 Jan. 1936, SMGC K13 p167, SJL.

69 Letter to the editor from 'Smaragdus', *Church of Ireland Gazette*, 20 Nov. 1953. Thanks to Dr Daithí Ó Corráin for this reference. It is questionable whether a priest could have organised a bishop to confirm children at such short notice.

70 Letter to the editor from 'Smaragdus', *Church of Ireland Gazette*, 20 Nov. 1953.

71 IFC 1255 p. 88, UCD.

72 Ibid., pp. 115–16.

73 Navan Travellers Heritage Teamwork, *Travellers . . . Their Life and Times* (Navan, July 1992), p. 3.

74 Navan Travellers Heritage Teamwork, *Now and Then* (Navan, 1996), p. 19.

75 Ibid., p. 20.

76 Ibid., p. 9.

77 *Report of the Council of Ireland 1934*, pp. 147–8, SSVP.

78 *Report of the Council of Ireland 1935*, p. 168, SSVP.

79 *Report of the Council of Ireland 1936*, p. 171, SSVP.

80 *Statistical Abstract of Ireland 1943*, p. 168; *Statistical Abstract of Ireland 1949*, p. 180.

81 *Statistical Abstract of Ireland 1949*, p. 180.

82 *Dáil Éireann Debates*, vol. 97, col. 1035 (29 May 1945).

83 *Dáil Éireann Debates*, vol. 126, col. 1831 (18 July 1951).

84 *Dáil Éireann Debates*, vol. 161, col. 419 (25 Apr. 1957).

85 *Statistical Abstract of Ireland 1958* (Dublin, 1958), p. 280.

86 George Gmelch, *The Irish Tinkers: The Urbanisation of an Itinerant People* (2nd edn, Illinois, 1985), p. 3.

87 Navan Travellers, *Travellers*, p. 6.

88 Nioclás Breatnach, *Ar Bóthar Dom* (Rinn Ó gCuanach, 1998), p. 95.

89 Chapter 15 in E. Estyn Evans, *Irish Folk Ways* (London, 1989).

90 See John C. O'Sullivan, 'The tools and trade of a tinker' in Caomhín Ó Danachair (ed.), *Folk and Farm: Essays in Honour of A. T. Lucas* (Dublin, 1976), pp. 208–17. We cannot, however, assume that tinsmithing was an exclusively Traveller occupation.

91 Gmelch, *The Irish Tinkers*, p. 4.

92 *Ireland's Own*, 27 Aug. 1913.

93 *Ireland's Own*, 17 Apr. 1937.

94 Mac Gréine, 'Irish Tinkers or "Travellers"', p. 171.

95 *Commission on Itinerancy*, Appendix XXIV, p. 137.

96 Evans, *Irish Folk Ways*, p. 200; Interview with John and Mary Quilligan, Northside Folklore Project (NFP) 96–004, Sound Recording (SR) 8; Travellers also made candle moulds, IFC S 289, p. 259.

97 Judith Okely, *The Traveller-Gypsies* (Cambridge, 1998 edn), pp. 46–65.

98 Navan Travellers, *Now and Then*, p. 7; Gmelch, *Nan*, p. 101.

99 Navan Travellers, *Now and Then*, p. 5.

100 *Commission on Itinerancy*, p. 72.

101 Ibid., p. 73.

102 Ibid., p. 36.

103 Author's interview with Mary Breatnach, 29 Dec. 2001.

104 Logan, *Fair Day*, p. 115.

105 IFC 1255, p. 113, UCD.

106 Ibid., p. 115.

107 *Irish Press*, 12 Mar. 1935, SMGC K13 p. 63, SJL.

108 Tim Leahy, *Memoirs of a Garda Superintendent* (County Clare, 1996), p. 110. See also, *Report of the Garda Commissioner on Crime for the year 1965*, Appendix D.

109 *Commission on Itinerancy*, p. 71.

100 See chapters 5 and 6 in Mark Holdstock, *The Great Fair: Horse Dealing in Ballinasloe* (London, 1999).

111 Mac Gréine, 'Irish Tinkers or "Travellers"', p. 172.

112 IFC 1255, p. 85, UCD.

113 Ibid., p. 108.

114 Ibid., p. 173.

115 Stowers Johnson, *Before and After Puck: Cork, Killarney and County Kerry* (London, 1953), p. 108.

116 Gmelch, *Nan*, p. 87.

117 Ibid., p. 130.

118 Joyce and Farmar, *Traveller*, p. 33.

119 Navan Travellers, *Now and Then*, p. 7.

120 Joyce and Farmar, *Traveller*, p. 31.

121 Ibid., p. 43.

122 Gmelch, *Nan*, p. 100.

123 Letter to the editor from 'Smaragdus', *Church of Ireland*, 20 Nov. 1953; *Irish Independent*, 29 Dec. 1933, SMGC k12 p. 26 no. 1, SJL; *Irish Times*, 4 Apr. 1934, SMGC k12 p. 28 no.2, SJL; *Irish Daily Independent*, 1 July 1910, SMGC k4 542–543 p. 153, SJL; IFC S 289, p. 259, UCD; author's interview with Nioclás Breatnach, 29 Dec. 2001.

124 IFC S 320, p. 191, UCD.

125 *Irish Independent*, 20 Mar. 1935, SMGC k13 p. 75, SJL.

126 Letter to the editor from 'Smaragdus', *Church of Ireland Gazette*, 20 Nov. 1953.

127 *Irish Independent*, 20 Mar. 1935, SMGC k13 p. 75, SJL.

128 Kevin C. Kearns, 'Irish Tinkers: an itinerant population in transition', *Annals of the Association of American Geographers* 67, 4 (1977), p. 540.

129 George Gmelch also cited the end of subsistence farming as an important change in the lives of Travellers (*Irish Tinkers*, p. 45). Tim Leahy noticed that 'no farmer to my knowledge in the dairying parts of County Kerry now cultivates any crop, not even vegetables or potatoes for his own domestic use, all farms being now set out in grass land', *Memoirs*, p. 46.

130 *Dáil Éireann Debates*, vol. 78, col. 727 (30 Nov. 1939).

131 In considering change in rural Ireland, regional disparities must not be forgotten. For example, 'By 1975 almost every farmer over 5 acres in Wexford had a tractor while at the other end of the scale less than 25% of farms in Mayo had made the transition', Tim O'Neill, 'Tools and things: machinery on Irish farms', in Alan Gailey and Daithí Ó hÓgáin (eds), *Gold under the Furze: Studies in Folk Tradition Presented to Caoimhín Danachair* (Dublin, 1982), p. 101.

132 Evans, *Irish Folk Ways*, p. 260.

133 Diarmuid Ó Giolláin, 'The pattern' in J. S. Donnelly and Kerby A. Miller (eds), *Irish Popular Culture 1650–1850* (Dublin, 1999), pp. 201–21.

134 Interview with Kitty O'Driscoll, NFP 98–023, SR 242.

135 Interview with shopkeeper in Peg Twomey's, NFP 98–023, SR 241; Interview with Kitty O'Driscoll, NFP 98–023, SR 242; *Cork Examiner*, 6 July 1926.

136 Evans, *Irish Folk Ways*, p. 262.

137 Ibid., p. 263. See also Seamus Ó Maithiú, *The Humours of Donnybrook: Dublin's Famous Fair and its Suppression* (Dublin, 1995).

138 See Patrick O'Donnell, *The Irish Faction Fighters of the Nineteenth Century* (Dublin, 1975).

139 Evans, *Irish Folk Ways*, p. 256.

140 Conrad M. Arensberg and Solon T. Kimball, *Family and Community in Ireland* (Cambridge, Mass., 1948), pp. 297–8.

141 Minutes of the Tolls and Markets Committee, cp/c/cm/tm 9 p. 280, Cork Archives Institute (CAI). The fairs were held in May and September.

142 Maher, *Road to God Knows Where*, p. 16.

143 IFC 1255, p. 89, UCD.

144 *Kerryman* (Cork edn), 16 Aug. 1930.

145 *Cork Examiner*, 14 July 1930.

146 *Kerryman* (Cork edn), 9 July 1955.

147 *Kerryman* (Cork edn), 8 July 1950.

148 *Kerryman* (Tralee edn), 17 Aug. 1935.

149 *Kerryman* (Cork edn), 26 July 1953.

150 *Kerryman* (Cork edn), 10 July 1954.

151 *Kerryman* (Cork edn), 23 July 1955.

152 *Kerryman* (Cork edn), 11 July 1953.

153 *Kerryman* (Kerry edn), 6 Aug. 1955.

154 John Healy, *The Death of an Irish Town* (Cork, 1968), p. 19; 'The tinkers free fights was a particular feature of the fair and one of the most spectacular', IFC 1255, p. 141, UCD.

155 Healy, *Death of an Irish Town*, pp. 19–20.

156 IFC S 351 p. 208, UCD. Maher describes how fights were quickly forgotten, *Road to God Knows Where*, p. 17.

157 *Reynolds Newspaper*, 28 May 1945, SMGC k15 p. 74 no.2, SJL.

158 *Connacht Tribune* (1st edn), 26 May 1945.

159 Although the photo of the crowning of Martin and Bridget Ward in *Illustrated*, 29 Sept. 1945, suggests any Traveller would do. SMGC k15 p. 70 no.3 and p. 71 no.1, SJL.

160 *Connacht Tribune*, 6 Oct. 1945.

161 Rathkeale Travellers celebrated a cluster of marriages in Buttevant, probably at Cahirmee Fair. O'Connor, *Rathkeale*, p. 138.

162 Maher, *Road to God Knows Where*, p. 20.

163 *Connacht Tribune* (1st edn), 26 May 1945. For a Traveller perspective on death and mourning see Ann O'Brien, 'Journey's end: customs around death' in Frank Murphy and Kathleen MacDonagh (eds), *Travellers Citizens of Ireland: Our Challenge to an Intercultural Irish Society in the 21st Century* (Dublin, 2000), pp. 80–6.

164 Houlihan, *Puck Fair*, p. 52.

165 Logan, *Fair Day*, p. 101.

166 Author's interview with Nioclás Breatnach, 29 Dec. 2001.

167 Arensberg and Kimball, *Family and Community*, p. 274.

TWO: INTIMATE STRANGERS

1   For a survey of the European context see Leo Lucassen, Annemarie Cottar and Wim Willems (eds), *Gypsies and Other Itinerant Groups: A Socio-historical Approach* (Basingstoke, 1998).

2   Nationalism is central to the arguments of some scholars. See Steve Garner, *Racism in the Irish Experience* (London, Dublin, Sterling Virginia, 2004); Bryan Fanning, *Racism and Social Change in the Republic of Ireland* (Manchester, 2002), especially pp. 30–58; Jim

MacLaughlin, *Travellers and Ireland: Whose Country? Whose History?* (Cork, 1995), pp. 23–38; Robbie McVeigh, 'Theorising sedentarism: the roots of anti-nomadism' in Thomas Acton (ed.), *Gypsy Politics and Traveller Identity* (Hertfordshire, 1997), pp. 7–25.

3   Caitríona Clear, 'Homelessness, crime, punishment and poor relief in Galway 1850–1914: an introduction', *Journal of the Galway Archaeological and Historical Society* 50 (1998), p. 126.

4   Ibid.,, p. 123.

5   *Report of the Commission on the Sick and Destitute Poor, Including the Insane Poor* (Dublin, 1927), p. 17.

6   Ibid.

7   Ibid., p. 61.

8   *Cork Examiner*, 10 Feb. 1926.

9   *Report of the Department of Local Government and Public Health 1922–25*, p. 52.

10 *Department of Local Government and Public Health 1922–25*, p. 52.

11 Department of Health, *Reconstruction and Improvement of County Homes* (Dublin, 1951), p. 14.

12 'Paddy Wheel About' lived in the neighbourhood of Kinsale for 30 years. After his death, it was discovered that he was an ex-soldier who, in the course of his military career, had led the desecration of a Roman Catholic Church, IFC S 320, pp. 76–8, UCD.

13 IFC S 288, p. 325, UCD.

14 IFC S 289, p. 261, UCD.

15 For instance, Johnny Walker, who lost a hand in battle IFC S 279, p. 65; John Collins, IFC S 279, p. 230, UCD.

16 IFC S 288, p. 327, UCD.

17 IFC S 337, p. 92, UCD.

18 IFC S 343, p. 33; IFC S 343, p. 388; IFC S 304, p. 18, UCD.

19 IFC S 289, p. 259, UCD.

20 IFC S 276, p. 101; IFC S 276, p. 102; IFC S 289, p. 259; IFC S 327, p. 318, UCD.

21 IFC S 353, p. 182, UCD.

22 See S. Ó Suilleabháin and R. T. H Christiansen, *The Types of the Irish Folktale* (Helsinki, 1967), no. 750 'Hospitality blessed', p. 147.

23 IFC S 326, p. 90, UCD.

24 IFC S 337, p. 93, UCD.

25 IFC S 326, p. 31, UCD.

26 Ó Suilleabháin and Christiansen, *Irish Folktale*, no. 751 'The greedy peasant woman', p. 147.

27 IFC S 343, p. 407, UCD.

28 IFC S 343, p. 33, UCD.

29 Superintendent M. Troy to Chief Superintendent, 28 Aug. 1925, DJ H207/4, NAI.

30 IFC S 347, p. 443, UCD.

31 IFC S 347, p. 441; IFC S 276, p. 101, UCD.

32 IFC S 304, p. 17, UCD.

33 The involvement of Ireland's Jews in the peddling trade has been documented in Dermot Keogh, *Jews in Twentieth-Century Ireland: Refugees, Anti-Semitism and the Holocaust* (Cork, 1998), p. 14.

34 Office of the Revenue Commissioners to Secretary Department of Justice, 5 Jan. 1925, DJ H207/1, NAI.

35 *Dáil Éireann Debates*, vol. 70, col. 131 (2 Feb. 1938).

36 *Dáil Éireann Debates*, vol. 70, col. 135 (2 Feb. 1938).

37 '. . . casual inmates of County Homes do not constitute a problem outside of cities and large towns' Department of Health, *County Homes*, p. 14.

38 *Report of the Annual Meeting of Presidents with the Council of Ireland 1925*, p. 11, SSVP.

39 *Commission on the Sick and Destitute Poor*, p. 17.

40 Ibid., p. 87.

41 See the annual *Report of the Department of Local Government and Public Health* up to 1949 for figures on indoor and outdoor relief.

42 Department of Health, *County Homes*, p. 9.

43 Sub-section (6) Section 49, *Dáil Éireann Debates*, vol. 140, col. 1184 (15 July 1953).

44 *Dáil Éireann Debates*, vol. 140, col. 1189 (15 July 1953).

45 *Dáil Éireann Debates*, vol. 140, col. 1190 (15 July 1953).

46 Deputies Dr Noel Browne, Dr ffrench-O'Carroll and Sean MacBride were vigorous in their opposition, *Dáil Éireann Debates*, vol. 140, col. 1196 (15 July 1953).

47 *Dáil Éireann Debates*, vol. 140, col. 1196 (15 July 1953).

48 *Dáil Éireann Debates*, vol. 140, col. 1200 (15 July 1953).

49 *Dáil Éireann Debates*, vol. 140, col. 1226 (15 July 1953).

50 Liam O'Flaherty, *The Informer* (New York and London, 1980), pp. 5–21.

51 George Orwell, *Down and Out in Paris and London* (Harmondsworth, 2001), pp. 130–3 recounts Orwell's first night in a lodging house.

52 Register of Common Lodging Houses 1910–48, 6 Sept. 1919, p. 30 CPLH/1, CAI.

53 Register of Common Lodging Houses 1910–48, Enclosures, 28 June 1943, CPLH/1, CAI.

54 Council of Ireland, *St Vincent's Glasnevin Centenary Record 1856–1956* (Dublin, 1956), p. 16, SSVP.

55 *The Origins and Objects of the St Vincent de Paul Society and its Workings in Ireland* (1923 edn, Dublin), p. 16, SSVP.

56 Council of Ireland, *St Vincent's Glasnevin*, p. 16, SSVP.

57 A report of the Dublin Union Commissioners noted a reduction in the number of 'casuals' seeking relief due to pressure at the Admissions Board, a more general knowledge of the Morning Star Hostel run by the Legion of Mary and the absence of army demobilisation. *Report of the Department of Local Government and Public Health 1929–30*, Appendix XLV, p. 253.

58 *Irish Times*, 4 Aug. 1922.

59 *Irish Times*, 5 Feb. 1924.

60 W. R. E. Murphy to Minister for Home Affairs, 31 Dec. 1924, DJ H207/4, NAI.

61 Sgt. R. O'Connell (Station Sgt. College Street) to Superintendent B Division, 21 Jan. 1921, DJ H207/4, NAI.

62 *Cork Examiner*, 22 Jan. 1926.

63 *Cork Examiner*, 22 Jan. 1926.

64 *Report of the Council of Ireland 1925*, pp. 36–7, SSVP.

65 *Report of the Council of Ireland 1926*, p. 24, SSVP.

66 *Cork Examiner*, 19 Feb. 1926.

67 A Sitting held by the Commissioner of the County Borough of Cork, 4 Feb. 1927, p. 408 CP/C/A 15, CAI ; A Sitting held by the Commissioner of the County Borough of Cork, 24 Sept. 1926, p. 379, CP/C/A 15, CAI.

68 *Report of the Council of Ireland 1941*, p. 33, SSVP.

69 Minutes of the meeting of the County Borough Council, 25 Sept. 1945 p. 568, CP/C/A 17, CAI.

70 Peter Hart, *The IRA and its Enemies* (Oxford: 1998), p. 150.

71 Ibid., p. 304.

72 Ibid., pp. 308–9.

73 Ibid., p. 304.

74 Ibid., p. 321.

75 George Gmelch and Sharon Bohn Gmelch, 'The emergence of an ethnic group: the Irish Tinkers', *Anthropological Quarterly* 49, 4 (Oct. 1976), pp. 225–38.

76 Sharon Bohn Gmelch, 'From poverty subculture to political lobby: the Traveller rights movement in Ireland' in Chris Curtin and Thomas Wilson, (eds), *Ireland from Below: Social Change and Local Communities* (Galway, 1989), pp. 301–19.

77 The fine distinction between tramps and Travellers is acknowledged in Gmelch and Gmelch, 'The emergence of an ethnic group', p. 236 n.7, but the mention of single mothers joining Travellers is on p. 232.

78 Nan Joyce and Anna Farmer, *Traveller: An Autobiography* (Dublin, 1986), pp. 1–2.

79 Patrick J. O'Connor, *All Ireland is in and about Rathkeale* (Newcastlewest, 1996), pp. 134–5. For a full history of the Palatine plantation see Patrick J. O'Connor, *People Make Places: The Story of the Irish Palatines* (Newcastlewest, 1989).

80 O'Connor, *Rathkeale*, p. 134.

81 Joyce and Farmar, *Traveller*, p. 1; Sean Maher, *The Road to God Knows Where: A Memoir of a Travelling Boyhood* (Dublin, 1998), p. 63.

82 Jane Helleiner, *Irish Travellers: Racism and the Politics of Culture* (Toronto, Buffalo, London, 2000), p. 50.

83 Ibid., p. 30.

84 Michael MacDonagh, 'Origins of the Travelling people' in Frank Murphy and Cathleen MacDonagh (eds), *Travellers: Citizens of Ireland: Our Challenge to an Intercultural Society in the 21st Century* (Dublin, 2000), pp. 21–5.

85 Ibid., p. 24. Eoin MacNeill made this assertion in *Phases of Irish History* (Dublin, 1937), p. 82.

86 MacLaughlin, *Travellers and Ireland*, pp. 23–38.

THREE: TRAVELLERS IN URBAN AREAS

1 In 1957, 2,170 convictions were secured under the Act and 27 children were sent to industrial schools, *Report of the Commissioner of the Garda Síochána on Crime for the year 1957*, p. 23.

2 David Rottman, *Crime in the Republic of Ireland: Statistical Trends and their Interpretation* (Dublin, 1980), p. 11.

3 Ibid., p. 33.

4 David Sibley, *Outsiders in Urban Societies* (Oxford, 1981), pp. 31–9.

5 Michael Verdon, *Shawlies, Echo Boys, the Marsh and the Lanes, Old Cork Remembered* (Dublin, 1993), p. 64.

6 Ibid., p. 65. See also P. H. Gulliver and M. Silverman, 'Hucksters and petty retailers in Thomastown 1880–1945', *Old Kilkenny Review* 4 (1993), pp. 1094–1100.

7 For more on pawnshops see Philip Doherty, 'The last pawnshops of Dublin City', *Dublin Historical Record* XLVII, 1 (1994), pp. 87–94 and Jim Fitzpatrick, *Three Brass Balls: The Story of the Irish Pawnshop* (Cork, 2001).

8 Verdon, *Shawlies*, p. 87.

9 *Cork Examiner*, 25 Sept. 1924.

10 Verdon, *Shawlies*, pp. 88–91.

11 See Daniel M. Bluestone, '"The pushcart evil" pedlars, merchants and New York's City Streets 1890–1940', *Journal of Urban History* 18, 1 (1991), pp. 68–92 and Andrew Brown-May, 'A charitable indulgence: street stalls and the transformation of public space in Melbourne *c.*1850–1920', *Urban History* 23, 1 (1996) pp. 48–71 for useful case studies on the evolution of street space.

12 The legislation in question was the Dublin Police Act 1842 and the Summary Jurisdiction (Ireland) Act 1851. See appendix.

13 Draft Street Trading Bill, first schedule, undated, DJ H207/1, NAI.

14 W. R. E. Murphy to Minister for Home Affairs, 6 Feb. 1924 DJ H207/1 NAI.

15 Pedlars Acts 1871 and 1881, and the Hawkers Act 1888 – see appendix.

16 *Dáil Éireann Debates*, vol. 14, col. 33 (19 Jan. 1926).

17 *Dáil Éireann Debates*, vol. 14, col. 44 (19 Jan. 1926).

18 *Dáil Éireann Debates*, vol. 14, col. 147 (27 Jan. 1926).

19 *Dáil Éireann Debates*, vol. 14, col. 147 (27 Jan. 1926).

20 *Dáil Éireann Debates*, vol. 14, col. 142 (19 Jan. 1926).

21 *Dáil Éireann Debates*, vol. 14, col. 413 (6 Feb.1926).

22 *Dáil Éireann Debates*, vol. 14, cols 418–19 (6 Feb. 1926).

23 *Dáil Éireann Debates*, vol. 14, col. 421 (6 Feb. 1926).

24 Street Trading Act 1926, Section 2 (5) (b).

25 *Dáil Éireann Debates*, vol. 18, col. 520–1, (16 Feb. 1927). Further appeals for an inquiry were put in *Dáil Éireann Debates*, vol. 19, cols 610–11 (31 Mar. 1927); *Dáil Éireann Debates*, vol. 29, col. 186–7 (30 June 1927).

26 *Dáil Éireann Debates*, vol. 55 col. 2471–2 (11 Apr. 1935).

27 Chief Superintendent to Philip Monahan, 3 Dec. 1928, CP/Files/41, CAI.

28 Interview with Kitty O'Driscoll, NFP 98–023, SR 242.

29 Minutes of Hackney Carriages Committee meeting, 25 Sept. 1924, in Minutes of the Meeting of the County Borough Council, 10 Oct. 1924, p. 169 CP/C/A 15, CAI. The meeting was also described in *Cork Examiner*, 25 Sept. 1924.

30 *Cork Examiner*, 1 Nov. 1924. The report is reproduced in full here, but could not be found in local or national archives.

31 *Statistical Abstract of Ireland 1931* (Dublin, 1931), p. 158. In 1947–48 there were an average of 817 cars a day parked in the city centre, though accommodation existed for only 560. Minutes of the Meeting of the County Borough Council, 23 Mar. 1948, CP/C/A 18, CAI.

32 *Cork Examiner*, 17 Dec. 1924.

33 A special sitting of the Commissioner, 4 Jan. 1929, CP/C/A 15, CAI.

34 Chief Superintendent to Philip Monahan, 3 Dec. 1928 CP/Files/41 CAI. The gender balance in the covered market, which eventually became the English Market, was not so favourable to women. Out of 78 stallholders, just 15 were women. Minutes of the Tolls and Markets Committee, 10 May 1920 p. 173, CP/C/CM/TM A 9, CAI.

35 S.A. Roche to Secretary, Department of Local Government and Public Health, 14 June 1929, CP/Files/41, CAI.

36 *The Garda Síochána Code 1928* (Dublin, 1928), p. 174.

37 Ibid., p. 174.

38 See the Minutes of the Hackney Carriages Committee, CP/C/CM/HCC/A 4, CAI.

39 Philip Monahan to Lord Mayor and Members of County Borough Council, 2 Oct. 1931, CP/Files/82, CAI.

40 Garda Commissioner, *Road Traffic Report 1937* (Dublin, 1937), p. 2.

41 *Report of the Department of Local Government and Public Health 1938–39*, p. 26.

42 Chief Superintendent to City Manager, 9 Apr. 1938, CP/Files/41, CAI.

43 Barry St. John Galvin to Philip Monahan, 28 Apr. 1938, CP/Files/41, CAI.

44 Minutes of County Borough Council Meeting, 24 Nov. 1942, CP/C/A 17, CAI.

45 Street Trading (County Borough of Cork) Order 1941, 11 Nov. 1941, CP/Files/41, CAI.

46 *Cork Examiner*, 1 Dec. 1924.

47 *Cork Examiner*, 21 Feb. 1925

48 *Cork Examiner*, 1 Dec. 1924.

49 Letter from the Cork Publicity Association Ltd in Minutes of the General Purposes Committee, 3 Apr. 1934, p. 312, CP/C/A 16, CAI.

50 Section 4 (3–4) School Attendance Act 1926.

51 Section 7 (1–4) School Attendance Act 1926.

52 Section 17 (4) School Attendance Act 1926.

53 *Report of the Department of Education 1925–27*, pp. 6–7.

54 For the nineteenth-century roots of this attitude see Maria Luddy, *Women and Philanthropy in Nineteenth-Century Ireland* (Cambridge, 1995), chapter 3.

55 *Irish Times*, 9 Feb. 1923.

56 Ibid.

57 B. Gilleece to C. Harrington, 24 Nov. 1932, CP/Files/141, CAI.

58 Philip Monahan to Stephen Roche, 30 May 1932, CP/Files/122, CAI.

59 Byelaws on 'Employment of Children and Street Trading by Persons under 16 years of age' passed on 26 Apr. 1937, CP/Files/143, CAI.

60 Philip Monahan to Lord Mayor and Members of County Borough Council, 18 Nov. 1938, CP/Files/143, CAI. Anti-litter byelaws were signed 28 Mar. 1939, see CP/Files/41, CAI.

61 Philip Monahan to Lord Mayor and Members of County Borough Council, 9 Dec. 1938, CP/Files/143, CAI.

62 For an overview of the period before independence, see Murray Fraser, *John Bull's Other Homes: State Housing and British Policy in Ireland, 1883–1922* (Liverpool, 1996).

63 Mary E. Daly, *The Buffer State: The Historical Roots of the Department of Environment* (Dublin, 1997), p. 221.

64 Ibid., p. 517.

65 Ibid., p. 223.

66 Note, undated, CP/Files/42, CAI.

67 George A. Byrne (Housing Superintendent) to Philip Monahan, 24 Sept. 1938, CP/Files/50, CAI.

68 Annual report of the Meat Inspector for the year ended 31 Dec. 1926, Minutes of the Public Health Committee, CP/C/CM/PH/A 31, CAI.

69 Acting City Manager to City Solicitor, 23 Oct. 1934, CP/Files/41, CAI.

70 Philip Monahan to Lord Mayor and Members, 8 Feb. 1935, CP/Files/142, CAI.

71 Author's interview with Dr Michael Flynn, 2 Feb. 2001.

72 Patrick J. O'Connor, *All Ireland is in and about Rathkeale* (Newcastlewest, 1996), p. 140.

73 Verdon, *Shawlies*, p. 45.

74 See Paul Grant, 'Producing Irish national space: the changing iconography of Irish street names in Munster 1885–1940' (Unpublished MPhil thesis, Department of Geography, UCC, 2000).

75 Richard Henchion, *Bishopstown, Wilton and Glasheen: A Picture of Life in the Three Western Suburbs of Cork from Early Days to Modern Times* (Cork, 2001), p. 40.

76 Micheal Lennon, 'Residential segregation in Cork city 1901–46' (Unpublished M.A. thesis, Department of Geography, UCC, 2000), p. 121.

77 Verdon, *Shawlies*, pp. 65–6.

78 *Report of the Annual Meeting of Presidents with the Council of Ireland 1936*, pp. 18–9, SSVP.

79 9 Mar. 1928 p. 523 CP/C/A 15, CAI.

80 Report of General Purposes Committee 14 Apr. 1958, in Minutes of the County Borough Council Meeting, 22 Apr. 1958, p. 466 CP/C/A 20, CAI.

81 Report of General Purposes Committee 5 Aug. 1958, in Minutes of the Meeting of the County Borough Council, 12 Aug. 1958, pp. 529–30 CP/C/A 20, CAI.

82 'The slum problem in Cork' in B. G. MacCarthy (ed.), *Some Problems of Child Welfare: University and Labour Series No. 6* (Cork, 1945), p. 73.

83 Minutes of Quarterly Meeting of Council, 11 Oct. 1955, p. 14, CP/C/A 20, CAI.

84 Minutes of the Meeting of the County Borough Council, 22 Apr. 1958 p. 469, CP/C/A 20, CAI.

85 Minutes of the Meeting of the County Borough Council, 12 Feb. 1957 CP/C/A 20, CAI.

86 Churchfield Tenants' Association, Minutes of the Meeting of the County Borough Council, 13 May 1958, pp. 478–9 CP/C/A 20, CAI.

87 Knockfree Housing Estate Protection and Development Committee, Minutes of the Meeting of the County Borough Council, 14 Nov. 1961 p. 496 CP/C/A 21, CAI.

88 Daly, *The Buffer State*, p. 341.

89 The 'pig in the parlour' was not confined to the countryside. A resident of Cork's crowded inner city recalled, 'I saw one house with the back rooms boarded off and a couple of pigs in it', Verdon, *Shawlies*, p. 87.

90 *Report of the Department of Local Government and Public Health 1934–35*, p. 16.

91 *Department of Local Government and Public Health 1934–35*, p. 17.

92 Ibid.

93 Ibid.

94 John Collins (2nd edn by Desmond Roche) *Local Government* (Dublin, 1963), p. 108.

95 Ibid.

96 *Report of the Department of Local Government and Public Health 1940–41*, pp. 17–18.

97 Explanatory memo, 3 Aug. 1939, DT s 11227, NAI.

98 M. Ó Múimhneacháin to Rúnaí Local Government and Public Health 18 Sept. 1940, DT s 11227, NAI.

99 Circular 88/40, Rúnaí to secretary of each board of public health and clerk of each UDC, 18 Sept. 1940, DT s 11227, NAI.

100 P. O Cinnéide, Rúnaí to Rúnaí Department of Local Government and Public Health, 28 Apr. 1941, DT s 11227, NAI.

101 See a defence of local authorities in Hurson to Secretary, Department of Taoiseach, 30 Sept. 1941, DT s 11227, NAI.

102 Circular 1/52 30 Sept. 1952, DT s 11227 B, NAI.

103 Minister to Taoiseach, 14 Oct. 1952, DT s 11227 B, NAI.

104 *Report of the Commission on Itinerancy* (Dublin, 1963), p. 52.

105 Minutes of the Municipal Council of the County Borough of Dublin 1953, p. 210; Minutes of County Borough Council Meeting, 14 Nov. 1961 p. 496, CP/C/A 21, CAI.

106 Minutes of County Borough Council Meeting, 14 Nov. 1961 p. 496, CP/C/A 21, CAI.

107 Report of the City Engineer, 13 Oct. 1964, p. 420, CP/C/A 22, CAI.

108 *Dáil Éireann Debates*, vol. 181, col. 427 (3 May 1960).

109 *Bord Fáilte Éireann Newsletter* 4 (1957). Thanks to Dr Eric Zuelow for this reference.

110 Thanks to Dr Eric Zuelow for this information.

111 *Report of the Department of Local Government 1958–59*, Appendix XXIII, p. 114.

112 Ibid., p. 115.

113 *Dáil Éireann Debates*, vol. 117, col. 1572 (21 July 1949).

114 *Dáil Éireann Debates*, vol. 163, col. 728 (4 July 1957); *Dáil Éireann Debates*, vol. 167, col. 158 (15 Apr. 1958).

115 Mr Fintan Coogan, *Dáil Éireann Debates*, vol. 167, col. 162 (15 Apr. 1958); *Dáil Éireann Debates*, vol. 174, col. 283 (9 Apr. 1959).

116 *Dáil Éireann Debates*, vol. 167, col. 165 (15 Apr. 1958).

117 *Kerryman* (Kerry edn), 23 July 1955.

118 Report of the General Purposes Committee, 20 Apr. 1956 p. 103, CP/C/A 20, CAI.

119 A complaint about begging vagrants from Galway Chamber of Commerce suggests that the tourist opinion which mattered was British or American. It is important to note that the 'vagrants' mentioned may not necessarily be Travellers, as the author assumes. Jane Helleiner, *Irish Travellers: Racism and the Politics of Culture* (Toronto, Buffalo, London, 2000), p. 53.

120 Rúnaí Aire Department of Justice to Rúnaí Príobháideach do'n Taoiseach, 10 Aug. 1940, DT 12039A, NAI.

121 Philippa Basset, *A List of the Historical Records of the Caravan Club of Great Britain and Ireland* (Birmingham and Reading, 1980), p. ii.

122 Some form of activity continued. A 1957 caravan rally was organised by the Munster centre of the Irish division of the Caravan Club. Yet most of the 35 caravans in the rally were from Belfast, indicating a lack of enthusiasm in the Republic for organised caravanning. *Kerryman* (Cork edn), 20 July 1957

123 *Dáil Éireann Debates*, vol. 107, col. 1013 (4 July 1947).

124 *Report of the Department of Local Government and Public Health 1928–29*, Appendix XVII p. 189.

125 *Report of the Department of Local Government and Public Health 1935–36*, Appendix XXVIII p. 299.

126 Helleiner, *Irish Travellers*, pp. 54–5.

127 Ibid., p. 54.

128 *Report of the Department of Local Government 1948–49*, p. 21.

129 Section 31 (1), Local Government (Sanitary Services) Act 1948.

130 Dominick Street and Lady's Lane were mentioned as camping sites in *Limerick Leader*, 9 Jan. 1952 and *Limerick Leader*, 16 Jan. 1952.

131 *Limerick Leader*, 9 Jan. 1952

132 *Limerick Leader*, 16 Jan. 1952.

133 *Limerick Leader*, 16 Feb. 1952.

134 *Irish Times*, 17 May 1952.

135 Exemptions to the powers of the local authorities are outlined in section 34 (12) Sanitary Services Act 1948. See appendix.

136 *Irish Times*, 17 May 1952.

137 *Limerick Leader*, 26 May 1952.

138 *Report of the Department of Local Government 1953–54*, Appendix XV, p. 94.

139 *Sunday Press*, 18 May 1952.

140 *Limerick Leader*, 12 Mar. 1955.

141 *Limerick Leader*, 14 Mar. 1955.

142 *Minutes of meeting*, 7 Sept. 1959, DH B132/372, NAI.

143 *Commission on Itinerancy*, p. 53.

144 Dublin Corporation felt it did not have the resources to provide playgrounds, nurseries, youth clubs, community centres etc. Ruth McManus, *Dublin 1919–1940: Shaping the City and Suburbs* (Dublin, 2002), p. 226.

FOUR: WELFARE AND ENTITLEMENT

1 *Irish Times*, 5 Feb. 1924.

2 For a detailed analysis of assistance offered to different groups see Mel Cousins, *The Birth of Social Welfare in Ireland, 1922–52* (Dublin, 2003).

3 Lynn Hollen Lees, *The Solidarities of Strangers: The English Poor Law and the People, 1700–1948* (Cambridge and New York, 1998).

4 Sinn Féin, *The Economic Programme of Sinn Féin which is founded on and to which is prefixed the Democratic Programme of Dáil Éireann* (1924).

5 Ibid.

6 See Joe Lee, *Modern Ireland: Politics and Society 1912–85* (Cambridge, 1989), pp. 124–5.

7 *Report of the Department of Local Government and Public Health 1922–25*, p. 64.

8 Ibid., p. 11.

9 Mary E. Daly, *The Buffer State: The Historical Roots of the Department of the Environment* (Dublin, 1997), pp. 116–17.

10 Mel Cousins, *The Birth of Social Welfare in Ireland, 1922–52* (Dublin, 2002), pp. 29–55.

11 *Irish Times*, 28 Mar. 1922.

12 *Report of the Department of Local Government and Public Health 1927–8*, p. 88.

13 *Cork Examiner*, 10 Feb. 1926.

14 The cost of the schemes was split between central government and rates-funded local government. That authorities were unwilling to fund these schemes is not surprising in the context of dissolutions of councils for excessive spending. *Department of Local Government and Public Health 1922–5*, p. 50.

15 *Department of Local Government and Public Health 1930–1*, p. 65. See also *Department of Local Government and Public Health 1935–6*, p. 87.

16 *Department of Local Government and Public Health 1932–3*, p. 123.

17 Ibid., p. 124.

18 *Department of Social Welfare 1947–49*, p. 49.

19 *Department of Local Government and Public Health 1922–5*, pp. 35–6.

20 *Department of Local Government and Public Health 1934–5*, p. 171.

21 *Department of Local Government and Public Health 1940–1*, p. 8.

22 Daly, *The Buffer State*, p. 180.

23 Humanitarian benevolence and Christian charity were two very different things. See Joseph E. Canavan SJ, 'Property and the Church', *Studies* 24 (Mar. 1923), pp. 395–6.

24 *Cork Examiner*, 17 Dec. 1925.

25 *Department of Social Welfare 1947–9*, p. 27.

26 *Report of the Commission on the Sick and Destitute Poor, Including the Insane Poor* (Dublin, 1927), p. 84.

27 In 1833 Frederick Ozanam, a Catholic student in the University of Paris, founded the Society of St Vincent de Paul. St Vincent de Paul is the patron saint of the poor and the society sought to aid the poor by visiting their homes. The first conference in Ireland was established in 1844.

28 Today, the parish conference remains though the other structures of the Society were reformed in the 1960s and 1970s. See *Report of the Task Force Approved by the President to Consider the Role and Structure of the Council of Ireland February 1978* (Dublin, 1978), SSVP.

29 In Cork, the Ladies Association of Charity of the St Vincent de Paul Society raised £400 in a sale of work, which they handed over to 'the gentlemen of the St Vincent de Paul Society', *74th Annual Report of the Ladies Association of Charity of the St Vincent de Paul Society, Year ending 31 December 1927* (Cork, 1928). The Ladies Association was revitalised in Dublin by Margaret Aylward, who subsequently founded the Sisters of the Holy Faith, Maria Luddy, *Women and Philanthropy in Nineteenth-Century Ireland* (Cambridge, 1995), p. 39.

30 *Origins and Objects of the St Vincent de Paul and its Workings in Ireland* (Dublin, 1923 edition), pp. 12–3, SSVP.

31 *67th Annual Meeting of the Presidents with the Council of Ireland* (Dublin, 1923), p. 23, SSVP.

32 *Report of the Council of Ireland 1926*, p. 12, SSVP.

33 Glynn also sat on the committee of inquiry into Health Insurance and Medical Services. See *Interim Report of Committee of Inquiry into Health Insurance and Medical Services* (Dublin, 1925).

34 *Commission on the Sick and Destitute Poor*, p. 84.

35 Ibid., p. 59.

36 Ibid., p. 87.

37 Ibid., p. 87.

38 Frank Duff had himself begun 'his social career' with the St Vincent de Paul. See Leon Ó Broin, *Just Like Yesterday: An Autobiography* (Dublin, n.d.), pp. 127–30.

39 *The Official Handbook of the Legion of Mary* (Dublin 1993), p. 9.

40 Ibid., p. 72.

41 Cecily Rosemary Hallack, *The Legion of Mary* (5th edn, London, 1950) p. 157. For a description of missionary work among 'gipsies or tinkers' see pp. 157–161.

42 *The Legion of Mary* (Dublin, 1937), p. 197.

43 Ibid., p. 199.

44 *Report of the Council of Ireland 1933*, p. 164, SSVP.

45 *Report of the Council of Ireland 1932*, p. 115, SSVP. Unfortunately, there is no corroborating evidence for this in the archives of the Jesuit community in Ireland.

46 *Report of the Annual Meeting of Presidents 1933*, pp. 26–7, SSVP.

47 *Report of the Council of Ireland 1933*, pp. 163, SSVP.

48 *Annual Meeting of Presidents 1933*, p. 37, SSVP.

49 Ibid., p. 41.

50 Ibid., p. 43.

51 Ibid., pp. 35–6.

52 Ibid., p. 44.

53 *Annual Meeting of Presidents 1934*, p. 16; *Annual Meeting of Presidents 1935*, p. 13, SSVP.

54 *Annual Meeting of Presidents 1936*, p. 30.

55 Ibid., p. 33.

56 The society was far from nationwide, being concentrated in cities and large regional towns. The establishment of new conferences was not trouble free; clerical resistance in County Cork frustrated efforts to expand into the regional towns of Kanturk and Midleton. Some local clergy believed that charity was the exclusive preserve of the female religious already present in the towns. *Report of the Annual Meeting of Presidents 1934*, p. 12.

57 *Report of the Council of Ireland 1933*, pp. 163–4.

58 *Report of the Council of Ireland 1934*, pp. 147–8.

59 *Report of the Council of Ireland 1935*, p. 168.

60 *Report of the Council of Ireland 1940*, p. 123.

61 For example, the well-known Traveller piper, Johnny Doran (1908–50) was based in Dublin during the winter but travelled during the summer months, see Fintan Vallely (ed.), *The Companion to Irish Traditional Music* (Cork, 1999), pp. 404–5.

62 *Report of the Council of Ireland 1936*, p. 171.

63 *Report of the Council of Ireland 1933*, p. 164.

64 *Report of the Council of Ireland 1936*, pp. 171–2.

65 *Report of the Council of Ireland 1937*, pp.174–5.

66 *Report of the Council of Ireland 1942*, p. 141. Also, *Report of the Council of Ireland 1947*, p. 77.

67 *Report of the Council of Ireland 1937*, pp. 174–5.

68 *Report of the Council of Ireland 1938*, p. 157.

69 *Report of the Council of Ireland 1937*, p. 175.

70 *Report of the Council of Ireland 1945*, p. 103.

71 *Report of the Council of Ireland 1943*, p. 169.

72 *Report of the Council of Ireland 1947*, p. 77. There was no reference to Travellers in the Corporation minutes of this year, nor any reason given for this closure of open spaces in the city centre. It is possible that Corporation officials decided to enforce or implement an order or byelaw passed before this date.

73 *Report of the Council of Ireland 1948*, p. 77.

74 *Report of the Council of Ireland 1947*, p. 77; *Report of the Council of Ireland 1948*, p. 77.

75 *Report of the Council of Ireland 1959*, p. 10.

76 *Report of the Council of Ireland 1960*, p. 8.

77 *Report of the Commission on Itinerancy* (Dublin, 1963), p. 88.

78 *Irish Independent*, 8 July 1961.

79 *Commission on Itinerancy*, pp. 87–8.

80 For example, the Ursuline convent in Thurles opened a school for one day a month in 1932, to prepare Traveller children for Holy Communion. Statement of the Church of Ireland Moral Welfare Society 'Memo on Itinerancy re Communication sent to RCB from Custom House', Feb. 1961, RCB. Thanks to Derek Philips, Synod Officer, who sent me this document.

81 *Annual Meeting of Presidents 1933*, p. 27, SSVP.

82 *Report of the Council of Ireland 1947*, p. 77.

83 *Commission on Itinerancy*, p. 60.

84 Ibid., p. 60.

85 Jane Helleiner, *Irish Travellers: Racism and the Politics of Culture* (Toronto, Buffalo, London, 2000), p. 56.

86 Sean Maher, *The Road to God Knows Where* (Dublin, 1972), p. 167.

87 Schedule of the Compulsory Purchase Order 1933, pp. 39–49, Minutes of the Municipal Council of the City of Dublin 1934, DCA.

88 Luan P. Cuffe and George J. Gmelch, 'Housing as a factor in social integration: the Traveller in Ireland' (Unpublished report, Apr. 1972), p. 12, Traveller Resource Centre.

89 Cuffe and Gmelch, 'Housing', p. 12.

90 Ibid., p. 15.

91 Ibid., p. 17.

92 Author's interview with Dr Michael Flynn, 2 Feb. 2001.

93 Cuffe and Gmelch, 'Housing', p. 17.

94 Ibid., p. 18.

95 Ibid.

96 Author's interview with Dr Michael Flynn, 2 Feb. 2001.

97 For example, 'without any legal authority' Dr James Deeny (Chief Medical Officer in the Department of Local Government and Public Health) closed a home for unmarried mothers and their children because the infant mortality rate was unacceptable, James Deeny, *To Cure and to Care: The Memoirs of a Chief Medical Officer* (Dublin, 1989), p. 85.

98 Jean Pierre Liegeois, *School Provision for Ethnic Minorities: The Gypsy Paradigm* (Hatfield, 1998); European Roma Rights Centre, *Stigmata: Segregated Schooling of Roma in Central and Eastern Europe, A Survey of Patterns of Segregated Education of Roma in Bulgaria, the Czech Republic, Hungary, Romania and Slovakia* (Budapest, 2003).

99 *Report of the Department of Education 1925–7*, p. 83.

100 The twentieth century has been neglected in favour of the eighteenth and nineteenth centuries. See Joseph Robins, *The Lost Children: A Study of Charity Children in Ireland 1700–1900* (Dublin, 1980), *Fools and Mad: A History of the Insane in Ireland* (Dublin, 1986) and Mark Finnane, *Insanity and the Insane in Post-Famine Ireland* (London, 1981).

101 *Report of the Department of Education 1925–7*, p. 91.

102 4,163 children remained in poor law institutions in 1926, compared to 6,012 in industrial schools. *Report of the Department of Education 1925–27*, p. 91.

103 *Report of the Department of Education 1925–7* Appendix 1, pp. 98–9.

104 *Report of the Department of Education 1930–1*, p. 81.

105 *Commission on the Sick and Destitute Poor*, p. 70.

106 Ibid., p. 71.

107 *Commission on Itinerancy*, p. 66.

108 Ibid.

109 *Report of the Council of Ireland 1948*, p. 77, SSVP.

110 Agenda, 27 July 1937, Box File Agendas, 15 Sept. 1926 to 15 Dec. 1949, GCCC.

111 Agenda and Minutes, 7 Dec. 1938 in ibid.

112 *Report of the Department of Education 1939–40*, p. 87. Perhaps more girls were committed owing to perceived female helplessness or vulnerability.

113 *Report of the Department of Education 1939–40*, p. 87.

114 *Report of the Department of Education 1936–7*, p. 118.

115 *Commission on Itinerancy*, p. 66.

116 *Dáil Éireann Debates*, vol. 88, col. 1540–5 (28 Oct. 1942).

117 Rúnaí Aire Department of Education to Rúnaí Príobháideach Department of Taoiseach, 28 Oct. 1958, DT s 12039 B, NAI.

118 *Dáil Éireann Debates*, vol. 88, col. 1543 (28 Oct. 1942). In the Dáil records, section 19 is cited, but it later became section 21.

119 Rúnaí Aire Department of Education to Rúnaí Príobháideach Department of Taoiseach, 28 Oct. 1958, DT s 12039 b, NAI.

120 *Dáil Éireann Debates*, vol. 88, col. 1543 (28 Oct. 1942).

121 Rúnaí Aire Department of Education to Rúnaí Príobháideach Department of Taoiseach, 28 Oct. 1958, DT s 12039 b, NAI.

122 *Dáil Éireann Debates*, vol. 88, col. 1543 (28 Oct. 1942).

123 *Dáil Éireann Debates*, vol. 88, col. 1544 (28 Oct. 1942).

124 Article 42 (1) states 'The State acknowledges that the primary and natural educator of the child is the Family and guarantees to respect the inalienable right and duty of parents to provide, according to their means, for the religious and moral, intellectual, physical and social education of their children.' See Michael Farry, *Education and the Constitution* (Dublin, 1996) for discussion on Article 42.

125 *Dáil Éireann Debates*, vol. 88, col. 1560 (28 Oct. 1942).

126 *Dáil Éireann Debates*, vol. 88, cols 1566–70 (28 Oct. 1942).

127 *Dáil Éireann Debates*, vol. 88, col. 1594 (28 Oct. 1942).

128 *Dáil Éireann Debates*, vol. 88, cols 1595–6 (28 Oct. 1942).

129 Full text of judgement can be found in R. A. Harrison, *The Irish Digest 1939–48* (Dublin, 1952), pp. 94–5.

130 'A child shall not be deemed for the purposes of this act to be receiving suitable education in a manner other than by attending a national school, a suitable school, or a recognised school unless such education and the manner in which such child is receiving it have been certified under this section by the Minister to be suitable' Section 4 (1), School Attendance Bill 1942, cited in the Chief State Solicitor, Judgement, In the matter of Article 26 of the Constitution and in the matter of the Schools Attendance Bill, DT s 12039 B, NAI.

131 Farry, *Education and the Constitution*, p. 68.

132 Rúnaí Aire Department of Education to Rúnaí Príobháideach Department of Taoiseach, 28 Oct. 1958, DT s 12039 B, NAI

133 Over 65 per cent of Traveller births were in hospital, *Commission on Itinerancy*, p. 48.

134 *Report of the Council of Ireland 1934*, p. 18, SSVP; *Report of Annual Meeting of Presidents 1936*, p. 17, SSVP.

135 *Report of the Department of Local Government and Public Health 1930–31*, p. 193. An outbreak in County Wicklow in 1930 was blamed on 'a band of itinerant tinkers', Brian Donnelly, *For the Betterment of the People: A History of Wicklow County Council* (Wicklow, 1999), p. 79.

136 *Report of the Department of Local Government and Public Health 1925–7*, p. 61.

137 *Report of the Department of Local Government and Public Health 1930–1*, p. 41.

138 A doctor was legally obliged to report a notifiable disease such as small pox or typhus to the Department of Local Government and Public Health, but deaths from common infections such as measles were not compiled annually until the threat of long-established epidemic diseases had receded.

139 *Report of the Department of Local Government and Public Health 1937–8*, p. 55.

140 'Ireland was the last country in Western Europe with louse-borne typhus', James Deeny, *To Cure and to Care: Memoirs of a Chief Medical Officer* (Dun Laoghaire, 1989), p. 77. Dr Robert C. Cummins believed that endemic rat typhus occasionally infected those humans who had not built up a resistance to it. See Cummins, 'The last reported case of typhus in Cork city' in his *Unusual Medical Cases: A Cork Physician's Memories* (Cork, 1962), pp. 11–23.

141 *Report of the Department of Local Government and Public Health 1937–8*, Appendix XII, p. 171.

142 *Report of the Department of Local Government and Public Health 1939–40*, p. 30.

143 Ibid., p. 138.

144 Ruth Barrington, *Health, Medicine and Politics in Ireland 1900–70* (Dublin, 1987), p. 139.

145 *Report of the Department of Local Government and Public Health 1940–1*, p. 34. Oddly, the Donegal County Medical Officer reported only one case of typhus in August 1940. Monthly report of Dr M. J. Bastible, County Medical Officer for Health, Aug. 1940, Minutes of Donegal County Council, Aug. 1940. Thanks to the Donegal County Council Archivist for sending me this report.

146 *Report of the Department of Local Government and Public Health 1940–1*, p. 35.

147 Proposal for an emergency powers order providing for precautions against the spread of infectious disease, 20 Aug. 1940, DT s 12047 A, NAI.

148 *Department of Local Government and Public Health 1940–41*, p. 35.

149 Ibid., p. 153.

150 Rúnaí Aire Department of Justice to Rúnaí Priobhaideach do'n Taoiseach 10 Aug. 1940, DT s 12039 A, NAI.

151 Health Bill 1947, Explanatory Memorandum, DT s 12047 A, NAI.

152 For a detailed examination of the 1947 Health Act and the Mother and Child scheme, see J. H. Whyte, *The Church and State in Modern Ireland 1923–79* (2nd edn, Dublin, 1980), pp. 120–272.

153 *Dáil Éireann Debates*, vol. 98, col. 1734 (12 Dec. 1945).

154 *Dáil Éireann Debates*, vol. 98, col. 1716 (12 Dec. 1945).

155 *Dáil Éireann Debates*, vol. 98, col. 1715–16 (12 Dec. 1945).

156 Whyte, *Church and State*, p. 133.

157 *Dáil Éireann Debates*, vol. 98, col. 1735 (12 Dec. 1945).

158 *Dáil Éireann Debates*, vol. 98, cols 1864, 1880, 1900 (13 Dec. 1945).

159 *Dáil Éireann Debates*, vol. 98, col. 2025 (13 Dec. 1945).

160 *Dáil Éireann Debates*, vol. 98, col. 2078 (13 Dec. 1945).

161 *Dáil Éireann Debates*, vol. 100, col. 953 (2 Apr. 1946).

162 *Dáil Éireann Debates*, vol. 100, col. 1268 (4 Apr. 1946).

163 *Department of Local Government and Public Health 1941–42*, p. 37.

164 Deeny, *To Cure and to Care*, p. 82.

165 Whyte, *Church and State*, p. 294.

166 See correspondence in DH B 135/30, NAI.

167 *Commission on Itinerancy*, pp. 50–1.

FIVE: SOME PRACTICAL SUGGESTIONS

1 John O'Connell, 'Travellers in Ireland: an examination of discrimination and racism', in Ronit Lentin and Robbie McVeigh (eds), *Racism and Anti-Racism in Ireland* (Belfast, 2002), pp. 49–62.

2 For a detailed analysis of this material see Jane Helleiner, *Irish Travellers: Racism and the Politics of Culture* (Toronto, Buffalo, London, 2000), pp. 58–68 and Jane Helleiner, '"Menace to the social order": anti-Traveller discourse in the Irish Parliament 1939–59', *Canadian Journal of Irish Studies* 24, 1 (July 1998), pp. 75–91.

3 *Dáil Éireann Debates*, vol. 74, cols 2108–9 (16 Mar. 1939); *Dáil Éireann Debates*, vol. 81, col. 40, (2 Oct., 1940); *Dáil Éireann Debates*, vol. 97, cols 1035–6 (29 May 1945); *Dáil Éireann Debates*, vol. 114, col. 995 (9 Mar. 1949).

4 *Dáil Éireann Debates*, vol. 123, cols 1066–7 (22 Nov. 1950).

5 *Dáil Éireann Debates*, vol. 123, cols 1067 (22 Nov. 1950). See Aoife Bhreatnach, The 'itinerant problem': the attitude of Dublin and Stormont governments to Irish Travellers, 1922–60' (*Irish Historical Studies*, forthcoming).

6 *Dáil Éireann Debates*, vol. 126, col. 1830 (18 July 1951).

7 *Dáil Éireann Debates*, vol. 159, cols 681–2 (11 July 1956). See also Captain Patrick Giles's contribution, col. 685.

8 *Dáil Éireann Debates*, vol. 167, col. 239 (16 Apr. 1958).

9 *Dáil Éireann Debates*, vol. 174, col. 783 (21 Apr. 1959).

10 *Dáil Éireann Debates*, vol. 174, cols 783–4 (21 Apr. 1959).

11 *Dáil Éireann Debates*, vol. 174, col. 784 (21 Apr. 1959).

12 *Dáil Éireann Debates*, vol. 174, cols 784–5 (21 Apr. 1959).

13 *Dáil Éireann Debates*, vol. 174, col. 785 (21 Apr. 1959).

14 Ibid.

15 Helleiner, *Irish Travellers*, p. 61.

16 *Commission on Itinerancy*, p. 36.

17 Joseph Lee, 'Centralisation and community' in Joseph Lee (ed.), *Ireland: Towards a Sense of Place* (Cork, 1985), pp. 84–102.

18 Ibid., p. 85.

19 *Report of the Commission on Itinerancy* (Dublin, 1963), p. 52.

20 Ibid., p. 53.

21 D. Finucane, 'Parking of caravans', *Iris an Gharda/Garda Review* 57, 9 (Aug. 1952), p. 709.

22 *Dáil Éireann Debates*, vol. 93, cols 971–2 (18 Apr. 1944).

23 *The Problem of the Mentally Handicapped* (1960); *The Report of the Commission on Mental Illness* (1967).

24 See, *Select Committee, Interim Report on the Health Services* (Dublin, 1962); *Health Services and their Future Development* (Dublin, 1963); *Investment in Education: Report of the Survey Team appointed by the Minister for Education in October 1962* (Dublin, 1965).

25 Lee, 'Centralisation and community', pp. 84–5.

26 Note 6 Aug. 1963, DT s 17506 A/63, NAI.

27 Ibid. Cabinet decision in Meeting of cabinet, 27 May 1960, GC 9/70 P. 221, DT CAB 2/20, NAI.

28 Meeting of cabinet, 27 May 1960 GC 9/70 P. 221, CAB 2/20, NAI.

29 Justice Walsh was a High Court Judge, appointed to the Supreme Court in 1961. He was also a member of the Commission on Workmen's Compensation, 1955–9. See G. W. Hogan, 'The early judgements of Mr Justice Brian Walsh' in James O'Reilly (ed.), *Human Rights and Constitutional Law: Essays in Honour of Brian Walsh* (Dublin, 1992), pp. 37–48.

30 As Limerick City Manager, Mathew Macken was responsible for the illegal application of the Sanitary Services Act. See chapter 2.

31 Author's interview with Fr Fehily, 8 May 2001.

32 *Irish Times*, 1 Oct. 1964.

33 Fr Fehily cited Haughey's personal support for the appointment of the Commission as crucial. Author's interview with Fr Thomas Fehily, 8 May 2001.

34 *Dáil Éireann Debates*, vol. 198, col. 1458 (13 Dec. 1962)

35 *Commission on Itinerancy*, Appendix 1, p. 110.

36 Ibid., p. 11.

37 Ibid., p. 13.

38 Ibid., p. 14.

39 Ibid., Appendix XLIII, p. 158.

40 For a list of all contributors see ibid., Appendix XLIII, pp. 158–9.

41 Department of External Affairs representatives submitted reports on France, Spain, Western Germany, Portugal, Belgium, Italy and Turkey. Ibid., p. 15.

42 Ibid., p. 15.

43 Ibid., p. 21.

44 Donald Kenrick, 'Irish Travellers – a unique phenomenon in Europe?' in May McCann, Séamas Ó Síocháin and Joseph Ruane (eds), *Irish Travellers: Culture and Ethnicity* (Belfast, 1996), p. 28.

45 *Commission on Itinerancy*, p. 27.

46 Ibid., p. 13

47 Ibid., p. 37.

48 Ibid., Appendix I, p. 114.

49 For criticism of its 'assimilationist' tone see Paul Noonan, 'Pathologisation and resistance: Travellers, nomadism and the state' in Paul Hainsworth (ed.), *Divided Society: Ethnic Minorities and Racism in Northern Ireland* (London, 1998), p. 158.

50 See *The Problem of the Mentally Handicapped* (1960) for outdated and now objectionable language.

51 Elisabeth Tonkin, Maryon Mac Donald and Malcolm Chapman, 'History and ethnicity' in John Hutchinson and Anthony D. Smith (eds), *Ethnicity* (Oxford and New York, 1996), p. 22.

52 *Dublin Opinion*, Mar. 1964, p. 12. Thanks to Dr Eric Zuelow for this reference.

53 In December 1960 just 783 Travellers, out of a total of 4,809 over the age of six years, were literate. *Commission on Itinerancy*, p. 64.

54 E. Estyn Evans to A. Robinson, 1 Oct. 1954, HA 8/1415, PRONI.

55 *Commission on Itinerancy*, p. 12.

56 Ibid., p. 29.

57 Ibid., p. 30.

58 Ibid., Appendices XL and XLI.

59 Ibid., p. 58.

60 Ibid., p. 35.

61 Ibid., p. 33.

62 For a small sample of this rhetoric see *Dáil Éireann Debates*, vol. 94, col. 1528 (19 Sept. 1944); *Dáil Éireann Debates*, vol. 93, col. 978 (18 Apr. 1944); *Dáil Éireann Debates*, vol. 100, col. 1200 (3 Apr. 1946); *Dáil Éireann Debates*, vol. 123, col. 1055 (22 Nov. 1950); *Dáil Éireann Debates*, vol. 123, cols 1099–7 (22 Nov. 1950).

63 *Statistical Abstract of Ireland 1966*, p. 21.

64 *Dáil Éireann Debates*, vol. 151, col. 1080 (14 June 1955).

65 *Statistical Abstract of Ireland 1966*, p. 24.

66 *Commission on Itinerancy*, p. 80.

67 Ibid., p. 82.

68 Ibid., p. 80.

69 Ibid., p. 79.

70 Ibid., p. 83.

71 Ibid., p. 82.

72 Cathleen MacDonagh, 'Origins' in Frank Murphy and Cathleen MacDonagh (eds), *Travellers, Citizens of Ireland: Our Challenge to an Intercultural Irish Society in the 21st Century* (Dublin 2000), p. 25.

73 *Commission on Itinerancy*, p. 84.

74 Ibid., p. 88.

75 Ibid., p. 89.

76 Ibid., p. 90.

77 Ibid.

78 Ibid., p. 106.

79 In 1956, four farmers from Bushy Park, County Galway were charged with attacking a Traveller encampment. *Cork Examiner*, 17 July 1956.

80 *Commission on Itinerancy*, p. 96.

81 Ibid., p. 96.

82 Ibid.

83 Ibid., p. 90.

84 Ibid., p. 102.

85 Ibid., p. 86.

86 Ibid., p. 87.

87 Ibid., p. 94.

88 Ibid., p. 102.

89 Ibid., p. 103.

90 Ibid.

91 Helleiner, *Irish Travellers*, p. 56; Brendan Corish told the Dáil, 'I know tinkers, itinerants, or whatever you like to call them, who have tried to stay put, who have got themselves jobs in factories or on building sites and who for years have been refused houses by local authorities', *Dáil Éireann Debates*, vol. 182, col. 512 (1 June 1960).

92 *Commission on Itinerancy*, p. 103.

93 Ibid., p. 106.

94 Ibid., p. 54.

95 Ibid., p. 55.

96 Ibid., p. 56.

97 Ibid., p. 55–6.

98 Ibid., p. 57.

99 Ibid., p. 62.

100 Ibid., p. 63.

101 Ibid., p. 67.

102 Ibid., p. 68.

103 Ibid., p. 69.

104 Ibid., p. 70.

105 Ibid., p. 73.

106 Ibid.

107 Ibid., p. 72.

108 Ibid., p. 74.

109 Ibid., p. 73.

110 Ibid., p. 75.

111 Ibid., p. 76.

112 Ibid., p. 88.

113 Ibid., p. 95.

114 Ibid., p. 100.

115 Ibid., p. 96.

116 Ibid., p. 97.

117 Ibid., p. 97.

118 Ibid., p. 92.

119 Ibid., p. 93.

120 Ibid., p. 101.

121 For the debate on the Summary Jurisdiction and Criminal Justice Bill 1958 and Travellers see *Northern Ireland Commons Debates*, vol. 41, cols 2891–9 (28 Jan. 1958). See appendix for details of Act.

122 *Commission on Itinerancy*, p. 104.

123 Ibid., p. 105.

124 Ibid., p. 107.

125 Ibid., p. 107.

126 Ibid., p. 108.

127 Ibid., p. 104.

128 Ibid., p. 104.

129 *Report of the Department of Local Government 1961–2*, p. 19.

130 Ibid., p. 20.

131 *Report of the Department of Local Government 1962–3*, p. 16.

132 *Commission on Itinerancy*, p. 87.

133 Con Lucey, 'The Beveridge Report and Éire', *Studies* 33 (Mar. 1943), p. 36.

134 Bryan Fanning, 'The mixed economy of welfare' in Gabriel Kiely, Anne O'Donnell, Patricia Kennedy and Suzanne Quin (eds), *Irish Social Policy in Context* (Dublin, 1999), pp. 53–5.

SIX: ASSIMILATION AND ABSORPTION

1 For a study of County Clare see Bryan Fanning, *Racism and Social Change in the Republic of Ireland* (Manchester, 2002), pp. 112–18; for the reaction in Galway city see Jane Helleiner, *Irish Travellers: Racism and the Politics of Culture* (Toronto, Buffalo, London, 2000), pp. 79–98

2 Note, 6 Aug. 1963, DT s 17506 A/63, NAI.

3 The most famous example of a failed report with ostensibly impeccable credentials was the report of the Commission on Vocational Organisation chaired by Bishop Michael Browne. See Dermot Keogh, *Twentieth-Century Ireland: Nation and State* (Dublin, 1994), pp. 147–9.

4 Oifig an Taoisigh, memorandum presented to government 16 Aug. 1963, DT s 17506 A/63, NAI.

5 *Dáil Éireann Debates*, vol. 242, cols 1703–5 (25 Nov. 1969).

6 *Dáil Éireann Debates*, vol. 232, col. 760 (8 Feb. 1968).

7 *Dáil Éireann Debates*, vol. 242, col. 892 (13 Nov. 1969).

8 Áine Hyland and Kenneth Milne (eds), *Irish Education Documents Vol. II: A Selection of Extracts of Documents Relating to the History of Education from 1922 to 1991 in the Irish Free State and the Republic of Ireland* (Dublin, 1992), p. 472.

9 *Dáil Éireann Debates*, vol. 229, col. 1202 (4 July 1967).

10 N. Ó Nualláin to Private Secretary, Department of Local Government, 16 Aug. 1963, D/T s 17506 A/63, 1994 release, NAI.

11 *Dáil Éireann Debates*, vol. 206, col. 1272 (12 Dec. 1963); *Dáil Éireann Debates*, vol. 207, cols 268–9, (30 Jan. 1964); *Dáil Éireann Debates*, vol. 207, cols 1791–2 (27 Feb. 1964); *Dáil Éireann Debates*, vol. 208, col. 949 (12 Mar. 1964); *Dáil Éireann Debates*, vol. 209, col. 1910 (21 May 1964); *Dáil Éireann Debates*, vol. 211, cols 511–12 (18 June 1964).

12 Minutes of the Quarterly meeting of the County Borough Council, 13 Oct. 1964, p. 422, cp/c/a 22, CAI.

13 *Dáil Éireann Debates*, vol. 206, col. 1272 (12 Dec. 1963).

14 Thomas Acton, *Gypsy Politics and Social Change* (London, 1974), p. 155; Grattan Puxon, 'The Romani movement: rebirth and the 1st Romani Congress in retrospect' in Thomas Acton (ed.), *Scholarship and the Gypsy Struggle: Commitment in Romani Studies* (Hertfordshire, 2000), p. 94.

15 MacDonald and Keenan were themselves Travellers, Acton, *Gypsy Politics and Social Change*, p. 156.

16 Puxon, 'The Romani movement' in Acton (ed.), *Scholarship*, p. 95. The Special Branch was a Garda unit that monitored subversive activities and political crime.

17 Author's interview with Fr Thomas Fehily, 8 May 2001.

18 Acton, *Gypsy Politics and Social Change*, p. 156.

19 *Report of the Commission on Itinerancy* (Dublin, 1963), p. 30.

20 *Irish Independent*, 31 Dec. 1963.

21 Note, Ó Nualláin to Taoiseach, 1 Jan. 1964, DT s 17506 A/63, 1994 release, NAI.

22 *Irish Times*, 8 Jan. 1964. The new camp was broken up a few days later, *Irish Times*, 15 Jan. 1964.

23 *Irish Independent*, 31 Dec. 1963. In the Dáil, the minister said the land was reserved for industrial use, *Dáil Éireann Debates*, vol. 206, col. 1272 (12 Dec. 1963).

24 *Irish Independent*, 31 Dec. 1963.

25 *Dáil Éireann Debates*, vol. 210, col. 394 (2 June 1964).

26 Secretary to each Sanitary Authority, Circular No. L.14/64, 4 Nov. 1964, GCCC files.

27 Rúnaí GCCC to Private Secretary to an Taoiseach, 8 June 1965, GCCC files.

28 Ibid.

29 *Irish Press*, 22 May 1965 and *Report of the Department of Local Government 1965–6*, p. 34.

30 Department of Local Government to Rúnaí GCCC, 3 Aug. 1965, GCCC files.

31 *Irish Press*, 22 May 1965.

32 Acton, *Gypsy Politics and Social Change*, p. 158.

33 Ibid.

34 Ibid., p. 157.

35 Ibid., p. 158.

36 Ibid., p. 157.

37 Puxon, 'The Romani movement' in Acton (ed.), *Scholarship*, p. 97. The crowning of 'The King of the Tinkers' described on p. 27 above may refer to the same Lawrence Ward.

38 Acton, *Gypsy Politics and Social Change*, p. 159.

39 Ibid.

40 Ibid., p. 160.

41 Acton claims that there was a diplomatic effort to prevent the international representatives from attending; Department of Foreign Affairs' files might contain some information on this. Acton, *Gypsy Politics and Social Change*, p. 160.

42 Ibid., p. 160.

43 Puxon, 'The Romani movement' in Acton (ed.), *Scholarship*, p. 97.

44 Acton, *Gypsy Politics and Social Change*, p. 160.

45 Signs outside the camp denied Puxon's authority to represent the camp residents, *Irish Times*, 10 Jan. 1966.

46 Acton, *Gypsy Politics and Social Change*, p. 161.

47 Puxon, 'The Romani movement' in Acton (ed.), *Scholarship*, p. 97.

48 Acton also dominates the academic discourse on Travellers and Gypsies, being Professor of Romani Studies at the University of Greenwich.

49 *Commission on Itinerancy*, p. 36.

50 Report of the Housing Committee, 3 Nov. 1964 p. 429 in Minutes of Meeting of the County Borough Council, 10 Nov. 1964, CP/C/A 22, CAI.

51 Report of the General Purposes Committee, 16 Mar. 1965, p. 492, in Minutes of Meeting of the County Borough Council, 23 Mar. 1965, CP/C/A 22, CAI; Minutes of the Quarterly Meeting of the County Borough Council, 13 Apr. 1965, p. 497, CP/C/A 22, CAI.

52 Report of the Housing Committee, 6 Apr. 1965 p. 501, in Minutes of Meeting of County Borough Council, 13 Apr. 1965, CP/C/A 22, CAI.

53 *Commission on Itinerancy*, p. 60.

54 A development plan for the city area was being drafted in accordance with the Local Government (Planning and Development) Act 1963. The first plan, published in 1969, made no reference to Traveller accommodation; see Cork Corporation *Cork City Development Plan 1969* (Cork, 1969).

55 Minutes of the Meeting of the County Borough Council, 22 June 1965, p. 542, CP/C/A 22, CAI.

56 Ibid., p. 543.

57 Ibid.

58 Minutes of the Meeting of the County Borough Council, 24 Aug. 1965, p. 573, CP/C/A 22, CAI.

59 Report of the Housing Committee, 2 Nov. 1965 p. 609, in Minutes of the Meeting of the County Borough Council, 9 Nov. 1965, CP/C/A 22, CAI.

60 Average number of Traveller families in Cork county calculated from figures in *Commission on Itinerancy*, Appendix 1. Cork city and county population figures for 1961 in W. E. Vaughan and A. J. Fitzpatrick (eds), *Irish Historical Statistics: Population 1821–1971* (Dublin, 1978), p. 20.

61 Report of the Housing Committee, 2 Nov. 1965 p. 609, in Minutes of the Meeting of the County Borough Council, 9 Nov. 1965, CP/C/A 22, CAI.

62 Report of the Housing Committee, 7 Dec. 1965 p. 628, in Minutes of the Meeting of the County Borough Council, 14 Dec. 1965, CP/C/A 22, CAI.

63 Minutes of the Meeting of the County Borough Council, 14 Dec. 1965 p. 629, CP/C/A 22, CAI.

64 Minutes of the Meeting of the County Borough Council, 25 Jan. 1966 p. 16, CP/C/A 23, CAI.

65 Minutes of the Preliminary Estimates Meeting, 22 Nov. 1966 p. 155, CP/C/A 23, CAI.

66 Adelaide Street was represented by Messrs Fitzpatrick, Webb and Peglar; Frenches Quay by Mr J. Forde, Miss O'Callaghan, Mrs Brennan and Mr H. Forde.

67 Report of the General Purposes Committee, 7 Feb. 1967 p. 188, CP/C/A 23, CAI.

68 *Commission on Itinerancy*, p. 61. See also chapter 4.

69 General Minutes, 7 Feb. 1967 p. 190, CP/C/A 23, CAI.

70 Ibid., p. 191.

71 *Irish Times*, 22 May 1968.

72 *Irish Times*, 23 May 1968.

73 For a well-researched outline of these boundaries see Michael J. Lennon, 'Residential segregation in Cork City 1901–46' (Unpublished MA thesis, UCC, 2000).

74 *Dáil Éireann Debates*, vol. 244, cols 297–8 (5 Feb. 1970).

75 Two hundred houses were built not far from Rossa Avenue in 1974, Richard Henchion, *Bishopstown, Wilton and Glasheen: A Picture of Life in the Three Western Suburbs of Cork from Early Days to Modern Times* (Cork, 2001), p. 66.

76 *Dáil Éireann Debates*, vol. 244, cols 297–8 (5 Feb. 1970).

77 Niall Bradley, 'Report on Travelling families in County Meath', 28 Feb. 1978. This report was kindly forwarded to me by the Meath County Librarian.

78 *Dáil Éireann Debates*, vol. 244, cols 297–8 (5 Feb. 1970).

79 Synopsis of address given by Justice Brian Walsh to the GCCC, 5 Aug. 1965, GCCC files.

80 Sharon B. Gmelch and George Gmelch, 'The Itinerant settlement movement', *Studies* 63 (Spring 1974), p. 2.

81 Victor Bewley was a Quaker and a member of the family that ran the famous Bewley Cafés in Dublin. His voluntary work was extensive though his involvement with Travellers was his most public activity. See Fiona Murdoch, *Victor Bewley's Memoirs* (Dublin, 2002), pp. 61–73.

82 Eleanor Clonmore, Countess of Wicklow was described as 'one of the leading figures in post-war Irish public affairs of her generation'. She was a Labour Party Senator and a prominent campaigner on housing, social issues and Northern Ireland. See her obituary in *Sunday Tribune*, 9 Mar. 1997. Thanks to Dr Niall Keogh for this reference.

83 Murdoch, *Victor Bewley's Memoirs*, p. 64.

84 Author's interview with Fr Thomas Fehily 8 May 2001.

85 Murdoch, *Victor Bewley's Memoirs*, p. 65.

86 Author's interview with Fr Thomas Fehily 8 May 2001.

87 The event ended when Travellers objected to being marked out as particularly needy. Author's interview with Fr Thomas Fehily, 8 May 2001.

88 Gmelch and Gmelch, 'The Itinerant settlement movement', p. 8. No trace of this newsletter survives.

89 *Northern Ireland Commons Debates*, vol. 69, cols 1472–3 (22 May 1968).

90 Gmelch and Gmelch, 'The Itinerant settlement movement', p. 3.

91 Ibid., p. 4.

92 Ibid., p. 3.

93 *Report of the Council of Ireland 1966*, p. 3, SSVP.

94 The conference was called St Benedict Joseph Labre, after the Beggar of Perpetual Adoration, patron saint of the homeless. *Report of the Council of Ireland 1968*, p. 9, SSVP.

95 *Report of the Council of Ireland 1969*, p. 2, SSVP.

96 Gmelch and Gmelch, 'The Itinerant settlement movement', p. 11.

97 *Dáil Éireann Debates*, vol. 233, cols 1035–6 (26 Mar., 1968).

98 *Dáil Éireann Debates*, vol. 242, cols 20–2 (4 Nov. 1969).

99 *Dáil Éireann Debates*, vol. 242, col. 528 (11 Nov. 1969).

100 Author's interview with Fr Thomas Fehily, 8 May 2001.

101 *Dáil Éireann Debates*, vol. 244, col. 298 (5 Feb. 1970).

102 Fr Fehily to Taoiseach, 26 Sept. 1969, DT 2000/6/340, NAI.

103 Author's interview with Dr Michael Flynn, 2 Feb. 2001. Boland resigned over what became known as the Arms Trial, see Keogh, *Twentieth-Century Ireland*, pp. 308–15.

104 Murdoch, *Victor Bewley's Memoirs*, pp. 65–6.

105 Gmelch and Gmelch, 'The Itinerant settlement movement', p. 11.

106 Ibid., p. 13.

107 Ibid., p. 14.

108 Seán Ó Riain, *Solidarity with Travellers: A Story of Settled People Making a Stand for Travellers* (Dublin, 2000), p. 17.

109 Ibid., p. 17.

110 Jim MacLaughlin, *Travellers and Ireland: Whose Country? Whose History?* (Cork, 1995), p. 82. See also Aoife Bhreatnach, 'Travellers and the print media: words and Irish identity' *Irish Studies Review* 6, 3 (1998), pp. 285–90.

111 According to Helleiner, the Galway ISC was composed of 'several influential and relatively well-off citizens of Galway', *Irish Travellers*, p. 82.

112 Helleiner, *Irish Travellers*, p. 83.

SEVEN: CONCLUSION

1 Christopher J. Smith, *Public Problems: The Management of Urban Distress* (New York and London, 1988), p. 4.

2 *Report of the Department of Local Government 1961–2*, p. 30.

EPILOGUE: RESETTLEMENT AND RESISTANCE SINCE 1970

1 See Bryan Fanning, *Racism and Social Change in the Republic of Ireland* (Manchester, 2002); Steve Garner, *Racism in the Irish Experience* (London, Dublin, Sterling Virginia, 2004); Jane Helleiner, *Irish Travellers: Racism and the Politics of Culture* (Toronto, Buffalo, London, 2000); Ronit Lentin and Robbie McVeigh (eds), *Racism and Anti-Racism in Ireland* (Belfast, 2002). Jim MacLaughlin, *Travellers and Ireland: Whose Country? Whose History?* (Cork, 1995).

2 For more on Rathkeale, County Limerick see Patrick J. O'Connor, *All Ireland is in and about Rathkeale* (Newcastlewest, 1996), p. 128–76.

3 MacLaughlin, *Travellers and Ireland*, p. 2.

4 See chapter 6 for the censorship of data collected from Travellers.

5 Cited in Sinéad Ní Shúinéir, 'The Association of Travelling People's vision of its educational mandate 1972–1995', (Unpublished conference paper, New Directions in Romani Studies, University of Greenwich, July 1996). Thanks to Sinéad for allowing me to use this material. Joyce Sholdice was National Coordinator for Settlement for NCTP from 1974–81. See her obituary in *Irish Times*, 15 Nov. 2003.

6 The NCTP was finally dissolved in the 1990s, *Report of the Task Force on the Travelling Community* (Dublin, 1995), p. 64.

7 The first Simon Community was established in Dublin in 1969. Seán Ó Riain, *Solidarity with Travellers: A Story of Settled People Making a Stand for Travellers* (Dublin, 2000), p. 19.

8 Ibid., p. 62.

9 Ibid., *Solidarity with Travellers*, p. 17.

10 Ní Shúinéir, 'The Association of Travelling People's vision'.

11 Mary Moriarty cited in Ní Shúinéir, 'The Association of Travelling People's vision'.

12 Mícheál Mac Gréil, *Prejudice and Tolerance in Ireland* (Dublin, 1977), p. 253, 315–31.

13 Mícheál Mac Gréil, *Prejudice in Ireland Revisited* (Maynooth, 1996), p. 323.

14 Ibid., p. 329.

15 Ibid., p. 344–7.

16 *Report of the Travelling People Review Body* (Dublin, 1983), p. 7.

17 *Report of the Task Force on the Travelling Community*, p. 57.

18 *Report of the Travelling People Review Body*, p. 8; see also George Gmelch and Sharon Bohn Gmelch, 'The cross-channel migration of Irish Travellers', *Economic and Social Review* 16, 4 (1985), pp. 287–290.

19 *Report of the Travelling People Review Body*, p. 38.

20 www.cso.ie/newsevents/pr_cen_02vol8.htm (accessed 6 Jan. 2006) The Traveller population was analysed in volume 8.

21 Disability and carers were analysed in volume 10.

22 Michelle Norris and Nessa Winston, 'Housing and accommodation of Irish Travellers: from assimilationism to multi-culturalism and back again' (Unpublished paper).

23 Ní Shúinéir, 'The Association of Travelling People's vision'.

24 See Helleiner, *Irish Travellers*, pp. 84–5 and *Irish Times*, 15 Nov. 2003. Attacks continued in the 1980s, Helleiner, *Irish Travellers*, pp. 3–4.

25 *Dáil Éireann debates*, vol. 511, col. 788 (24 Nov. 1999).

26 Fanning, *Racism and Social Change*, pp. 133–5.

27 The apocalyptic vision of contemporary society presented by some in the media, 'the Commentariat', is mocked in David MacWilliams, *The Pope's Children: Ireland's New Elite* (Dublin, 2005), pp. 18–27.

28 *Report of the Travelling People Review Body*, p. 36.

29 Ibid., p. 35.

30 Norris and Winston, 'Housing and accommodation of Irish Travellers'.

31 Gerry Whyte, *Social Inclusion and the Legal System: Public Interest Law in Ireland* (Dublin, 2001), p. 233.

32 Fanning, *Racism and Social Change*, pp. 129–30.

33 Helleiner, *Irish Travellers*, pp. 229–36.

34 *Irish Times*, 17 Oct. 2003.

35 Cases were approximately 60/40 in favour of the complainant, *Irish Times*, 28 June 2002.

36 *Irish Times*, 30 June 2003. For a list of groups involved see www.iccl.ie/minorities/03_equalitycoalitionpconf.html (Accessed 18 Jan. 2006).

37 For example, see Judith Walkowitz, *City of Dreadful Delight: Narratives of Sexual Danger in Late-Victorian London* (London, 1992) and Judith Knelman, *Twisting in the Wind: The Murderess and the English Press* (Toronto, 1998).

38 The innovative project of Dr Anthony Keating, IRCHSS Post-Doctoral Fellow 2003, 'The appearance and reality in the documentation of sex offences in the Irish Free State and Republic 1930–59', has proved this form of censorship.

39 The incident in New Ross in 1961 was not mentioned in the *New Ross Standard*, only covered in the *Cork Examiner*. For more on this see Aoife Bhreatnach, 'Policing the community: homicide and violence in Traveller and settled society', *Irish Economic and Social History* (forthcoming, 2007).

40 The identification was based on garda intelligence rather than arrests and convictions. *Irish Times*, 11 Jan. 1996. See also *Sunday Independent*, 4 Feb. 1996.

41 The national print and broadcast media in November 2005 covered Nally's case and his sentencing extensively.

42 Nora Casey, 'The print media as an influence on attitudes to Travellers: an example from North Tipperary' (MPhil, TCD, 2005).

43 *First Progress Report of the Committee to monitor and co-ordinate the implementation of the reccommendations of the Task Force on the Travelling Community* (Dublin, 2000), p. 10.

44 Niamh Hardiman, 'Inequality and representation of interests' in William Crotty and David E. Schmitt (eds), *Ireland and the Politics of Change* (London, 1998), pp. 122–43.

APPENDIX

1   Office of the Revenue Commissioners to Secretary D/J, 5 January 1925 D/J H207/1, NAI.

Bibliography

—

PRIMARY SOURCES

NATIONAL ARCHIVES OF IRELAND, DUBLIN
Cabinet minutes
Department of Foreign Affairs, PMUN series
Department of Health
Department of Justice
Department of Taoiseach

CORK ARCHIVES INSTITUTE, CORK CITY
Records of Cork Corporation:
    CP/Files Series: City Manager's correspondance and miscellaneous files
    Minutes of the Borough Council of Cork Corporation
    Minutes of the Hackney Carriages committee
    Minutes of the Public Health committee
    Minutes of the Tolls and Markets committee
    Register of Common Lodging Houses, 1910–48

Records of Cork County Council:
    Minutes of Cork County Council

GENERAL COUNCIL OF COUNTY COUNCILS, DUBLIN
Agendas of Annual meetings, 1920–89
General Council of County Councils general files
Minute Book, 1946–63

DUBLIN CITY ARCHIVES, DUBLIN
Dublin Corporation Reports, 1930–70
Minutes of the Municipal Corporation of the City of Dublin, 1930–70

GARDA SÍOCHÁNA ARCHIVES, DUBLIN CASTLE
Iris an Gharda/Garda Review

REPRESENTATIVE CHURCH BODY LIBRARY, DUBLIN
Statement of the Church of Ireland Moral Welfare Society, 'Memo on Itinerancy re
    Communication sent to RCB from Custom House', February 1961.

DUBLIN DIOCESAN RECORDS, DUBLIN
Archbishop McQuaid Papers

CENTRAL CATHOLIC LIBRARY, DUBLIN
Irish Catholic Directory, 1917–67.

SOCIETY OF ST VINCENT DE PAUL, HEADQUARTERS, DUBLIN
Annual Report of the Council of Ireland, 1920–69
Eucharistic Congress Week Ireland 1932 – General Meeting of the Society in Dublin (Dublin, 1932).
Origins and Object of the St Vincent de Paul Society and its workings in Ireland (Dublin, 1923 edition).
Report of the Task Force appointed by the President to consider the Role and Structure of the Council of Ireland February 1978 (Dublin, 1978).
Report of the Annual Meeting of Presidents with the Council of Ireland, 1920–44
St. Vincent's Glasnevin Centenary Record 1856–1956 (Dublin, 1956).
The Society of St Vincent de Paul and a Centenary of Catholic Charitable Activity in Ireland (Dublin, 1929).

NORTHSIDE FOLKLORE PROJECT, CORK
Northside Folklore Project, Sound Recordings

ROINN BHÉALOIDEAS ÉIREANN/DEPARTMENT OF IRISH FOLKLORE, UNIVERSITY COLLEGE DUBLIN
Bailiúchán na Scol/Schools Collection, 1937–8
Main Manuscript Collection

SIDNEY JONES LIBRARY, UNIVERSITY OF LIVERPOOL
Gypsy Lore Society Archive
Scott Macfie Gypsy Collection

TRAVELLER RESOURCE CENTRE, DUBLIN
Cuffe, Luan P. and Gmelch, George J., 'Housing as a factor in social integration: the Traveller in Ireland' (Unpublished report, April 1972), Traveller Resource Centre.

INTERVIEWS
8 May 2001, Fr Thomas Fehily, member of the Commission on Itinerancy, Chairman of the National Committee for Itinerant Settlement.
2 February 2001, Dr Michael Flynn, County Medical Officer for Westmeath, Midlands Area Health Board Programme Manager, member of the Travelling People Review Body.
29 December 2001, Nioclás Breatnach, collector for the Déise area, Folklore Commission (1935–37), with a special interest in Shelta.
29 December 2001, Mary Breatnach.

REPUBLIC OF IRELAND GOVERNMENT PUBLICATIONS

Annual Reports of the Commissioner of the Garda Síochána on Crime, 1947–69
Annual Reports of the Department of Education
Annual Reports of the Department of Local Government and Public Health, 1925–47
Annual Reports of the Department of Local Government, 1947–69
Census of Population 1926, 1936, 1946, 1951, 1961
Statistical Abstracts of Ireland, 1930–69

REPUBLIC OF IRELAND GOVERNMENT REPORTS

First Progress Report of the Committee to monitor and co-ordinate the implementation of the recommendations of the Task Force on the Travelling Community (Dublin, 2000).
First Report of the Department of Health, 1945–9 (Dublin, 1949).
First Report of the Department of Social Welfare, 1947–9 (Dublin, 1949).
Housing: A Review of Past Operations and Immediate Requirements (Department of Local Government, 1947).
Interim Report of Committee of Inquiry into Health Insurance and Medical Services (Dublin, 1925).
Investment in Education: Report of the Survey Team appointed by the Minister for Education in October 1962 (Dublin, 1965).
Health Services and their Future Development (Dublin, 1963).
Outline of Proposals for the Improvement of the Health Services (Department of Health, White Paper, 1947).
Reconstruction and Improvement of County Homes (Department of Health, 1951).
Report of the Commission on Emigration and Other Population Problems 1948–54 (Dublin, 1956).
Report of the Commission on Itinerancy (Dublin, 1963).
Report of the Commission on the Relief of the Sick and Destitute Poor, including the Insane Poor (Dublin, 1927).
Report of the Conference between the Department of Local Government and Public Health and Representatives of local Public Health and Public Assistance Authorities, 8, 9 July 1930 (Dublin, 1930).
Report of the Inter-Departmental Committee on Seasonal Migration to Britain 1937–38 (Dublin, 1938).
Report of the Local Government (Dublin) Tribunal (Dublin, 1938).
Report of the Task Force on the Travelling Community (Dublin, 1995).
Report of the Travelling People Review Body (Dublin, 1983).
The Problem of the Mentally Handicapped (Department of Health, 1960).
The Report of the Commission on Mental Illness (Department of Health, 1967).

BRITISH GOVERNMENT PUBLICATIONS

Report on the Employment of Children (Ireland) 1902 Cd 1144 vol. xlix.

PARLIAMENTARY DEBATES

Dáil and Seanad Éireann Debates
Debates of the Northern Ireland House of Commons and Senate

NEWSPAPERS

Church of Ireland Monthly
Church of Ireland Gazette
Republican Congress
The Connacht Tribune
The Cork Examiner
The Donegal Democrat
The Irish Independent
The Irish Press
The Irish Times
The Kerryman
The Limerick Leader
The Sunday Tribune

PERIODICALS

Administration
Annals of the Association of American Geographers
Archivium Hibernicum
Art History
Capuchin Annual
Crane Bag
Dublin Historical Record
Dublin Review
Ireland's Own
Iris an Gharda/Garda Review
Irish Catholic Directory
Irish Economic and Social History
Irish Geography
Irish Historical Studies
Irish Medical Journal
Irish Studies Review
Journal of Modern History
Journal of the Cork Historical and Archaeological Society
Journal of the Gypsy Lore Society
Journal of Ulster Folklife
Journal of Urban History
Mallow Field Club Journal
National Geographic
New Ireland Review
Old Kilkenny Review
Past and Present
Social Studies, Irish Journal of Sociology
Studia Hibernica
Studies
The Annual Observer

Economic and Social Review
Historical Review
History Review: Journal of the UCD Historical Society
Time
Urban Geography
Urban History Yearbook/Urban History
Women's Studies International Forum

SECONDARY SOURCES

PUBLISHED WORKS ON TRAVELLERS

Acton, Thomas, *Gypsy Politics and Social Change: The Development of Ethnic Ideology and Pressure Politics among British Gypsies from Victorian Reformism to Romany Nationalism* (London, Boston; 1974).

Acton, Thomas (ed.), *Gypsy Politics and Traveller Identity* (Hertfordshire, 1997).

Acton, Thomas (ed.), *Scholarship and the Gypsy Struggle: Commitment in Romani Studies, a Collection of Papers and Poems to Celebrate Donald Kenrick's 70th year* (Hertfordshire, 2000).

Adams, Barbara; Okely, Judith; Morgans, David; Smith, David, 'Gypsies: current policies and practices', *Journal of Social Policy* 4, 2 (1975), pp. 129–50.

Allen, Diana, 'Gypsies and planning policy' in Thomas Acton (ed.), *Scholarship and the Gypsy Struggle: Commitment in Romani Studies, a collection of papers and poems to celebrate Donald Kenrick's 70th year* (Hertfordshire, 2000), pp. 114–18.

Barnes, Bettina, 'Irish Travellers', in Farnham Rehfisch (ed.), *Gypsies, Tinkers and other Travellers* (London, 1975), pp. 231–55.

Bewley, Victor E. H., *The Travelling People, Christianity in Action 3* (Dublin, 1971).

Bewley, Victor E. H., *Discrimination: Christianity in Action 9* (Dublin, 1972).

Bewley, Victor E. H. *Travelling People* (Dublin, 1974).

Bhreatnach, Aoife, 'Travellers and the print media: words and Irish identity', *Irish Studies Review* 6, 3 (1998) pp. 285–90.

Bhreatnach, Aoife, 'The "itinerant problem": the attitude of Dublin and Stormont governments to Irish Travellers, 1922–60', *Irish Historical Studies* (forthcoming, 2006).

Bhreatnach, Aoife, 'Policing the community: homicide and violence in Traveller and settled society', *Irish Economic and Social History* (forthcoming, 2007).

Bhreatnach, Aoife, 'Planning and philanthropy: Travellers and class boundaries in urban Ireland', in Maria Luddy and Fintan Cullen (eds), *Politics and the Middle Class in Modern Ireland* (forthcoming, 2007).

Bhreatnach, Aoife, '"Clear out, clear out of here!": trespass, land ownership and Irish Travellers' in Aoife Bhreatnach and Ciara Breathnach (eds), *Portraying Irish Travellers: Histories and Representations* (forthcoming, 2007)

Binchy, Alice, 'Travellers language: a sociolinguistic prespective' in May McCann, Séamas Ó Síocháin, and Joseph Ruane, *Irish Travellers: Culture and Ethnicity* (Belfast, 1996), pp. 134–54.

Breatnach, Nioclás, 'Big Jim's lore and language', *The Annual Observer* 1 (1979).

Burke, Mary, 'Eighteenth-century European scholarship and nineteenth-century Irish literature: Synge's *Tinker's Wedding* and the orientalizing of "Irish gypsies"' in Betsey Taylor Fitzsimon and James H. Murphy (eds), *The Irish Revival Reappraised* (Dublin, 2004), pp. 205–16.

Clifford, Sigerson, *Travelling Tinkers* (Dublin, 1951).

Cnúasach Andeas, 'Tadgh agus an Túincéir', *Béaloideas* 29 (1961), pp. 59–61.

Cusack, Tricia, 'Migrant travellers and touristic idylls: the paintings of Jack B. Yeats and post-colonial identites', *Art History* 21, 2 (1998), pp. 201–18.

Delaney, Paul, 'Representations of Travellers in the 1880s and 1900s', *Irish Studies Review* 9, 1 (2001), pp. 53–68.

Delaney, Paul, 'A marginal footnote': O'Faoláin, the subaltern and Irish Travellers', *Irish Studies Review* 11, 2 (2003), pp. 155–64.

Dempsey, M. and Geary, R. C., *The Irish Itinerants: Some Demographic, Economic and Educational Aspects* (Dublin, 1976).

European Roma Rights Centre, *Stigmata: Segregated Schooling of Roma in Central and Eastern Europe, a survey of patterns of segregated education of Roma in Bulgaria, the Czech Republic, Hungary, Romania and Slovakia* (Budapest, 2003).

Fanning, Bryan, *Racism and Social Change in the Republic of Ireland* (Manchester, 2002).

Farrell, Fintan and Watt, Philip (eds), *Responding to Racism in Ireland* (Dublin, 2001).

Fay, Ronnie, 'Health and racism: a Traveller perspective', in Fintan Farrell and Philip Watt (eds), *Responding to Racism in Ireland* (Dublin, 2001), pp. 99–114.

Finucane, D., 'Parking of caravans', *Iris an Gharda/Garda Review* 57, 9 (Aug. 1952), p. 709.

Flynn, Michael, 'Mortality, morbidity and marital features of travellers in the Irish midlands', *Irish Medical Journal* 79, 11 (1986), pp. 308–10.

Flynn, Michael, 'Rates of consanguineous marriages among Travellers disputed', *Irish Medical Journal* 90, 7 (1997), p. 276.

Fraser, Angus M., 'The Tinkers of Ireland', *Journal of the Gypsy Lore Society* 44 (1965), pp. 38–48.

Garner, Steve, *Racism in the Irish Experience* (London, 2004).

Geary, R. and O'Shea, C., 'Defining the traveller: from legal theory to practical action', *Journal of Social Welfare and Family Law* 17, 2 (1995), pp. 167–78.

Gmelch, George, 'The effects of economic change on Irish Travellers sex roles and marriage patterns' in Farnham Rehfisch (ed.), *Gypsies, Tinkers and other Travellers* (London, 1975), pp. 257–69.

Gmelch, George, *The Irish Tinkers: the Urbanization of an Itinerant People* (2nd edn, Illinois, 1985).

Gmelch, George and Gmelch, Sharon Bohn, 'The itinerant settlement movement', *Studies* 63 (Spring 1974), pp. 1–16.

Gmelch, George and Gmelch, Sharon Bohn, 'The emergence of an ethnic group: The Irish Tinkers', *Anthropological Quarterly* 49, 4 (October 1976), pp. 225–38.

Gmelch, George and Gmelch, Sharon Bohn, 'Ireland's travelling people: a comprehensive bibliography', *Journal of the Gypsy Lore Society* series 4, 1, 3 (1977), pp. 159–69.

Gmelch, George and Gmelch, Sharon Bohn, 'Begging in Dublin: the Strategies of a Marginal Urban Occupation', *Urban Life* 6, 4 (1978), pp. 439–54.

Gmelch, George and Gmelch, Sharon Bohn, 'The cross-channel migration of Irish Travellers', *Economic and Social Review* 16, 4 (1985), pp. 287–90.

Gmelch, George and Kroup, Ben (eds), *To Shorten the Road: Essays and Biographies* (Dublin, 1978).

Gmelch, Sharon, *Tinkers and Travellers* (Dublin, 1979).

Gemlch, Sharon, *Nan: the Life of an Irish Travelling Woman* (London, 1987).

Gmelch, Sharon, 'From poverty subculture to political lobby: the Traveller rights movement in Ireland' in Chris Curtin and Thomas Wilson (eds), *Ireland from Below: Social Change and Local Communities* (Galway, 1989), pp. 301–19.

Gow, J., 'The Irish Tinkers', *Journal of Ulster Folklife* 17 (1971), pp. 90–2.

Gregory, Lady (Augusta), *The Travelling Man* (Dublin, London, n.d.).

Gregory, Lady (Augusta), 'The wandering tribe' in Lady (Augusta) Gregory, *Poets and Dreamers: Studies and Translations from the Irish by Lady Gregory including Nine Plays by Douglas Hyde* (New York, 1974), pp. 94–7.

Helleiner, Jane, '"The tinker's wedding" revisited: Irish Traveller marriage' in Matt T. Salo (ed.), *One Hundred Years of Gypsy Studies* (Publication no. 5 Gypsy Lore Society, Maryland, 1990), pp. 77–86.

Helleiner, Jane, 'Traveller settlement in Galway city: politics, class and culture' in Chris Curtin, Hastings Donnan and Thomas M. Wilson (eds), *Irish Urban Cultures* (Belfast, 1993), pp. 181–201.

Helleiner, Jane, 'Gypsies, Celts and tinkers: colonial antecedents of anti-traveller racism in Ireland', *Ethnic and Racial Studies* 18, 3 (1995), pp. 532–54.

Helleiner, Jane, '"Women of the itinerant class": gender and anti-Traveller racism in Ireland', *Women's Studies International Forum* 20, 2 (1997), pp. 275–87.

Helleiner, Jane, '"Menace to the social order": anti-Traveller discourse in the Irish Parliament 1939–59', *Canadian Journal of Irish Studies* 24, 1 (July 1998), pp. 75–91.

Helleiner, Jane, *Irish Travellers: Racism and the Politics of Culture* (Toronto, Buffalo, London, 2000).

Helleiner, Jane and Szuchewcz, Bohdan, 'Discourses of exclusion: the Irish press and Travelling people' in Stephen Riggins (ed.), *The Language and Politics of Exclusion: Others in Discourse* (London, 1997), pp. 109–30.

Heuss, Herbert, 'Anti-Gypsyism research: the creation of a new field of study' in Thomas Acton (ed.), *Scholarship and the Gypsy Struggle: Commitment in Romani Studies, a Collection of Papers and Poems to Celebrate Donald Kenrick's 70th year* (Hertfordshire, 2000), pp. 52–67.

Hopper, Keith, '"A Gallous story and a dirty deed": word and image in Neil Jordan and Joe Comerford's *Traveller* (1981)', *Irish Studies Review* 9, 2 (2001), pp. 179–92.

Hyde, Douglas, 'The Tinker and the Sheeog' in Lady (Augusta) Gregory, *Poets and Dreamers: Studies and Translations from the Irish by Lady Gregory including Nine Plays by Douglas Hyde* (New York, 1974), pp. 194–204.

Joyce, Nan and Farmer, Anna, *Traveller: An Autobiography* (Dublin, 1986).

Keane, Hawley, *National Council for Travelling People 1969–85: A Short History* (Dublin, 1989).

Kearns, Kevin C., 'Irish Tinkers: an itinerant population in transition', *Annals of the Association of American Geographers* 67, 4 (1977) pp. 538–48.

Kearns, Kevin C., 'Population shift and settlement patterns of Irish Travellers', *Irish Geography* 11 (1978), pp. 23–34.

Kenrick, Donald, 'Irish Travellers – A unique phenomenon in Europe?' in May McCann, Séamas Ó Síocháin and Joseph Ruane (eds), *Irish Travellers: Culture and Ethnicity* (Belfast, 1996), pp. 20–35.

Lentin, Ronit and McVeigh, Robbie (eds), *Racism and Anti-Racism in Ireland* (Belfast, 2002).

Lewy, Guenter, *The Nazi Persecution of the Gypsies* (Oxford, 2000).

Liegeois, Jean-Pierre, *Gypsies and Travellers: Socio-Cultural Data* (Strasbourg, 1987).

Liegeois, Jean-Pierre, *School Provision for Ethnic Minorities: The Gypsy Paradigm* (Hatfield, 1998)

Mac Énrí, Mícheál, '"Ceant" agus Saoghal na dTincéirí', *Béaloideas* 9, 2 (1939), pp. 219–29.

Mac Gréine, Pádraig, 'Further notes on tinkers "cant"', *Béaloideas* 4, 3 (1934), pp. 259–63.

Mac Gréine, Pádraig, 'Irish Tinkers or "Travellers": some notes on their manners and customs, and their secret language or "cant"', *Béaloideas* 3, 2 (1931), pp. 170–186.

Macalister, R. A. Stewart, *The Secret Languages of Ireland: with Special Reference to the Origin and Nature of the Shelta Language Partly Based upon the Collections and Manuscripts of the late John Sampson* (Cambridge, 1937).

MacDonagh, Michael, 'Origins of the Travelling people' in Frank Murphy and Cathleen MacDonagh (eds), *Travellers: Citizens of Ireland: Our Challenge to an Intercultural Irish Society in the 21st Century* (Dublin, 2000), pp. 21–5.

MacLaughlin, Jim, 'Nation building, social closure and anti-Traveller racism in Ireland', *Sociology* 33, 1 (1999), pp. 129–51.

MacLaughlin, Jim, 'The political geography of anti-Traveller racism in Ireland: the politics of exclusion and the geography of closure', *Political Geography* 17, 4 (1998), pp. 417–35.

McLaughlin, Jim, *Travellers and Ireland: Whose Country? Whose History?* (Cork, 1995).

Maher, Sean, *The Road to God Knows Where: A Memoir of a Travelling Boyhood* (Dublin, 1998).

Mayall, David, *Gypsy-Travellers in Nineteenth-Century Society* (Cambridge, 1988).

Mayall, David, *English Gypsies and State Policies* (Hertfordshire, 1995).

Mayall, David, *Gypsy Identities 1500–2000: from Moon-Men to the Ethnic Romany* (London, 2003).

McCann, May, Ó Síocháin, Séamas and Ruane, Joseph (eds), *Irish Travellers: Culture and Ethnicity* (Belfast, 1996).

McCarthy, Patricia, 'The sub-culture of poverty reconsidered' in May McCann, Séamas Ó Síocháin and Joseph Ruane (eds), *Irish Travellers: Culture and Ethnicity* (Belfast, 1996), pp. 121–9.

McKeown, Kieran and McGrath, Bríd, *Accommodating Travelling People: a Study of Accommodation for Travelling People in the Greater Dublin Area* (Dublin, 1996).

McVeigh, Robbie, 'Irish Travellers and the logic of genocide' in Michel Peillon and Eamonn Slater (eds), *Encounters with Modern Ireland* (Dublin, 1998), pp. 155–62.

McVeigh, Robbie, 'Theorising sedentarism: the roots of anti-nomadism' in Thomas Acton (ed.), *Gypsy Politics and Traveller Identity* (Hertfordshire, 1997), pp. 7–25.

Mercier, Vivian, 'The tinker's wedding' in S. B. Bushru (ed.), *Sunshine and Moon's Delight: A Centenary Tribute to J. M. Synge 1871–1909* (n.p., 1972), pp. 75–90.

Munnelly, Tom, *Songs of the Irish Travellers 1967–75* (Dublin, 1983).

Murphy, Frank and MacDonagh, Cathleen (eds), *Travellers: Citizens of Ireland: Our Challenge to an Intercultural Irish Society in the 21st Century* (Dublin, 2000).

Navan Travellers Heritage Teamwork, *Now and Then* (Navan, 1996).

Navan Travellers Heritage Teamwork, *Travellers… Their Life and Times* (July 1992, Navan).

Ní Fhloinn, Bairbre, 'Irish Travellers and the oral tradition' in Pavee Point, *A Heritage Ahead: Cultural Action and Travellers* (Dublin, 1995), pp. 63–85.

Ní Fhloinn, Bairbre, 'Storytelling traditions of Irish Travellers', *The Field Day Anthology of Irish Writing: Irish Women's Writing and Traditions*, vol. IV (Cork, 2002), pp. 1263–83.

Ní Nualláin, Sinéad and Forde, Mary, *Changing Needs of Irish Travellers: Health, Education and Social Issues* (Galway, 1992).

Ní Shúinéir, Sinéad, 'Irish Travellers, ethnicity and the origins question' in May McCann, Séamas Ó Síocháin and Joseph Ruane (eds), *Irish Travellers: Culture and Ethnicity* (Belfast, 1996), pp. 54–77.

Ní Shúinéir, Sinéad, 'Why do Gaujos hate Gypsies so much anyway? A case study' in Thomas Acton (ed.), *Gypsy Politics and Traveller Identity* (Hertfordshire, 1997), pp. 26–53.

Ní Shúinéir, Sinéad, 'Othering the Irish (Travellers)' in Ronit Lentin and Robbie McVeigh (eds), *Racism and Anti-Racism in Ireland* (Belfast, 2002), pp. 177–92.

Ní Shúinéir, Sinéad, 'Travellers or the travelling people' in Brian Lalor (ed.), *The Encyclopedia of Ireland* (Dublin, 2003), pp. 1071–3

Ní Shúinéir, Sinéad, 'From apocrypha to canon: inventing Traveller history', *History Ireland* 12, 4 (2004), pp. 15–19.

Noonan, Paul, 'Pathologisation and resistance: Travellers, nomadism and the state' in Hainsworth, Paul (ed.), *Divided Society: Ethnic Minorities and Racism in Northern Ireland* (London, 1998), pp. 152–83.

Ó Baoill, Dónall P., 'Travellers' Cant: language or register?' in May McCann, Séamas Ó Síocháin, and Joseph Ruane (eds), *Irish Travellers: Culture and Ethnicity* (Belfast, 1996), pp. 155–69.

Ó Riain, Sean, *Solidarity with Travellers: A Story of Settled People Making a Stand for Travellers* (Dublin, 2000).

O'Brien, Ann, 'Journey's end: customs around death' in Frank Murphy and Kathleen MacDonagh (eds), *Travellers Citizens of Ireland: Our Challenge to an Intercultural Irish Society in the 21st century* (Dublin, 2000), pp. 80–6.

O'Connell, John, 'Travellers in Ireland: an examination of discrimination and racism', in Ronit Lentin and Robbie McVeigh (eds), *Racism and Anti-Racism in Ireland* (Belfast, 2002), pp. 49–62.

O'Malley, Mary, 'Emigration of Irish Travellers', in Mary Clancy (ed.), *The Emigrant Experience* (Galway, 1991), pp. 102–10.

O'Sullivan, John C., 'The tools and trade of a tinker' in Caomhín Ó Danachair (ed.), *Folk and Farm: Essays in Honour of A. T. Lucas* (Dublin, 1976), pp. 208–17.

Okely, Judith, *The Traveller-Gypsies* (Cambridge, 1983).

Pavee Point, *A Heritage Ahead: Cultural Action and Travellers* (Dublin, 1995).

Puxon, Grattan, 'The Romani movement: rebirth and the first World Romani Congress in retrospect' in Thomas Acton (ed.), *Scholarship and the Gypsy Struggle: Commitment in*

Romani Studies, a Collection of Papers and Poems to Celebrate Donald Kenrick's 70th year (Hertfordshire, 2000), pp. 94–113.

Rehfisch, Farnham, *Gypsies, Tinkers and other Travellers* (London, 1975).

Rottman, David B., Tussing, A. Dale and Wiley, Miriam, W., *The Population Structure and Living Circumstances of Irish Travellers: Results from the 1981 Census of Travelling Families* (Dublin, 1986).

Salo, Matt T.(ed.), *One Hundred Years of Gypsy Studies* (Publication No. 5, Gypsy Lore Society, Maryland, 1990).

Sibley, David, *Outsiders in Urban Societies* (Oxford, 1981).

Smith D., and Broomfield, J., 'Romani and Shelta useage by house-dwelling children', *Journal of the Gypsy Lore Society* series 4, 1, 2 (1977), p. 153.

Starkie, Walter, *Raggle-Taggle: Adventures with a Fiddle in Hungary and Roumania* (London, 1933).

Weldon, Helen, 'Tinkers, sorners and other vagabonds', *New Ireland Review* 26, 1 (1906), pp. 43–7.

Whyte, Gerry, *Social Inclusion and the Legal System: Public Interest Law in Ireland* (Dublin, 2001).

Wiedel, Janine, *Irish Tinkers* (London, 1976).

Wren, Maev-Ann, 'The Travelling people – racialism in Ireland', *Crane Bag* 5, 1 (1981), pp. 17–21.

OTHER PUBLISHED WORKS

Abercrombie, Patrick, 'The Dublin town plan', *Studies* 31 (June 1942), pp. 155–60.

Adler, Jeffrey, '"Vagging the demons and scondrel": vagrancy and the growth of St Louis, 1830–61' *Journal of Urban History* 13, 1 (1986), pp. 3–30.

Arensberg, Conrad M., *The Irish Countryman* (New York, 1937).

Arensberg, Conrad M, and Kimball, Solon T., *Family and Community in Ireland* (Cambridge Mass., 1948).

Bannon, Michael J. (ed.), *The Evolution of Irish Planning* (Dublin, 1985).

Bannon, Michael J., 'Irish planning from 1921–1945: an overview' in Michael J. Bannon, Kevin I. Nowlan, John Hendry and Ken Mawhinney (eds), *Planning the Irish Experience 1920–88* (Dublin, 1989), pp. 13–70.

Bannon, Michael J., Nowlan, Kevin I., Hendry, John and Mawhinney, Ken (eds), *Planning the Irish Experience 1920–88* (Dublin, 1989).

Barrington, Ruth, *Health, Medicine and Politics in Ireland 1900–70* (Dublin, 1987).

Barrington, T. J., *The Irish Administrative System* (Dublin, 1980).

Basset, Philippa, *A List of the Historical Records of the Caravan Club of Great Britain and Ireland* (Centre of Urban and Regional Studies, University of Birmingham and Institute of Agricultural History, University of Reading, 1980).

Beecher, Seán, *A Dictionary of Cork Slang* (Cork, 1999).

Beiner, Guy, 'The invention of tradition?', *History Review: Journal of the UCD Historical Society* 12 (2001), pp. 1–10.

Bhreatnach, Nioclás, *Ar Bóthar Dom* (Rinn Ó gCúanach, 1998).

Bluestone, Daniel M., '"The pushcart evil" pedlars, merchants and New York's city streets 1890–1940', *Journal of Urban History* 18, 1 (1991), pp. 68–92.

Boll, Heinrich, *Irish Journal* (London, New York, Toronto, Sydney, 1967).

Boyce, George D. and O'Day, Alan (eds), *The Making of Modern Irish History: Revisionism and the Revisionist Controversy* (London and New York, 1996).

Bradley, Dan, *Farm Labourers: Irish Struggle 1900–76* (Belfast, 1988).

Breathnach, M., 'The Department of Education' in F. C. King (ed.), *Public Administration in Ireland*, vol. III (1954), pp. 87–108.

Breathnach, Seamus, *The Irish Police* (Dublin, 1974).

Breen, Richard, 'Social class, schools and society' in Joe Mulholland and Dermot Keogh (eds), *Education in Ireland: For What and For Whom?* (Cork and Dublin, 1990) pp. 40–48.

Breen, Richard, Hannan, D., Rottman, D. B. and Whelan, C. T., *Understanding Contemporary Ireland: State, Class and Development in the Republic of Ireland* (Dublin, 1990).

Breen, Richard and Whelan, C. T., *Social Mobility and Social Class in Ireland* (Dublin, 1996).

Brett, David, 'The construction of heritage' in Michael Cronin and Barbara O'Connor (eds), *Tourism in Ireland: A Critical Analysis* (Cork, 1993), pp. 183–202.

Brown, Stewart J., and Miller, David W. (eds), *Piety and Power in Ireland 1760–1960: Essays in Honour of Emmet Larkin* (Belfast and Notre Dame, 2000).

Brown, Terence, *Ireland: A Social and Cultural History* (London, 1985).

Browne, M. J., *The Synod of Maynooth: Decrees which Affect the Catholic Laity* (Dublin, 1930).

Brown-May, Andrew, 'A charitable indulgence: street stalls and the transformation of public space in Melbourne *c.*1850–1920', *Urban History* 23, 1 (1996) pp. 48–71.

Burke, Helen, *The People and the Poor Law in Nineteenth-Century Ireland* (Dublin, 1987).

Burke, Helen, 'Foundation stones of Irish social policy 1831–1951' in Gabriel Kiely, Anne O'Donnell, Patricia Kennedy, and Suzanne Quin (eds), *Irish Social Policy in Context* (Dublin, 1999), pp. 11–32.

Burke, Joanna, *Husbandry to Housewifery: Women, Economic Change and Housework in Ireland 1890–1914* (Oxford, 1993).

Burke, Peter, *Popular Culture in Early Modern Europe* (Aldershot, 1978).

Burke, Peter, *History and Social Theory* (Cambridge, 1999).

Burke, Peter (ed.), *New Perspectives on Historical Writing* (2nd edn, Cambridge, 2001).

Butler Cullingford, Elizabeth, *Ireland's Others: Ethnicity and Gender in Irish Literature and Popular Culture* (Cork, 2001).

Butlin, R. A. (ed.), *The Development of the Irish Town* (London, 1977).

Callan, T., Nolan, B., Whelan, B. J., Hannan, D. F. with Creighton, S., *Poverty, Income and Welfare in Ireland* (Dublin, 1989).

Canavan, Joseph E., 'Property and the Church', *Studies* 24 (Mar.1923), pp. 391–405.

Canavan, Joseph E., 'The Poor Law Report', *Studies* 16 (Dec. 1927), pp. 631–40.

Carroll, Patrick, *The Garda Síochána Guide* (3rd edn, Tralee, 1956).

Casey, Joanne, *Bowling Down London Way* (Essex, 1994).

Ceallacháin, Seán C. N., *Na Spailpíní* (Dublin, 1992).

City and County Managers Association, *City and County Management 1929–90: A Retrospective* (Dublin, 1991).

Clancy, P., Drudy, S., Lynch, K., and O'Dowd, L. (eds), *Ireland: A Sociological Profile* (Dublin, 1986).

Clarke, Howard B. (ed.), *Irish Cities* (Dublin, 1995).

Clear, Caitríona, 'Homelessness, crime, punishment and poor relief in Galway 1850–1914: An Introduction', *Journal of the Galway Archaeological and Historical Society,* 50 (1998), pp. 118–34.

Clear, Caitríona, *Nuns in Nineteenth-Century Ireland* (Dublin, 1987).

Collins, John (2nd edn by Desmond Roche), *Local Government* (Dublin, 1963).

Collins, Neil, *Local Government Managers at Work: The City and County Manager System of Local Government in the Republic of Ireland* (Dublin, 1987).

Comerford, James J., *My Kilkenny IRA Days 1916–22* (Kilkenny, 1978)

Connolly, S. J. (ed.), *The Oxford Companion to Irish History* (Oxford, 1998).

Conroy, Pauline, 'From the fifties to the nineties: social policy comes out of the shadows' in Gabriel Kiely, Anne O'Donnell, Patricia Kennedy and Suzanne Quin (eds), *Irish Social Policy in Context* (Dublin, 1999), pp. 33–50.

Convery, Frank J., and Schmid, A. Allan, *Policy Aspects of Land-Use Planning in Ireland* (Dublin, 1983)

Cook, Geoffrey, 'Britain's legacy to the Irish social system' in P. J. Drudy (ed.), *Irish Studies 5: Ireland and Brtain since 1922* (Cambridge, 1986), pp. 65–86.

Coolahan, John, *Irish Education: History and Structure* (Dublin, 1981).

Corish, Patrick J., *The Irish Catholic Experience: A Historical Survey* (Dublin, 1985).

Cork Corporation, *Cork City Development Plan 1969* (Cork, 1969).

Cork Town Planning Association, *Cork: A Civic Survey* (Liverpool, 1926).

Cormack, Bill, *A History of Holidays 1812–1990* (London, 1998).

Coughlan, Anthony, 'The social scene', *Adminstration* 14, 3 (1966), pp. 204–15.

Coyne, E. J., 'Cooperative organisation of society', *Studies* 23 (June 1934), pp. 185–202.

Coyne, E. J., 'Health Bill 1952', *Studies* 42 (Mar. 1953), pp. 1–22.

Cronin, Denis A., 'The great horse-fair of Cahirmee County Cork' in Denis A. Cronin, Jim Gilligan and Karina Holton (eds), *Irish Fairs and Markets: Studies in Local History* (Dublin, 2001), pp. 124–42.

Cronin, Denis A., Gilligan, Jim and Holton, Karina (eds), *Irish Fairs and Markets: Studies in Local History* (Dublin, 2001).

Cronin, Maura, 'From the 'flat 'o the city' to the top of the hill': Cork since 1700' in Howard B. Clarke (ed.), *Irish Cities* (Dublin, 1995), pp. 55–68.

Cronin, Michael, 'City administration in Ireland', *Studies*, 12 (September 1923), pp. 345–56.

Cronin, Michael, 'Fellow Travellers: contemporary travel writing and Ireland' in Michael Cronin and Barbara O'Connor (eds), *Tourism in Ireland: A Critical Analysis* (Cork, 1993), pp. 51–67.

Cronin, Michael and O'Connor, Barbara (eds), *Tourism in Ireland: A Critical Analysis* (Cork, 1993).

Crossman, Virginia, *Local Government in Nineteenth-Century Ireland* (Belfast, 1994).

Cullen, Mary, 'Breadwinners and providers: women in the household economy of labouring families 1835–6' in Maria Luddy and C. Murphy (eds), *Women Surviving: Studies in Irish Women's History in the Nineteenth and Twentieth Centuries* (Dublin, 1989), pp. 85–116.

Cullen, Paul, *Refugees and Asylum Seekers in Ireland* (Cork, 2000).

Cummins, Robert C., *Unusual Medical Cases: A Cork Physicians Memories* (Cork, 1962).

Curtain, Chris, Donnan, Hastings and Wilson, Thomas M. (eds), *Irish Urban Cultures* (Belfast, 1993).

Curtin, Chris, and Wilson, Thomas M. (eds), *Ireland from Below: Social Change and Local Communities* (Galway, 1989).

Dalton, R. J., 'The slum problem in Cork' in B. G. MacCarthy (ed.), *Some Problems of Child Welfare, University and Labour Series* no. 6 (Cork, 1945), pp. 71–83.

Daly, Mary E., *Social and Economic History of Ireland since 1800* (Dublin, 1981).

Daly, Mary E., *Dublin, the Deposed Capital: A Social and Economic History 1860–1914* (Cork, 1984).

Daly, Mary E., 'Irish Urban History: a Survey', *Urban History Yearbook* (1986), pp. 61–72.

Daly, Mary E., *Industrial Development and Irish National Identity 1922–39* (New York, 1992).

Daly, Mary E., *The Buffer State: the Historical Roots of the Department of the Environment* (Dublin, 1997).

Daly, Mary E., *The Spirit of Earnest Inquiry: the Statistical and Social Inquiry Society of Ireland 1847–1997* (Dublin, 1997).

Daly, Mary E. and Dickson, D. (eds), *The origins of popular literacy in Ireland: Language Change and Educational Development 1700–1920* (Dublin, 1990).

Daunton, M. J., 'Payment and participation: welfare and state formation in Britain 1900–51', *Past and Present* 150 (1996), pp. 169–216.

Davis, E. E., Grube, Joel E. and Morgan, Mark, *Attitudes towards poverty and related social issues in Ireland* (ESRI, Dublin, 1984).

Davis, John (ed.), *Rural Change in Ireland* (Belfast, 1999).

Deakin, Nicholas, *The Politics of Welfare: Continuities and Change* (New York and London, 1994).

Deeny, James, *To Cure and to Care: the Memoirs of a Chief Medical Officer* (Dublin, 1989).

Devane, Rev. R.S., *A Guide for Parish Councils in Ireland* (Dublin, 1940).

Devlin, John, 'The state of health in Ireland', in Joseph Robins (ed.), *Reflections on Health: Commemorating 50 years of the Department of Health 1947–97* (Dublin, 1997), pp. 10–28.

Dillon, T. W. T., 'Public health planning', *Studies* 33 (Dec. 1944), pp. 433–9.

Dillon, T. W. T., 'The social services in Éire', *Studies* 34 (Sept. 1945), pp. 325–36.

Dillon, T. W. T., 'The Society of St Vincent de Paul in Ireland 1845–1945', *Studies,* 34 (Dec. 1945), pp. 515–21.

Doherty, Philip, 'The last pawnshops of Dublin City', *Dublin Historical Record,* 47, 1 (1994), pp. 87–94.

Donnelly, Brian, *For the Betterment of the People: A History of Wicklow County Council* (Wicklow, 1999).

Donnelly, J. S., *Landlord and Tenant in Nineteenth-Century Ireland* (Dublin, 1973).

Donnelly, J. S., *The Land and the People of Nineteenth-Century Cork: The Rural Economy and the Land Question* (London and Boston, 1975).

Donnelly, J. S. and Miller, Kerby A. (eds), *Irish Popular Culture 1650–1850* (Dublin, 1999).

Drudy, P.J. (ed.), *Irish Studies 5: Ireland and Britain since 1922* (Cambridge, 1986).

Dunne, Eamonn, 'Action and reaction: Catholic lay organisations in Dublin in the 1920s and 1930s', *Archivium Hibernicum* XLVIII (1994), pp. 107–18.

Dyos, H. T. and Wolff, M. (eds), *The Victorian City: Images and Realities* (London and Boston, 1973).

Ellis, Peter Berresford, *A History of the Irish Working Class* (London, 1972).

English, Richard, *Radicals and the Republic: Socialist Republicanism in the Irish Free State 1925–37* (Oxford, 1994).

English, Richard and Walker, Graham (eds), *Unionism in Modern Ireland: New Perspectives on Politics and Culture* (London and New York, 1996).

Evans, E. Estyn, *Irish Folkways* (London, 1989).

Fahey, Tony and Watson, Dorothy, *An Analysis of Social Housing Need* (Dublin, 1995).

Fanning, Bryan, 'The mixed economy of welfare' in Gabriel Kiely, Anne O'Donnell, Patricia Kennedy and Suzanne Quin (eds), *Irish Social Policy in Context* (Dublin, 1999), pp. 51–69.

Farmar, Tony, *Ordinary Lives: Three Generations of Irish Middle-Class Experience, 1907, 1932, 1962* (Dublin, 1991).

Feehan, James A., *A Fool for Christ: the Priest with the Trailer* (Cork, 1993).

Ferriter, Diarmaid, *Cuimhnigh ar Luimneach: A History of Limerick County Council 1898–1998* (Limerick, 1999).

Finnane, Mark, *Insanity and the Insane in Post-Famine Ireland* (London, 1981).

Finnegan, Francis, *A Study of Irish Immigrants in York 1840–75* (Cork, 1982).

Fitzpatrick, A. J, and Vaughan, W. E. (eds), *Irish Historical Statistics: Population 1821–1971* (Dublin, 1978).

Fitzpatrick, David, *Politics and Irish Life 1913–1921: Provincial Experience of War and Revolution* (Cork, 1998).

Fitzpatrick, Diarmuid, *The Active Service Unit: A Guide to Catholic Action in the Sphere of Social Reconstruction* (Dublin, 1933).

Fitzpatrick, Jim, *Three Brass Balls: the Story of the Irish Pawnshop* (Cork, 2001).

Foley, Tadhg and Ryder, Seán (eds), *Ideology and Ireland in the Nineteenth Century* (Dublin, 1998).

Ford, P. and G., *A Select List of Reports of Inquiries of the Irish Dáil and Senate 1922–70* (Dublin, 1974).

Fyfe, Nicholas R. (ed.), *Images of the Street: Planning, Identity and Control in Public Space* (London, 1998).

Gailey, Alan and Ó hÓgáin, Daithí (eds), *Gold under the Furze: Studies in Folk Tradition Presented to Caoimhín Danachair* (Dublin, 1982).

Galvin, Patrick, *The Raggy Boy Trilogy* (Dublin, 2002).

Garda Síochána, *Garda Síochána Code 1928* (Dublin, 1928).

Garda Síochána, *Manual of Law and Police Duties* (1st edn, Dublin, 1942).

Gibbon, P., 'Arensberg and Kimball revisited', *Economy and Society* 2, 4 (1973), pp. 479–98.

Gibbons, Luke, *Transformations in Irish Culture* (Cork, 1996).

Giddens, Anthony and Held, David (eds), *Classes, Power and Conflict: Classical and Contemporary Debates* (London, 1992).

Gillespie, Raymond and Hill, Myrtle (eds), *Doing Irish Local History: Pursuit and Practice* (Belfast, 1998).

Glynn, Sean, 'Irish immigration to Britain 1911–1951: patterns and policy', *Irish Economic and Social History* 8 (1981), pp. 50–69.

Goldstorm, J. M., and Clarkson, L. A. (eds), *Irish Population, Economy and Society: Essays in Honour of the Late K. H. Connell* (Oxford, 1981).

Goldthorpe, J. H., and Whelan, C. T. (eds), *The Development of Industrial Society in Ireland* (Oxford, 1992).

Graham, B. J. and Proudfoot, L. J. (eds), *An Historical Geography of Ireland* (London and San Diego, 1993).

Gray, Breda, 'Longings and belongings – gendered spatialities of Irishness', *Irish Studies Review* 7, 2 (1999), pp. 193–210.

Gray, Breda, 'Gendering the Irish diaspora: questions of enrichment, hybridisation and return', *Womens Studies International Forum* 23, 2 (2000), pp. 167–185.

Gregory, Lady (Augusta), *Poets and Dreamers: Studies and Translations from the Irish by Lady Gregory including nine plays by Douglas Hyde* (New York, 1974).

Gulliver, P. H., and Silverman, M., *Approaching the Past: Historical Anthropology through Irish Case Studies* (New York, 1992).

Gulliver, P. H., and Silverman, M., 'Hucksters and petty retailers in Thomastown 1880–1945', *Old Kilkenny Review,* 4 (1993), pp. 1094–1100.

Gulliver, P. H. and Silverman, M., *Merchants and Shopkeepers: An Historical Anthropology of an Irish Market Town 1200–1991* (Toronto, 1995).

Hainsworth, Paul (ed.), *Divided Society: Ethnic Minorities and Racism in Northern Ireland* (London, 1998)

Hallack, Cecily Rosemary, *The Legion of Mary* (5th edn, London, 1950).

Hannan, Damian, *Displacement and Development: Class, Kinship and Social Change in Irish Rural Communities* (Dublin, 1979).

Hannon, Philip, and Gallagher, Jackie (eds), *Taking the Long View: 70 years of Fianna Fáil* (Dublin, 1996).

Hardiman, Niamh, 'Inequality and representation of interests' in William Crotty and David E. Schmitt (eds), *Ireland and the Politics of Change* (London, 1998), pp. 122–43.

Harrison, R. A., *The Irish Digest 1939–48* (Dublin, 1952).

Hart, Peter, *The IRA and its Enemies: Violence and Community in Cork, 1916–23* (Oxford, 1998).

Hazelkorn, Ellen, 'Class, clientelism and the political process in the Republic of Ireland' in P. Clancy, S. Drudy, K. Lynch and L. O'Dowd (eds), *Ireland: A Sociological Profile* (Dublin, 1986), pp. 326–43.

Healy, John, *The Death of an Irish Town* (Cork 1968).

Henchion, Richard, *Bishopstown, Wilton and Glasheen: A Picture of Life in the Three Western Suburbs of Cork from Early Days to Modern Times* (Cork, 2001).

Hensey, Brian, *The Health Services of Ireland* (Dublin, 1959).

Herman Rice, John, *The Irish Police Guide for the Use of the Civic Guard* (11th edn, Dublin, 1926).

Hickey, D. J., and Doherty, J. E., *A Dictionary of Irish History* (Dublin, 1987).

Hobsbawm, Eric, *On History* (London, 1999).

Hogan, G. W., 'The early judgements of Mr Justice Brian Walsh' in James O'Reilly (ed.), *Human Rights and Constitutional Law: Essays in Honour of Brian Walsh* (Dublin, 1992), pp. 37–48.

Holdstock, Mark, *The Great Fair: Horse Dealing at Ballinasloe* (London, 1993).

Horgan, J. J., 'Local government developments at home and abroad', *Studies,* 15 (Dec. 1926), pp. 529–541.

Horgan, Michael and Carroll, Patrick, *The Garda Síochána Guide* (Dublin, 1934).

Horowitz, Irving Louis, *The Decomposition of Sociology* (New York, Oxford, 1994).

Houlihan, Michael, *Puck Fair: History and Traditions* (Limerick, 1999).

Hourihan, Kevin, 'The evolution and influence of town planning in Cork' in P. O'Flannagan and C. G. Buttimer (eds), *Cork History and Society: Interdisciplinary Essays on the History of an Irish County* (Dublin, 1993), pp. 941–61.

Hourihan, Kevin, 'Urban population density patterns and change in Ireland, 1901–1979', *Economic and Social Review* 13, 2 (1982), pp. 125–47.

Hout, M., *Following in Fathers Footsteps: Social Mobility in Ireland* (London and Cambridge, Mass., 1989).

Hughes, J. G and Walsh B. M., *Internal Migration Flows in Ireland and their Determinants* (Dublin, 1980)

Humphreys, Robert, *No Fixed Abode: A History of Responses to the Roofless and the Rootless in Britain* (London and New York, 1999).

Hunter, Stephen (ed.), *Life Journeys: Living Folklore in Ireland Today* (Cork, 1999).

Hutchinson, John and Smith, Anthony D. (eds), *Ethnicity* (Oxford and New York, 1996).

Hyland, Áine and Milne, Kenneth (eds), *Irish Education Documents Volume II: A Selection of Extracts of Documents Relating to the History of Education from 1922 to 1991 in the Irish Free State and the Republic of Ireland* (Dublin, 1992).

Inglis, Tom, *Moral Monopoly: The Catholic Church in Modern Irish Society* (Dublin, 1987).

Irish Country Women's Association, *Eadrainn: a History of the Cork Federation 1936–94* (Cork, 1994)

Irish priest, *A Manual of Catholic Action: Its Nature and Requirements* (Dublin, 1933).

Johnson, Stowers, *Before and After Puck: Cork, Killarney and County Kerry* (London, 1953),

Jordan, Alison, *Who Cared: Victorian and Edwardian Charity in Belfast* (Belfast, n.d.).

Kaim-Caudle, P. R., *Social Security in Ireland and Western Europe* (Dublin, 1964).

Kaim-Caudle, P. R., *Housing in Ireland: Some Economic Aspects* (Dublin, 1965).

Kearney, Timothy, 'Editorial – Minorities in Ireland', *Crane Bag,* 5, 1 (1981), pp. 3–4.

Keenan, Desmond J., *The Catholic Church in Nineteenth-Century Ireland: A Sociological Study* (Dublin, 1983).

Kelly, Adrian, 'Catholic action and the development of the Irish welfare state in the 1930s and 1940s', *Archivium Hibernicum* 53 (1999), pp. 107–17.

Keogh, Dermot, *Jews in Twentieth Century Ireland: Refugees, Anti-Semitism and the Holocaust* (Cork, 1998).

Keogh, Dermot, *The Rise of the Irish Working Class: The Dublin Trade Union Movement and Labour Leadership 1890–1914* (Belfast, 1982).

Kiely, Gabriel, O'Donnell, Anne, Kennedy, Patricia, and Quin, Suzanne (eds), *Irish Social Policy in Context* (Dublin, 1999).

Kinealy, Christine, 'The workhouse system in County Waterford 1838–1923' in William Nolan and Thomas P. Power (eds), *Waterford: Interdisciplinary Essays on the History of an Irish County* (Dublin 1992), pp. 579–612.

King, F. C. (ed.), *Public Administration in Ireland Volume III* (1954).

Kuhling, Carmen, 'New age travellers on cool mountain' in Michel Peillon and Eamonn Slater (eds), *Encounters with Modern Ireland* (Dublin, 1998), pp. 147–53.

Lalor, Brian (ed.), *The Encyclopedia of Ireland* (Dublin, 2003)

Lankford, Siobhán, *The Hope and the Sadness: Personal Recollections of Troubled Times in Ireland* (Cork, 1980).

Larkin, Emmet, *The Historical Dimensions of Irish Catholicism* (Washington and Dublin, 1997).

Leahy, Tim, *Memoirs of a Garda Superintendent* (County Clare, 1996).

Lee, Joseph, *Modernisation of Irish Society 1848–1918* (Dublin, 1973).

Lee, Joseph (ed.), *Ireland: Towards a Sense of Place* (Cork, 1985).

Lee, Joseph, 'Centralisation and community' in Lee, Joseph (ed.), *Ireland: Towards a Sense of Place* (Cork, 1985) pp. 84–102.

Lee, Joseph, *Ireland 1912–85: Politics and Society* (Cambridge, 1989).

Lees, Lynn Hollen, *The Solidarities of Strangers: The English Poor Law and the People 1700–1948* (New York and Cambridge, 1998).

Legion of Mary, *The Legion of Mary* (Dublin, 1937).

Legion of Mary, *The Official Handbook of the Legion of Mary* (Dublin, 1993).

Leonard, Fr CP., *The Legion of Mary* (London, 1933).

Logan, Patrick, *Fair Day: the Story of Irish Fairs and Markets* (Belfast, 1986).

Lucey, Con, 'The Beveridge Report and Éire', *Studies,* 33 (March 1943), pp. 36–44.

Luddy, Maria, *Women and Philanthropy in Nineteenth-Century Ireland* (Cambridge, 1995).

Luddy, Maria and Murphy, C. (eds), *Women Surviving: Studies in Irish Women's History in the Nineteenth and Twentieth Centuries* (Dublin, 1989).

Mac Cárthaigh, David, *The Gurranabraher Story: A History of its Place and its People* (Cork, 1997).

MacCarthy, B. G. (ed.), *Some Problems of Child Welfare University and Labour Series No. 6* (Cork, 1945).

MacNeill, Eoin, *Phases of Irish History* (Dublin, 1937).

Malcolm, Elizabeth, *Ireland Sober, Ireland Free: Drink and Temperance in Nineteenth-Century Ireland* (Dublin, 1986).

Malcolm, Elizabeth and Jones, Greta (eds), *Medicine, Disease and the State in Ireland 1650–1940* (Cork, 1999).

Marnane, J., *Cork County Council: the First Hundred Years* (Cork, 1999).

Marwick, Arthur, *The Sixties: Cultural Revolution in Britain, France, Italy and the US c.1958–1974* (Oxford and New York, 1998).

Mc Cormack, W. J. (ed.), *The Blackwell Companion to Modern Irish Culture* (Oxford and Mass., 1999).

McCullagh, Ciaran, *Crime in Ireland: A Sociological Introduction* (Cork, 1996).

McKibbin, Ross, *Classes and Cultures: England 1918–1951* (Oxford, 2000).

McMahon, Deirdre, 'John Charles McQuaid: Archbishop of Dublin 1940–72' in Kelly, James and Keogh, Dáire (eds), *History of the Catholic Diocese of Dublin* (Dublin, 2000).

McManus, Ruth, *Dublin, 1910–1940: Shaping the City and Suburbs* (Dublin, 2002)

McNiffe, Louis, *A History of the Garda Síochána: A Social History of the Force, 1922–52 with an Overview of the Years, 1952–97* (Dublin, 1997).

Mitchell, Arthur, *Revolutionary Government in Ireland: Dáil Éireann 1919–22* (Dublin, 1995).

Morgan, Austen and Purdie, Bob (eds), *Ireland, Divided Nation, Divided Class* (London, 1980).

Mulholland, Joe and Dermot Keogh, *Education in Ireland: For What and For Whom?* (Cork and Dublin, 1990).

Murdoch, Fiona, *Victor Bewley's Memoirs* (Dublin, 2002).

Murphy, Charles K., *The Spirit of Catholic Action* (London, 1943).

Murray Fraser, *John Bull's Other Homes: State Housing and British Policy in Ireland, 1883–1922* (Liverpool, 1996).

Newman, Jeremiah, *The State of Ireland* (Dublin, 1977).

Nolan, Brian, Callan, Tim, Whelan, Christopher T. and Williams, James, *Poverty and Time: Perspectives on the Dynamics of Poverty* (Dublin, 1994).

Nowlan, Kevin I., 'The evolution of Irish planning' in Michael J. Bannon, Kevin I. Nowlan, John Hendry and Ken Mawhinney (eds), *Planning the Irish Experience 1920–88* (Dublin, 1989), pp. 71–85.

Nolan, William (ed.), *The Shaping of Ireland: The Geographical Perspective* (Cork and Dublin, 1986).

Nolan, William and McGrath T. G. (eds), *Tipperary: History and Society* (Dublin, 1985).

Nolan, William and O'Neill, Timothy P. (eds), *Offaly History and Society: Interdisciplinary Essays on the History of an Irish County* (Dublin, 1998).

Nolan, William and Power, Thomas P. (eds), *Waterford: Interdisciplinary Essays on the History of an Irish County* (Dublin 1992).

Nolan, William, Ronayne, Liam and Dunleavy, Mairead (eds), *Donegal History and Society: Interdisciplinary Essays on the History of an Irish County* (Dublin, 1995).

Nolan, William and Whelan, Kevin (eds), *Kilkenny: Interdisciplinary Essays on the History of an Irish County* (Dublin, 1990).

Ó Broin, Leon, *Just Like Yesterday: An Autobiography* (Dublin, 1985?)

O'Callaghan, Antóin, *The Lord Mayors of Cork 1900–2000* (Cork 2000).

Ó Cinnéide, Seamus, *A Law for the Poor: A Study of Home Assistance in Ireland* (Dublin, 1970).

Ó Ciosáin, Niall, 'Boccoughs and God's poor: deserving and undeserving poor in Irish popular culture' in Tadhg Foley and Sean Ryder (eds), *Ideology and Ireland in the Nineteenth Century* (Dublin, 1998), pp. 93–9.

O'Connell, Maurice R. (ed.), *Decentralisation of Government: Proceedings of the Fourth Annual Daniel O'Connell Workshop* (Dublin, 1994).

O'Connor, B., 'Myths and mirrors: tourist images and national identity' in Michael Cronin and Barbara O'Connor (eds), *Tourism in Ireland: A Critical Analysis* (Cork, 1993), pp. 68–85.

O'Connor, Emmet, *A Labour History of Ireland 1824–1960* (Dublin, 1992).

O'Connor, Patrick J., *All Ireland is in and about Rathkeale* (Newcastlewest, Co. Limerick, 1996).

Ó Crualaoich, Gearóid, 'County Cork folklore and its collection' in P. O'Flannagan, P. and C. G. Buttimer (eds), *Cork History and Society: Interdisciplinary Essays on the History of an Irish County* (Dublin, 1993), pp. 919–40.

O'Day, Alan and Stevenson, John (eds), *Irish Historical Documents since 1800* (Dublin 1992).

O'Donnell, Anne, 'Comparing welfare states: considering the case of Ireland's welfare' in Gabriel Kiely, Anne O'Donnell, Patricia Kennedy and Suzanne Quin (eds), *Irish Social Policy in Context* (Dublin, 1999), pp. 70–89.

O'Donnell, E. E., *Fr. Browne's Cork: People and Places 1912–54* (Dublin, 1995).

O'Donnell, Patrick, *The Irish Faction Fighters of the Nineteenth Century* (Dublin, 1975).

O'Dowd, Anne, *Common Clothes and Clothing 1860–1930* (Dublin, 1990).

O'Dowd, Anne, *Spalpeens and Tattie Hokers: History and Folklore of the Irish Migratory Agricultural Worker in Ireland and Britain* (Dublin, 1990).

O'Flaherty, Liam, *The Informer* (UK, 1980).

O'Flanagan, P., and Buttimer, C. G., *Cork History and Society: Interdisciplinary Essays on the History of an Irish County* (Dublin, 1993).

O'Flanagan, P, Ferguson, P. and Whelan, K. (eds), *Rural Ireland 1600–1900: Modernisation and Change* (Cork, 1987).

Ó Giolláin, Diarmuid, 'The Pattern' in J. S. Donnelly and Kerby A. Miller (eds), *Irish Popular Culture 1650–1850* (Dublin, 1999), pp. 201–21.

Ó Giolláin, Diarmuid, *Locating Irish Folklore: Tradition, Modernity and Identity* (Cork, 2000).

Ó Gráda, Cormac, 'Seasonal migration and post-famine adjustment in the west of Ireland', *Studia Hibernica*, 13 (1973), pp. 48–76.

O'Hanlon, Michael, *Hiring Fairs and Farm Workers in North-West Ireland* (Derry, 1992).

O'Leary, Don, *Vocationalism and Social Catholicism in Twentieth-Century Ireland* (Dublin, 2000).

O'Mahony, Colmán, *In the Shadows: Life in Cork 1750–1930* (Cork, 1997).

O'Mahony, Paul, *Prison Policy in Ireland: Criminal Justice versus Social Justice* (Cork, 2000).

Ó Maithiú, Seamus, *The Humours of Donnybrook: Dublin's Famous Fair and its Suppression* (Dublin, 1995).

O'Neill, Tim, 'Tools and things: machinery on Irish farms' in Alan Gailey and Daithí Ó hÓgáin (eds), *Gold under the Furze: Studies in Folk Tradition Presented to Caoimhín Danachair* (Dublin, 1982), pp. 101–14.

O'Reilly, James (ed.), *Human Rights and Constitutional Law: Essays in Honour of Brian Walsh* (Dublin, 1992).

Ó Suilleabháin, Seán, *A Handbook of Irish Folklore* (Detroit, 1970).

Ó Suilleabháin, Seán and Christiansen, R. T. H., *The Types of the Irish Folktale* (Helsinki, 1967)

O'Sullivan, Denis, 'Pre-existing acquaintance and friendship among industrial school boys', *Social Studies, Irish Journal of Sociology* 3, 1 (1974), pp. 13–24.

O'Sullivan, J. J., 'The new social welfare scheme', in F. C. King (ed.), *Public Administration in Ireland Vol. III* (1954), pp. 129–47.

Orwell, George, *Down and Out in Paris and London* (Harmondsworth, 2001).

Pahl, R. E., *Whose City? And Other Essays on Sociology and Planning* (Harlow, 1970).

Peillon, Michel and Slater, Eamonn (eds), *Encounters with Modern Ireland* (Dublin, 1998).

Pfretzschner, Paul A., *The Dynamics of Irish Housing* (Dublin, 1965).

Philpin, C. H. E. (ed.), *Nationalism and Popular Protest in Ireland* (Cambridge, 1987).

Porter, Roy, *The Social History of Madness, Stories of the Insane* (London, 1999).

Prunty, Jacinta, 'From city slums to city sprawl: Dublin from 1800 to the present' in Howard B. Clarke (ed.), *Irish Cities* (Dublin, 1995), pp. 109–22.

Prunty, Jacinta, *Dublin Slums 1800–1925 A Study in Urban Geography* (Dublin, 1998).

Regan, John M., *The Irish Counter-Revolution 1921–1936: Treatyite Politics and Settlement in Independent Ireland* (Dublin, 1999).

Robertson, Manning, *County Borough of Cork and Neighbourhood Planning Report* (Cork, 1941).

Robins, Joseph, *Fools and Mad: A History of the Insane in Ireland* (Dublin, 1986).

Robins, Joseph, *The Lost Children: A Study of Charity Children in Ireland 1700–1900* (Dublin, 1987).

Robins, Joseph, *Custom House People* (Dublin, 1993).

Robins, Joseph, *The Miasma: Epidemic and Panic in Nineteenth-Century Ireland* (Dublin, 1995).

Robins, Joseph (ed.), *Reflections on Health: Commemorating 50 years of the Department of Health 1947–97* (Dublin, 1997).

Rottman, David B., *Crime in the Republic of Ireland: Statistical Trends and their Interpretation* (Dublin, 1980).

Rouse, Paul, *Ireland's Own Soil: Government and Agriculture in Ireland 1945–65* (2000).

Samuel, Raphael, 'Comers and goers' in H. T. Dyos and M. Wolff (eds), *The Victorian City: Images and Realities* (London and Boston, 1973), pp. 123–60.

Shiel, M. J., *The Quiet Revolution: the Electrification of Rural Ireland 1946–76* (Dublin, 1984).

Silverman, Marilyn, *An Irish Working Class: Explorations in Political Economy and Hegemony 1800–1950* (Toronto, 2001).

Silverstone, Roger, *Visions of Suburbia* (London and New York, 1997).

Sinn Féin, *The Economic Programme of Sinn Féin* (Dublin, 1924).

Smith, Christopher J., *Public Problems: The Management of Urban Distress* (New York and London, 1988).

Thompson, E. P., 'Time, work-discipline and industrial capitalism' in Anthony Giddens and David Held (eds), *Classes, Power and Conflict: Classical and Contemporary Debates* (London, 1992), pp. 299–309.

Tomes, Nancy, *The Gospel of Germs: Men, Women and the Microbe in American Life* (Cambridge, Mass. and London, 1998).

Vallely, Fintan (ed.), *The Companion to Irish Traditional Music* (Cork, 1999).

Verdon, Michael, *Shawlies, Echo Boys, the Marsh and the Lanes, Old Cork Remembered* (Dublin, 1993).

Walsh, B. M., *The Structure of Unemployment in Ireland 1954–72* (Dublin, 1974).

Walsh, Dermot P. J., *The Irish Police: A Legal and Constitutional Perspective* (Dublin, 1998).

Whelan, Brendan J., 'Changing work patterns', in K. A. Kennedy (ed.), *From Famine to Feast, Economic and Social Change in Ireland 1847–1997: Lectures on the Occasion of the 150th anniversary of the Statistical and Social Inquiry Society of Ireland* (Dublin, 1998), pp. 111–22.

Whiteman, William M., *The History of the Caravan* (London, 1973).

Whyte, J. H., *Church and State in Modern Ireland 1923–1979* (Dublin, 1984).

Williams, J. D., *Donegal County Council: 75 years* (Donegal, 1974).

UNPUBLISHED MATERIAL

Fennell, Mary B., 'Travellers: assimilation and the education system' (MSocSc, UCC, 1995).

Casey, Nora, 'The print media as an influence on attitudes to Travellers: an example from North Tipperary' (MPhil, TCD, 2005).

Grant, Paul, 'Producing Irish national space: the changing iconography of Irish street names in Munster 1885–1940' (MPhil, UCC, 2000).

Grindley, Geraldine, 'An exploratory study of management practice in voluntary organisations' (MSc, Dublin City University, 1991).

Keane, Liam, 'Irish Travellers and ethnic mobilisation: a study of Travellers in Kilkenny' (MA, UCC, 1992).

Lennon, Michael J., 'Residential segregation in Cork city 1901–46' (MA, UCC, 2000).

Ní Shúinéir, Sinéad, 'Solving itinerancy: thirty-five years of Irish government commissions' (Unpublished conference paper, New Directions in Romani Studies, University of Greenwich, June 1998).

Ní Shúinéir, Sinéad, 'The Association of Travelling People's vision of its educational mandate 1972–1995' (Unpublished conference paper, New Directions in Romani Studies, University of Greenwich, July 1996).

Norris, Michelle and Winston, Nessa, 'Housing and accommodation of Irish Travellers: From assimilationism to multi-culturalism and back again' (Unpublished paper).

Turton, Brian J., 'Touring caravanning and the changing geography of leisure in Britain: a case study of the Caravan Club' (Department of Geography, University of Keele, Occasional Paper 12, 1987).

Index

—